I0823253

Marianne North

Northern Lights

Series Editor: Walter Melion, Asa Griggs Candler Professor of Art History, Emory University, and Foreign Member, KNAW, Royal Netherlands Academy of Arts and Sciences

The 'Northern Lights' book series profiles Northern art in its infinite variety, including paintings, sculptures, objects and architecture. Often the phrase 'Northern art' conjures iconic works of the Northern Renaissance and the 'Dutch Golden Age'. While welcoming contributions about such works, this series also looks beyond 'the usual suspects'. The extended time period – from the Middle Ages to the 19th century – invites authors to explore themes in Northern art without the constraint of conventional chronological boundaries. The expansive geographical coverage offers the potential to highlight the names and works of artists and movements that haven't been privileged in art-historical publishing up until now.

The series publishes illustrated thematic surveys, artist monographs and histories of Northern art collections in museums. It incorporates a range of volumes, from more specialized studies for scholars, to books that are accessible to art enthusiasts.

Marianne North

A Victorian Painter for the 21st Century

Lynne Howarth-Gladston

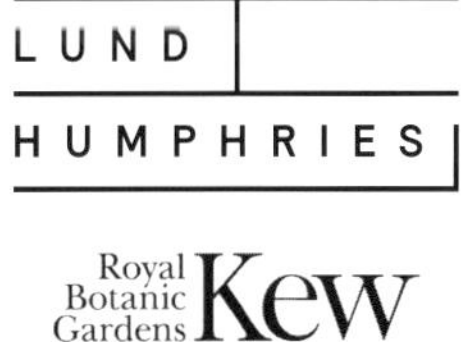

For Dorothy & Lissy

First published in 2024
by Lund Humphries in association with The Royal Botanic Gardens, Kew

Lund Humpries
Huckletree Shoreditch
Alphabeta Building
18 Finsbury Square
London EC2A 1AH
www.lundhumphries.com

ISBN 978–1–84822–625–8

A Cataloguing-in-Publication record for this book is available from the British Library.

Copy edited by Julie Gunz
Project managed and designed by Crow Books
Set in Adobe Jenson Pro
Printed in Bosnia and Herzegovina

Front Cover: Marianne North, 192, *Wild Flowers from the Neighbourhood of New York*, oil on board, 35 × 25 cm, Royal Botanic Gardens, Kew

Contents

Acknowledgements

Quotes with the kind permissions of the Trustees of the Royal Botanic Gardens, Kew, Surrey, UK. The Royal Botanic Gardens, Kew, Library and Archive team, and Conservation team, past and present, including Marilyn Ward, James Kay, Jonathan Farley, Julia Buckley, and Kew photographer Andy McRob. The Royal Botanic Gardens, Kew, Publishing team. Dr Shirley Sherwood, The Shirley Sherwood Gallery, at The Royal Botanic Gardens, Kew. Annie Farrer, botanical illustration teacher at Kew, 2002.

Tom and Sally North for the North family archive.

Australian artist Pip & Pop, aka Tanya Schultz.

Peter Aaron, photographer.

Will Coleman, Wyeth Foundation, previously at The Olana Partnership.

The Lund Humphries team, especially Erika Gaffney.

Professor Paul Gladston.

Jon at 'The Genius Bar', Leicester City, Leicestershire, UK.

The late Laura Ponsonby.

In the UK: The Ashmolean Picture Gallery, Oxford. The Birmingham City Art Gallery, Birmingham Museum Trust. The Royal Geographical Society, London. Tate Gallery, London. The Fitzwilliam Museum, Cambridge. The Courtauld Collection, London. The Victoria & Albert Museum, London. Horace Walpole's Strawberry Hill House, Twickenham, Surrey. Leighton House Museum, Holland Park Road, London. Alexander Pope's Grotto, Radnor House, Twickenham, Surrey. Ham House, London Borough of Richmond upon Thames. Painshill, near Cobham, Surrey.

In the USA: Cooper Hewitt Gallery, Smithsonian Design Museum, Washington, DC, especially Janice Hussein. The Smithsonian American Art Museum and Renwick Gallery, Washington, DC. The Olana Partnership, New York State. The Metropolitan Museum, New York City.

In Australia: Queensland Museum, Brisbane, Queensland. University of Queensland, Brisbane, Queensland. Art Gallery of New South Wales Collection, Sydney, New South Wales.

In Germany: The Alte Pinakothek – Alte Munich Galerie, Munich. Wörlitz Garden Realm, Dessau, Saxony.

In China: The Summer Palace, Beijing. The Temple of Heaven, Beijing.

The Poggi Museum, Bologna, Italy.

Rijksmuseum, Amsterdam, The National Gallery of Amsterdam, Netherlands.

Note on the Figures

Marianne North's paintings are not dated by the artist, although they were all produced within the period 1871–85. They are traditionally left undated, which is the style followed in the figure captions here. In the text I have related certain paintings to places and dates where North is known to have travelled. The captions given are North's original descriptions, and as such they reflect the language of North's day and use plant names that may now have changed. They also use North's own spellings, which may now be deemed incorrect and are occasionally inconsistent. All North image titles are preceded in the text and figure captions with the 3-digit code assigned to her paintings by North.

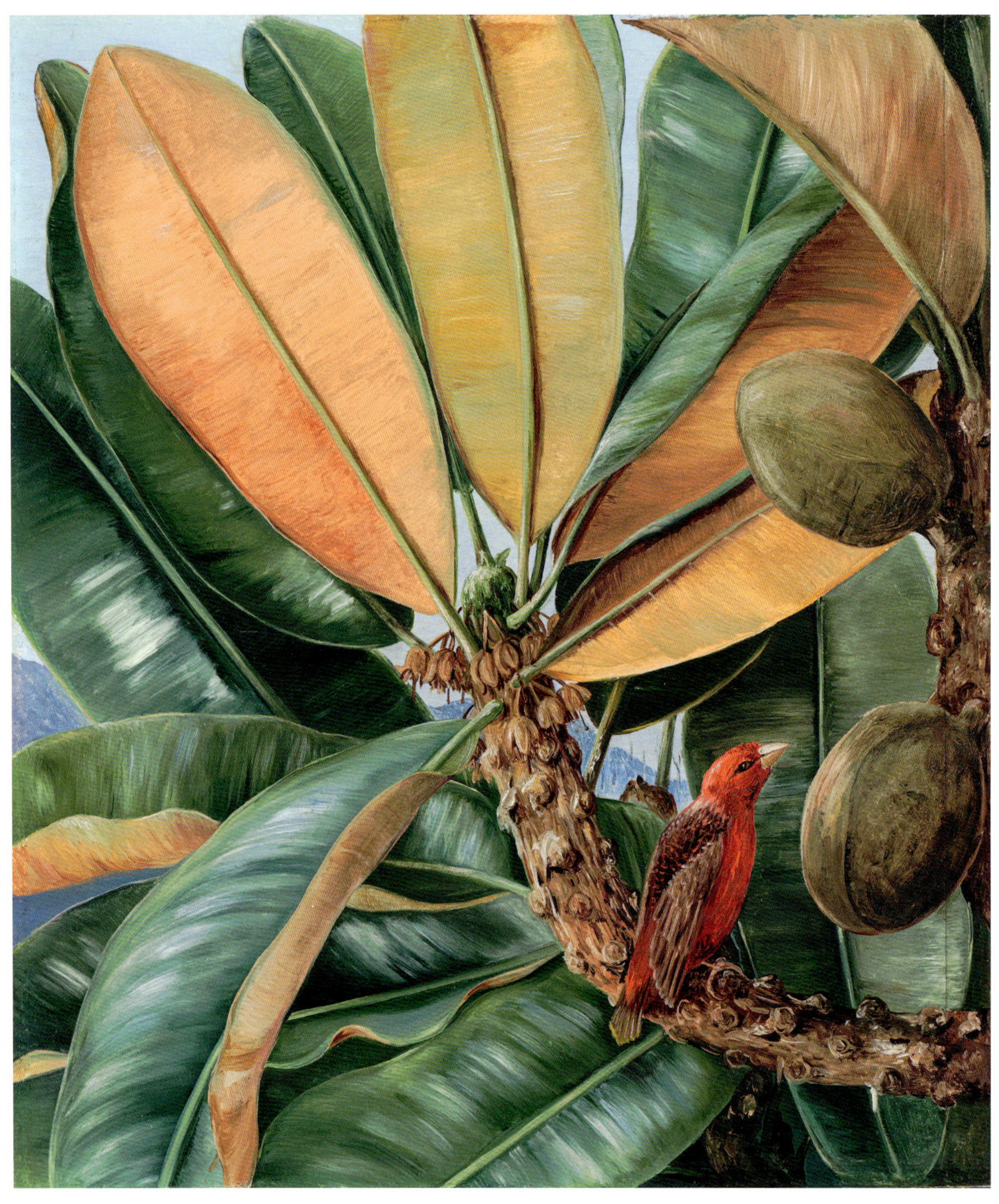

1 Marianne North, 501, *Foliage, Flowers, and Fruit of the Capucin Tree of the Seychelles*, oil on board, 43.6 × 37.9 cm, Royal Botanic Gardens, Kew.

Introduction

Marianne North, a Victorian Botanical Painter for the 21st Century

Marianne North (1830–90) was a significant contributor to 19th-century science and culture, not only as a botanical painter but also a global traveller, plant finder and diarist. North's paintings added to the field of botanical illustration by representing plants accurately in their natural settings based on direct observations in 170 countries and territories across six continents. The Marianne North Gallery at the Royal Botanic Gardens, Kew – self-funded and purpose-built to permanently display more than 800 of North's paintings – was established in 1881 and is still open to the public today. Paintings on display at the gallery, which include topographical landscapes as well as studies of plants from around the world, were produced by North over a remarkably brief period between 1871 and 1885; prior to which North had been a largely unknown amateur painter. Many of North's paintings, while conservative to contemporary eyes, were highly innovative during the 19th century because of their unusual combination of scientific rigour and artistic imagination.

In addition to completing a major body of botanical painting and establishing the North Gallery, as contributions to botanical science North also discovered four flower species previously unknown to science, for which a new *Northia* genus was named: *Northia seychellana* (a tree in the Seychelles; fig.1). Other species names reflect North as the plant's credited discoverer: *Nepenthes northiana* (the large pitcher-plant of Borneo; fig.2); *Crinum northianum* (a relative of the amaryllis; fig.3); and *Kniphofia northiae* (a member of the African torch lilies or poker plants; fig.4). A fifth species, *Areca northiana* (a feather palm), was later removed from North's plant-finding record. North's diaries, which are still in print today, were edited by the artist's sister Catherine Addington Symonds and published posthumously in three volumes between 1892 and 1893. The diaries contain detailed information about North's life and social circle in Britain, in addition to travels across Europe, the Americas, Africa, Asia and Australasia. North also left a large body of correspondence, some with major figures of the 19th century, that gives insights into the artist's opinions, relationships, personal life and work. Quotations of North's writing included in this book are mostly taken directly from the diaries and correspondence.

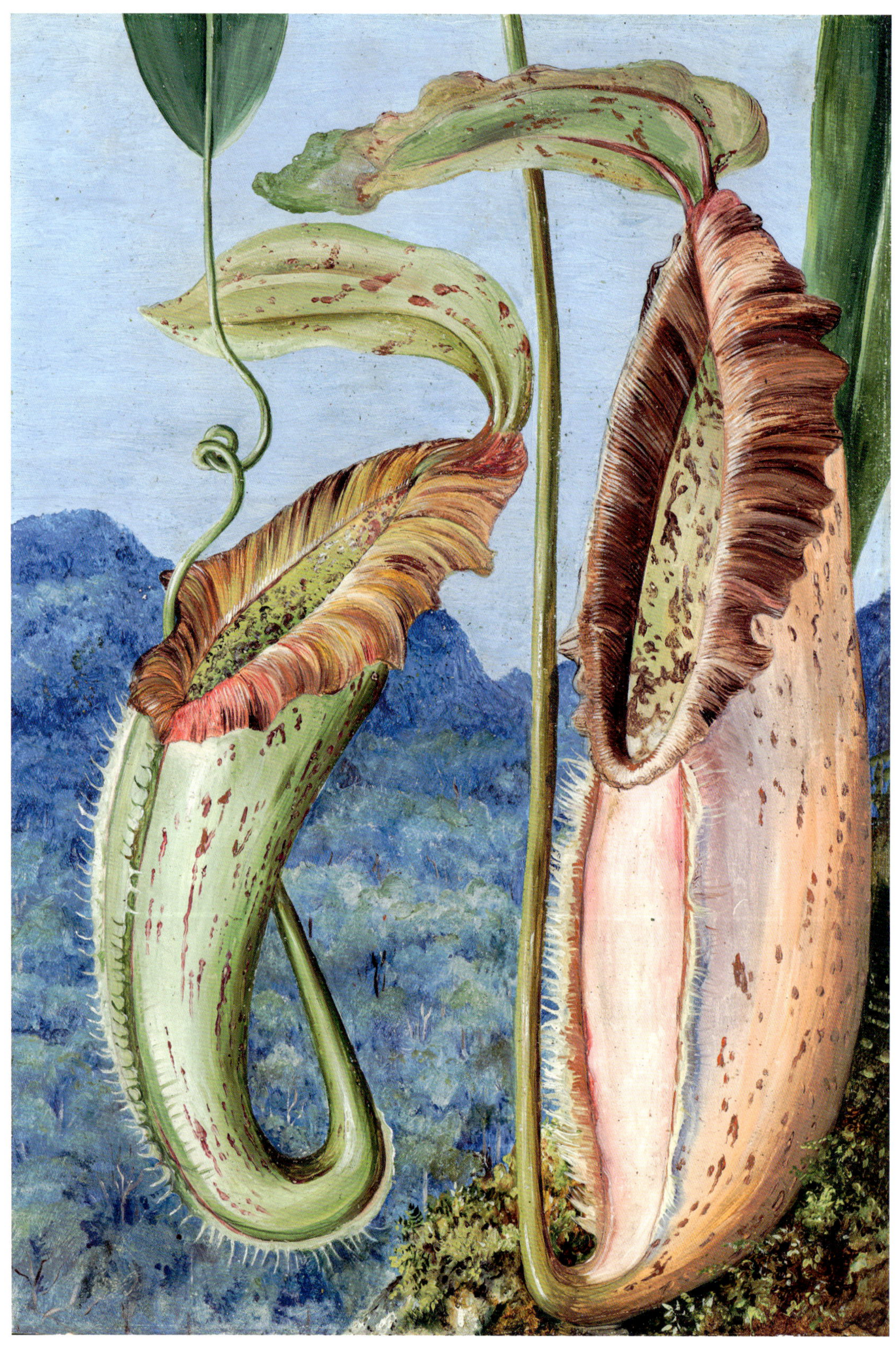

2 Marianne North, 561, *A New Pitcher Plant from the Limestone Mountains of Sarawak, Borneo*, oil on board, 50.6 × 34.8 cm, Royal Botanic Gardens, Kew.

North was born into a comfortably off upper-middle-class family with aristocratic connections which provided the advantages of established wealth and recognised social status. North's father Frederick was a Liberal member of the British parliament who had a lifelong interest in the natural sciences and foreign travel. The North family travelled to Europe and lived there for an extended period between 1847 and 1850. North was especially close to Frederick, and they became constant companions after the death of North's mother, Janet, in 1855. Frederick and North travelled together several times to Europe and the Middle East from the second half of the 1850s until Frederick's death in 1869. Despite approaches from suitors, North chose not to marry. Substantial wealth inherited by Frederick – some of which Janet most likely brought to the marriage – enabled North to pursue a career as a travelling botanical painter in earnest. North did not identify as a feminist but is in many ways a role model for women's independence.

Frederick introduced North to a wide circle of notable figures in 19th-century British and European society, among them the father and son William and Joseph Hooker, successive directors of Kew Gardens. This circle provided social and professional connections that, along with inherited wealth, enabled North to travel and pursue a career, and eventually to build the North Gallery at Kew. Living at a time in which the world had become far more intensely connected, North's, at times, arduous global travels were facilitated by an expanding worldwide rail, road and steamship network as well as emerging telecommunications, developed as part of the spread of 19th-century Euro-American colonialism.

North's considerable, albeit unorthodox, achievements as a botanical painter were recognised during the 19th century by both the scientific community and the wider public – leading British newspapers reported constantly on the painter's travels abroad. North had artistic as well as scientific aspirations and was closely connected to some of the major artists of the 19th century, including the British painter and writer Edward Lear and the American Luminist and member of the Hudson River School, Frederic Edwin Church. North's work was exhibited at prestigious London art galleries – the Kensington Gallery in 1877 and the Conduit Street Gallery in 1879 – and reviewed positively by major journals and newspapers of the day. North's paintings do not conform exactly to the specialist conventions of botanical illustration and are therefore, in many ways, unhelpful to scientific classification. They are nevertheless a unique testament to scientific and artistic endeavour during the late 19th century. North continues to attract a loyal, almost cult following among those interested in botanical painting and early feminism.

The reception of North's botanical painting and the North Gallery since the 19th century has been decidedly mixed. Some (usually with a knowledge of, or interest in, botanical illustration) admire the aesthetic qualities and exactness of North's work. Others have described it as gaudy and amateurish. The North Gallery has also been criticised for being overcrowded and in bad taste. Such views – which coincide with a more general dismissal of a supposedly antiquated Victorian society and culture – do not take into consideration the genuinely innovative nature of North's paintings and their display within the North Gallery. This book situates North's work as a travelling botanical painter and diarist in relation to the prevailing social, political, cultural and scientific conditions of the mid- to late 19th century. At that time, the boundaries between art and science were not as precisely drawn as they were subsequently. Indeed, through the work of the scientist Alexander von Humboldt and others, art was seen as an important adjunct to science. North's hybrid scientific/artistic approach to botanical painting – which involves numerous technical and stylistic innovations including the possible use of photography as a visual aid – and the extraordinary panoramic spectacle housed at the North Gallery were thoroughly progressive in their immediate late 19th-century historical setting. That

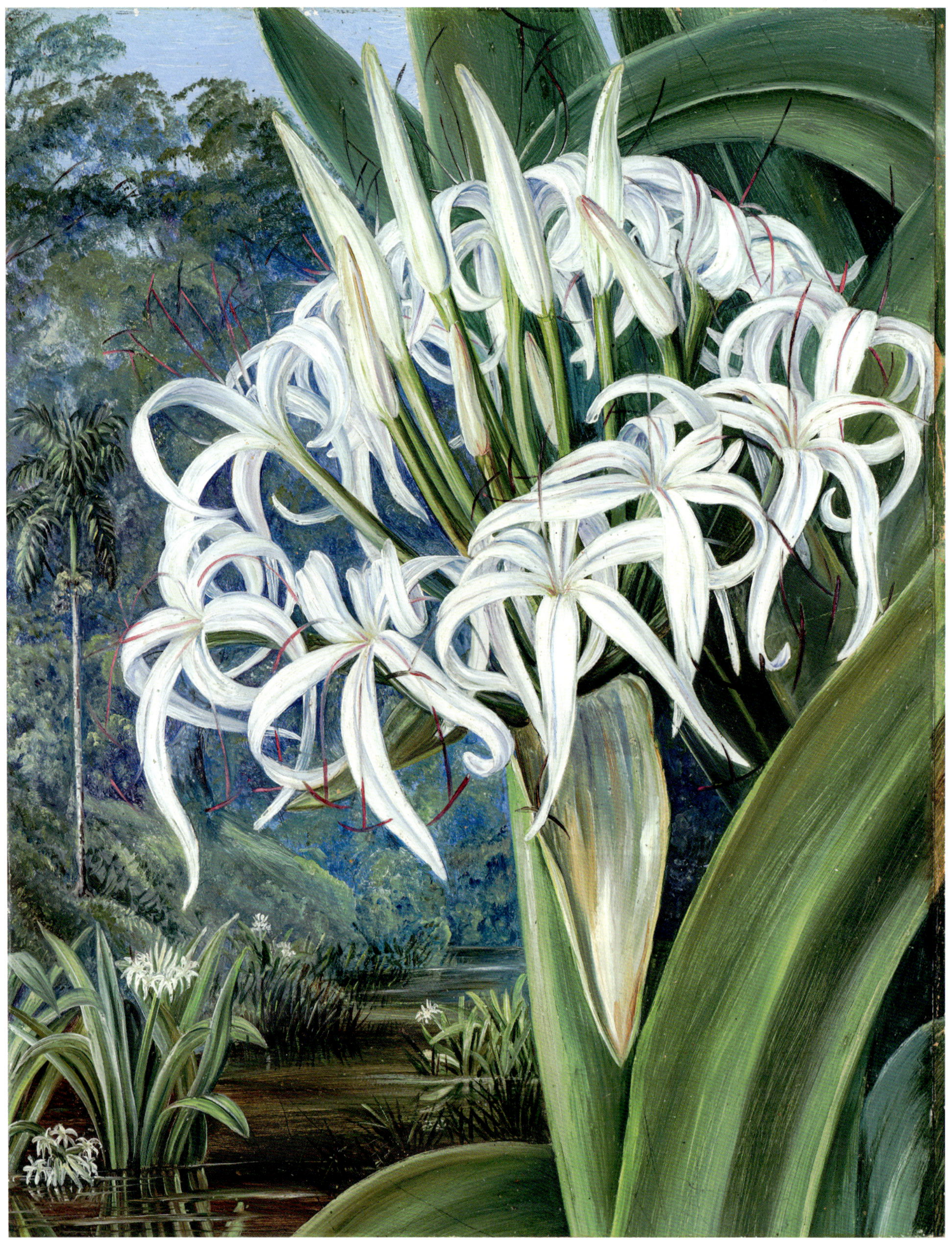

3 Marianne North, 602, *A Bornean Crinum*, oil on board, 45.7 × 36.4 cm, Royal Botanic Gardens, Kew.

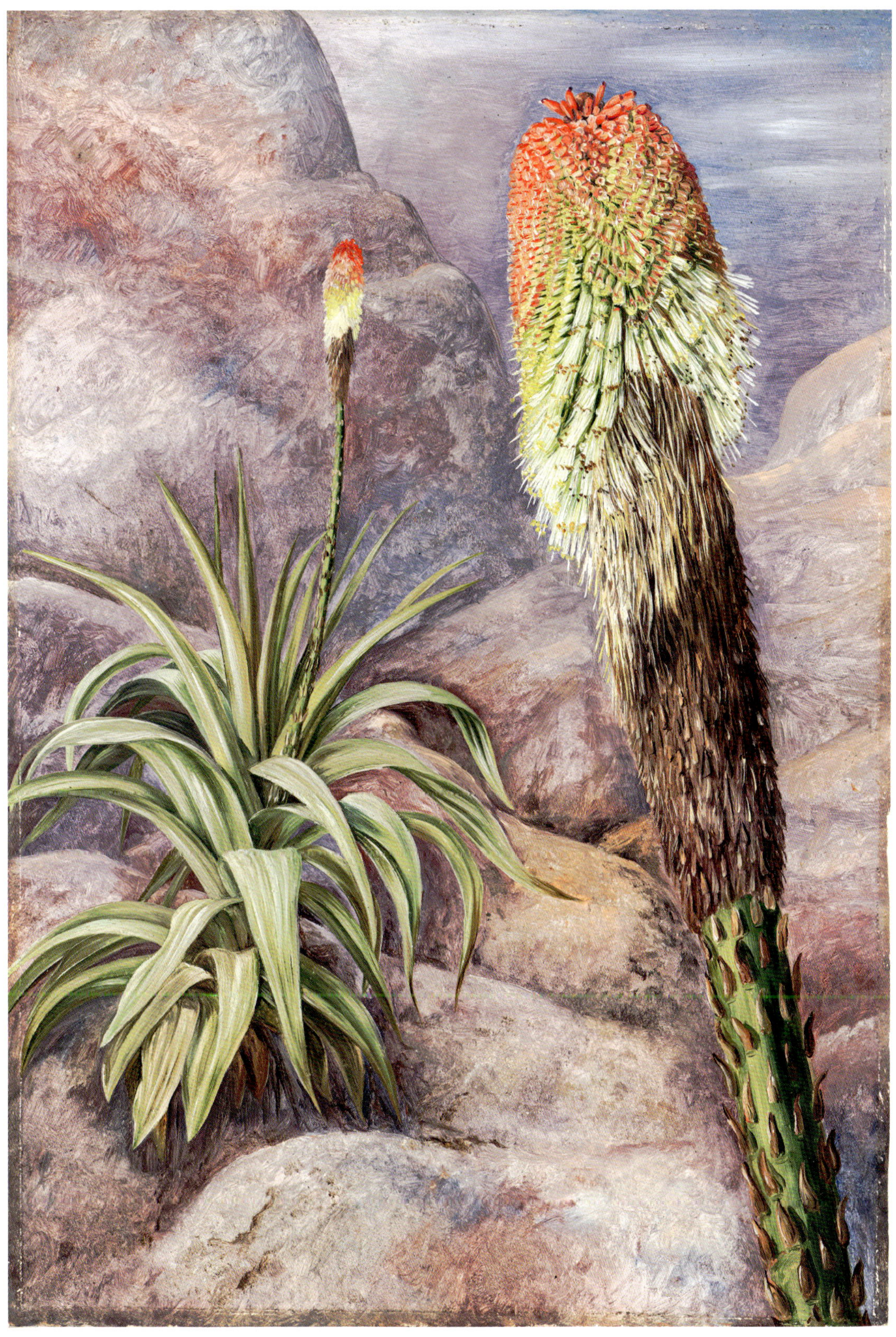

4 Marianne North, 367, *A Giant Kniphofia near Grahamstown*, oil on board, 50.5 × 35.2 cm, Royal Botanic Gardens, Kew.

progressiveness intersects with North's agency as a financially independent woman in a still intensely patriarchal Victorian society, as well as North's close family and social connections to others at the forefront of social reform, animal welfare, environmentalism and libertarianism. While travelling North also took an interest in indigenous cultures which was unusual for the time.

North's legacy has recently been reappraised as part of celebrations surrounding the reopening of the North Gallery after substantial renovations in 2009, and through a BBC 4 television documentary first broadcast in 2016, to which the present author was a contributor. Both sought to interpret North from the standpoint of current feminist and decolonial discourses. This reappraisal is only partially accurate, however. North was, like many upper-middle-class British Victorians, a direct beneficiary of colonialist capitalism as well as being indifferent to feminism. North's paintings and the indeterminate scientific/artistic outlook they embody are nevertheless highly prescient of contemporary concerns. North was critical of the negative impact of capitalism on the natural environment during the 19th century, both in Britain and abroad. Moreover, the North Gallery at Kew, with its permanent panoramic display of North's paintings, is resonant with current ideas related to the bringing together of art and science, as well as the development of an aesthetically sublime postmodernist installation and site-specific art. North is presented here as someone whose painting points well beyond, while being bound up with, the established scientific and cultural conventions of the 19th century.

I

Early Life

Marianne North – known affectionately to close family members as 'Pop' – was born in the English seaside town of Hastings on 24 October 1830. North was a sibling to three other children: an older half-sister, Janet (1817–72; product of North's mother's first marriage), an older brother, Charles (1828–1906), and a younger sister, Catherine (1837–1913). North's ancestor, Edward North (1496–1564), was the 1st Baron North of Kirtling in the English county of Cambridgeshire; the family's ancestral seat had been at Rougham, in the English county of Norfolk. The 2nd Baron North, Roger North (1531–1600), who was a member of parliament for Cambridgeshire, wrote about the North family's history and gained Marianne's admiration because of a shared love of painting and music.[1] Another Roger North – brother to Dudley North, the 3rd Baron North (*c.*1582–*c.*1652) – was a seafaring adventurer and privateer who, according to Marianne, decided to have the family's ancestral home 'blown up with gunpowder' and the contents dispersed. North writes that the 'sailor squire cared only for the sea, and in his old age settled himself [. . .] in the first lodging-house ever let in Hastings'.[2] North's father, Frederick (1800–1869), reconnected the family with Rougham by spending time there during holidays away from school at Harrow, one of England's leading private schools, and undergraduate study at St John's College, Cambridge.

After graduating from Cambridge University, Frederick, who had developed an interest in geology, lived for a time at Mont Blanc in Switzerland, amassing a large collection of rock crystals. The collecting of rocks became fashionable in Europe during the 18th century and remained so during the early 19th century, developing out of an esoteric interest in geology among natural historians. Natural history was envisaged in Christian terms as a way of expanding knowledge of God. Natural historians believed that such knowledge could be gained not just from the study of scripture but also of the nearby countryside, the seashore and the garden. English naturalists, such as Parson Gilbert White (1720–93), believed that natural history 'customarily offered no threat to orthodox creationism'.[3] The fashion for collecting rocks in 18th-century Europe was also associated with a contemporaneous neoclassical revival of the art and architecture of Graeco-Roman antiquity. The poet and translator

Alexander Pope (1688–1744), for example, collected rocks to decorate a grotto inspired by examples from classical antiquity as part of the undercroft of the poet's home at Twickenham on the River Thames, close to London. By the early 1800s, a scientific approach to the study of geology had begun to supersede that of natural history. Building on ideas first posited by the Scottish geologist James Hutton (1726–97) in 1795, writing in the book *Principles of Geology* (1830–33), Scottish geologist Charles Lyell (1797–1875) argued that the earth had been shaped by natural forces over immensely long periods of time. Lyell's uniformitarian theory of the earth's development and its challenge to received ideas of creationism would go on to influence Charles Darwin's (1809–82) theory of evolution, first published in full in *On the Origin of Species* (1859).

During the 19th century, the study of nature was closely aligned with ideas of self-improvement and redemption through honest work put forward by the Scottish essayist, philosopher and historian Thomas Carlyle (1795–1881). North is likely to have been influenced, through Frederick's interest in geology, by Lyell's uniformitarian theory and Carlyle's redemptive view of the study of nature. Study of the natural world was also encouraged by the English writer and Christian socialist Charles Kingsley (1819–75). Kingsley was the author of several books, including *Glaucus* (1855), a treatise on natural history, as well as the novels *Yeast* (1848), which addresses relationships between the landed gentry and rural poor, *Westward Ho!* (1855) and *The Water-Babies* (1863). In *Glaucus*, Kingsley develops the idea of redemption through observation put forward by the art critic, environmental campaigner and writer on social reform John Ruskin (1819–1900), by arguing that natural history as a form of knowledge production depends not on extraordinary human abilities but simple acts of looking, available to all with sight. Kingsley was an avid campaigner on conditions relating to public sanitation and animal rights.[4] North's travels in later life were inspired in part by Kingsley's novel, *At Last: A Christmas in the West Indies* (1871).[5] Kingsley was a friend of Charles Darwin and responded positively to Darwin's theory of evolution.

On returning to England, Frederick initially intended to study law but instead married Marianne North's mother, Janet, and with the likely support of Janet's family connections embarked on a political career. Janet was the widow of Robert Shuttleworth of Gawthorpe Hall near Burnley in Lancashire, and the eldest daughter of Sir John Marjoribanks, Baronet of Lees and member of parliament for Berwickshire on the borders between Scotland and England.[6] Marriage to Janet enhanced Frederick's social standing and probably provided sufficient financial independence to avoid the need to pursue a salaried profession. Frederick was elected as a Liberal member of parliament for the town of Hastings in 1830 and became a freeman of the town after having been voted in by an electorate of 11 voters, of which Frederick was one.

Restricted election practices of the sort that installed Frederick as a freeman of Hastings were a matter of increasing public concern in late Georgian Britain, eventually leading to the passing into law of the Great Reform Act (1832). The Act, which was supported by Britain's Liberals in the teeth of fierce opposition from socially conservative Tories, brought about major changes to the electoral system of England and Wales that would have significant repercussions for the whole of British society. Those changes included the abolition of small constituencies, so-called 'rotten boroughs' – districts with tiny electorates – and the representation of more than one constituency by a single member of parliament. The Reform Act extended suffrage to a wider property-owning and mercantile electorate, as well as to households with a yearly rental of £10 or more, and to some of their lodgers. Non-property-owning working people were excluded from voting. The Act also formally excluded women voters for the first time – although very few women voted in parliamentary elections before 1832, there had previously been no legal restrictions barring them from doing so. Frederick voted in favour of the Great Reform Act in support of the Liberal party. North writes of 'the heated divisions' stirred up by parliamentary debates on the Act and how, after it was passed, Frederick's 'health broke down and he had to give up parliament for awhile [*sic*].'[7] North also writes, 'My first recollections relate to my father. He was from first to the last the one idol and friend of my life, and apart from him I had little pleasure and no secrets', adding, 'We had much variety in our life, spending winter at Hastings, the spring in London, and dividing the summers between my half-sister's old Hall in Lancashire and a farmhouse in Rougham.'[8] North was happiest when Frederick was not 'consumed with Parliamentary responsibilities.'[9]

Another significant figure in North's early life was Lucie Austin (1821–69), who became a regular guest of the family. North comments that Austin 'inspired me with the most profound respect and admiration, as one raised above ordinary mortals.'[10] Lucie married Sir Alexander Cornewall Duff-Gordon (1811–72), 3rd Baronet of Halkin, after Duff-Gordon had proposed while Lucie was staying with the North family.[11] The couple eventually settled in Egypt. Lucie's book *Letters from Egypt* (1865) describes their experiences there. Lucie's life almost certainly influenced North's own desire to travel beyond British shores. North's older half-sister Janet was married to Dr James Kay (1804–77), an educationalist and social reformer.[12] On their marriage, James took Janet's family arms and surname to become James Kay-Shuttleworth, the 1st Baronet of Gawthorpe Hall. James wrote *The Moral and Physical Condition of the Working Classes Employed in the Cotton Manufacture in Manchester* (1832), which was cited in the German industrialist and political philosopher Friedrich Engels's (1820–95) *The Condition of the Working Class in England* (1845) – a book that in turn impacted on the writings of Karl Marx (1818–83). What we would now see as contradictory relationships between hereditary social privilege, involvement in colonialism and a desire for liberal social reform were a prominent and largely accepted feature of British Victorian society. Active participation in public life at the time was limited for the most part to the professional and upper classes.

In youth and young adulthood, North was acutely aware of the damaging impact on the British landscape of the Industrial Revolution of the late 18th and early 19th centuries. As well as causing environmental change, industrialisation also introduced agricultural machinery which replaced human labour, creating poverty that forced many to relocate to industrial cities in search of employment. North alludes euphemistically to those changes, stating that in Rougham 'I knew every big tree, pretty garden, or old farmhouse, with the wooden patterns let into the walls, and yews and box trees cut into cocks and hens, and I sadly missed them when the days of "improvement and restoration" came.'[13] During a visit to Gawthorpe, North saw how the nearby River Calder was 'spoilt by the number of factories which threw in their surplus dyes, and its colour varied from orange to scarlet or purple', commenting that '[t]he noise, smoke, and general griminess of every body and thing in that country were most unattractive to me, and I was always glad to move from it to clean dull Norfolk.'[14] Those early life experiences would go on to inform North's later concerns with the global impact of colonialism on the natural world.

Although connected closely by family ties to the politics of social reform, North's response to the impact of industrialisation would appear to have been inspired in large part by lingering 18th-century Romantic ideas of the picturesque inspired by the painter Claude Lorrain (1600–1682; fig.5) as well as fashionable 19th-century literary representations of a pristine, Eden-like, pre-industrial nature. At Rougham, North 'would follow [Frederick] about from field to field, [...] while he was busy with his axe, and devouring Cooper's novels under the trees he had planted, till I fancied myself in the virgin forests of America.'[15] The writer to whom North refers is most likely the American James Fenimore Cooper (1789–1851), author of the novel *The Last of the Mohicans* (1826). North's concerns regarding the impact of industrialisation on the natural

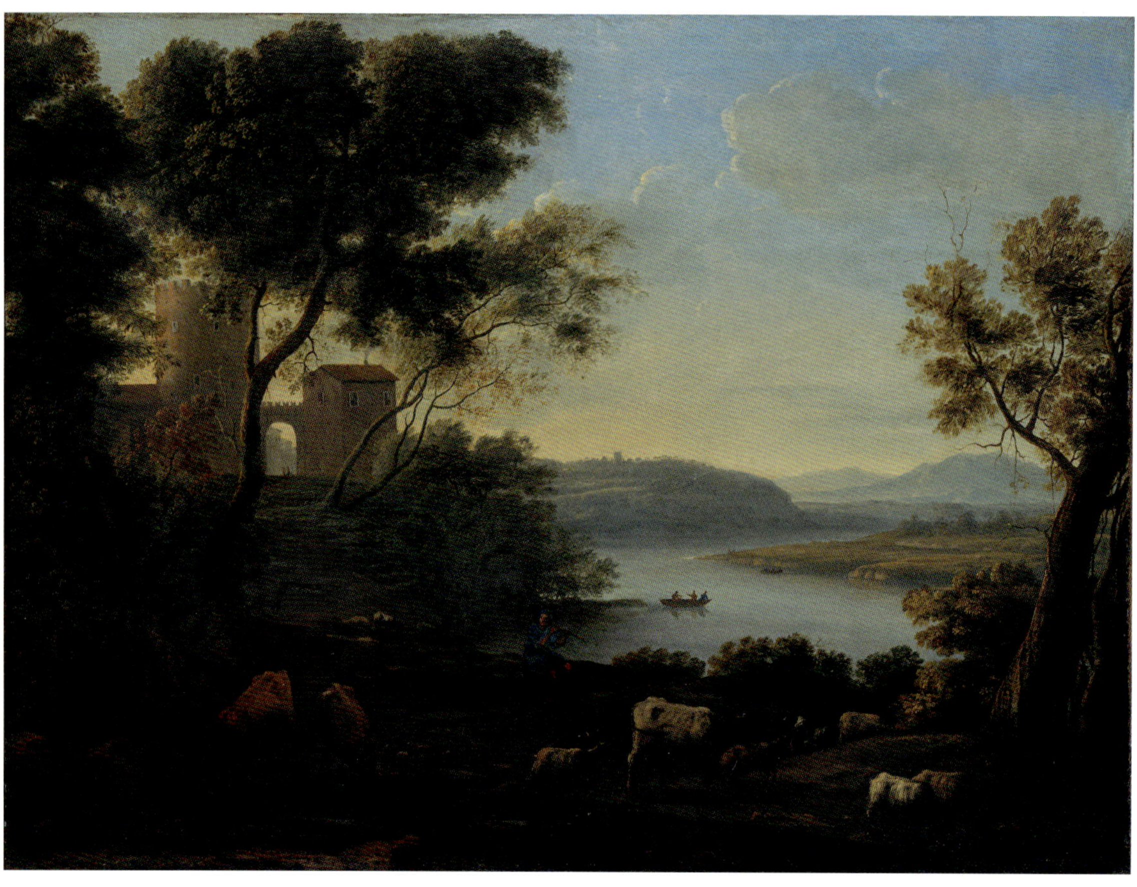

5 Claude Lorrain (Claude Gellée), *Pastoral Landscape: The Roman Campagna*, c.1639, oil on canvas, 101.6 × 135.9 cm, The Metropolitan Museum of Art, New York.

environment may also have been informed by Ruskin's environmental campaigning and criticism of unbridled capitalism.

Romantic ideas of the picturesque – the depiction of nature and rural life as beautiful, charming and quaint – were prominent in British cultural life during the late 18th and early 19th centuries. The Scottish engineer James Nasmyth (1808–90), who surveyed the industrialised Black Country in the English county of Worcestershire, describes 'blazing furnaces, the smoke of which blacked the country as far as the eye could reach', commenting 'We pay a heavy price for it in the loss of picturesqueness and beauty.'[16] Many artists in Britain during the early 19th century, however, chose not to concentrate on the poverty of working people in the countryside. The art historian John Gage writes that 'Although there was some talk in the late eighteenth century of the morality of landscape, there is little indication that landscape painters, working as they did for a wealthy market, were much concerned with the acute deprivation suffered by Industrial or agricultural workers' and that 'It was not until the social reform movements of the Victorian period that artists began to look with greater sympathy at the humble inhabitants of their scenes.'[17]

British aesthetic sensibilities of the late 18th and early 19th centuries were not entirely averse to scenes reshaped by industrialisation. Gage also writes that 'the appearance of mills, mines and furnaces in often mountainous areas of the British Isles could easily be accompanied with the familiar concept of the Sublime'[18] – that is to say, the terror and then heightened pleasure felt in the face of the unimaginably vast and powerful, first described with philosophical rigour by Edmund Burke's (1729–97) treatise, *A Philosophical Enquiry into the Origin of our Ideas of the Sublime and the Beautiful* (1757).[19] A Romantic interest in the sublime had developed in Britain during the 17th and 18th centuries as a critical foil to classical ideas of well-formed beauty. Notable 18th-century exponents of ideas of the sublime include the architect, garden designer and friend of Edmund Burke, Sir William Chambers (1723–96), whose *A Dissertation on Oriental Gardening* (1772) includes accounts of 'horrid' Chinese gardens and landscapes. Chambers writes of how the Chinese 'conceal in cavities, on the summits of the highest mountains, foundries, lime-kilns, and glass-works, which send forth large volumes of flame, and continued columns of thick smoke, that give these mountains the appearance of volcanoes'.[20] Chambers, who visited China as a young man on at least two occasions as an employee of the Swedish East India Company, used Chinese stylings and aesthetics as part of the redesigning of Kew Gardens in the late 1750s and early 1760s. Chambers's work at Kew contrasted oriental sublimity with classical European beauty and became a strong influence on garden design throughout Europe.

The English artist Joseph Wright of Derby (1734–97) produced several paintings depicting the impact of industrialisation on the Derbyshire landscape, including *Arkwright's Cotton Mills by Night* (*c.*1783), that resonate strongly with Chambers's description of 'horrid Chinese landscapes'. The English industrialist and inventor Richard Arkwright's (1732–92) factory at Cromford Mill in Derbyshire was the world's first water-powered cotton mill. Arkwright would later go on to own and operate mills in Manchester. The Alsatian-born artist Philippe-Jacques de Loutherbourg (1740–1812) painted similar scenes, such as *Iron Works, Coalbrook Dale* (1805), which depicts a furnace set upon a hill, belching orange smoke, next to the River Severn in the English county of Shropshire. A worker, accompanied by a dog, travels towards the furnace on horseback, dragging industrial wares while passing a heap of ruined Greek columns. This symbolic juxtaposition, which also appears in paintings by Wright, maintains a relationship with then-dominant neoclassical sensibilities while simultaneously indicating a progressive Romantic breaking with the restrictions of the past. Such visions form a backdrop to North's own later excursions into landscape painting.

North may have had a Romantic aversion to the impact of industrialisation on the British landscape, but was also a privileged beneficiary of the improvements that the Industrial Revolution brought to travel across the country. North writes of journeying south on the newly established railway line 'somewhere beyond York', adding 'There were only bits of railways in those days, and we generally drove a long way to reach them, and then used to sit in our own carriage, which was tied on a truck, surrounded by all our own luggage.' This, as North tells us, was 'a long week's work'.[21] Rail travel in early 19th-century England was depicted as a sublime combination of overwhelming mechanical power and, for the time, exhilarating speed by the artist J.M.W. Turner's (1775–1851) painting *Rain, Steam, and Speed – The Great Western Railway* (1844).

As a child, North received little in the way of formal education, writing that 'Governesses hardly interfered with me in those days. Walter Scott [author of the acclaimed historical novels *Waverley* (1814) and *Ivanhoe* (1820)] or Shakespeare gave me their versions of history, and Robinson Crusoe and some other old books my ideas of geography.'[22] From an early age North began to develop ambitions towards botanical painting, which in Britain during the mid-19th century was considered appropriate to 'female polite culture'.[23] While middle-class women were not generally trained as artists, they were encouraged, as the art historian Tabitha Barber makes clear, to produce technical illustrations as a

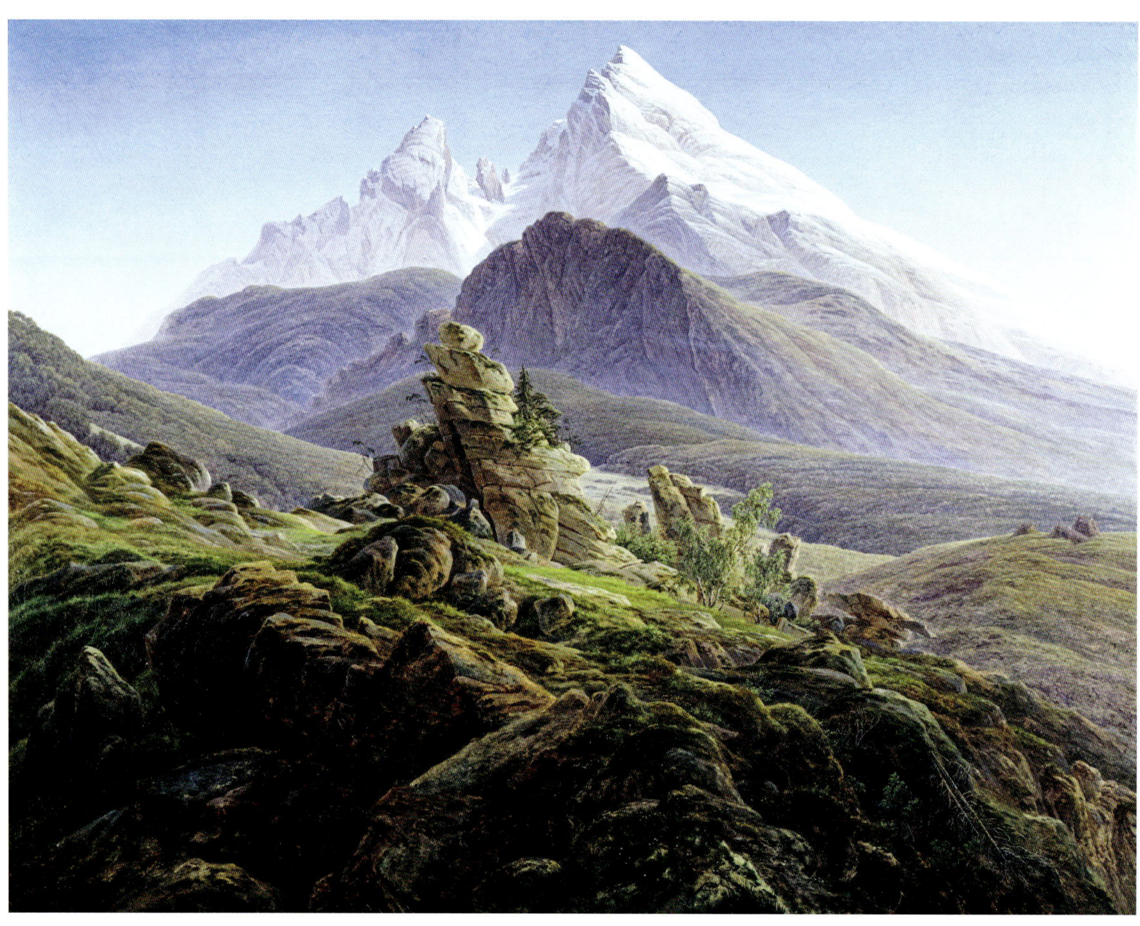

6 Caspar David Friedrich, *Der Watzmann*, also known as *The Watzmann*, 1824–5, oil on canvas, 136 × 170 cm, Alte Nationalgalerie, Berlin.

'useful source of scientific information.'[24] North acquired two volumes on British fungi from a nearby library, commenting that they

> started me collecting and painting all varieties I could find at Rougham, and for about a year they were my chief hobby [. . .] One [of the fungi] I remember, had a most horrible smell; [. . .] and I was very anxious to see the change, I put it under a tumbler in my bedroom window [. . .] and next morning [. . .] the tumbler was broken into bits and the fungus standing up about five inches high [. . .] having hatched itself free [. . .] and smelling most vilely.

North concludes that 'Good and bad smells are merely a matter of taste, for it soon attracted crowds of a particular kind of fly, which seemed thoroughly to enjoy themselves on it.'[25] North complained to Frederick and Janet of being uneducated and was sent to a school in the nearby city of Norwich under the tutelage of a 'Madame de Whal'. However, North found that 'school-life was hateful to me' and that the teaching was 'purely mechanical routine', with the 'only bright days' being when Frederick rode over for business and they went out for the day. Although lacking in formal education, North grew up in an area of England where there were many radical Protestants, known as 'Dissenters', 'ranters'

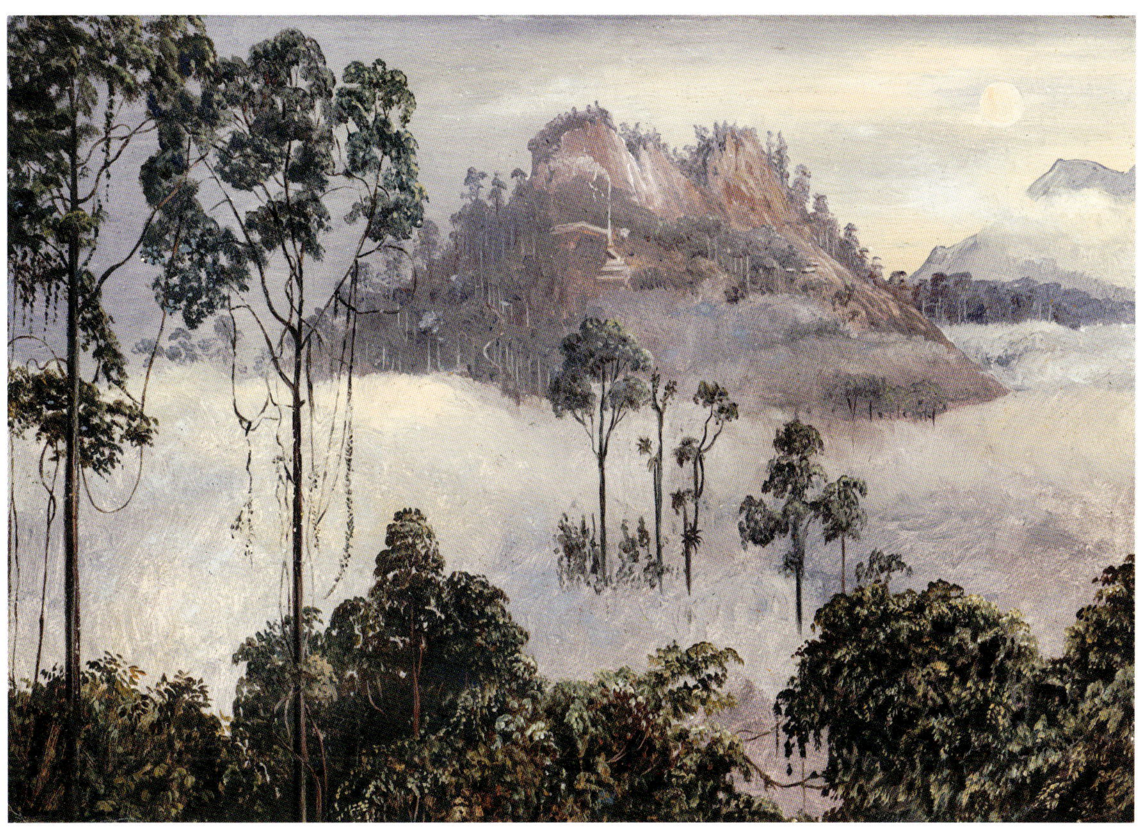

7 Marianne North, 584, *The Quicksilver Mountain of Tegora, Sarawak, by Moonlight*, oil on board, 34.9 × 49.7 cm, Royal Botanic Gardens, Kew.

or Primitive Methodists, 'whose chief preachers were women'.[26]

North's formal schooling came to an end when Frederick failed to be re-elected to parliament and decided to take the family travelling across Europe for the next three years, first settling in the Prussian city of Heidelberg for a period of eight months from August 1847.[27] North writes of how Frederick would lead the family on expeditions throughout Prussia, which started by rail. Their peripatetic life was interrupted by the political upheavals that took place across Europe in 1848. North writes of the 'revolutionary ideas' that forced France's King Louis Philippe (1773–1850) to flee the country. Revolutionary fervour soon crossed the Rhine to Prussia. Ideas of a united Germany were proclaimed, with North noting a meeting of radicals in Heidelberg on 26 March 1848. Soon afterwards the family decided to flee Heidelberg, eventually taking a flat in the Bavarian city of Munich.[28] They then moved on again, arriving in Dresden, the capital of Saxony, the day after revolution had broken out there.

The Norths later moved to Vienna, then capital of the Austro-Hungarian empire. While visiting the Austrian city of Gratz, North writes of 'soldiers, mostly raw recruits, border men and Croats, [. . .] brought there to be drilled' before being sent to fight in the Hungarian and Italian wars. North sympathised with the men, writing, 'These poor creatures came from their homes in picturesque sheepskin coats, with the wool inside and embroidery outside; their well-shaped sandalled feet

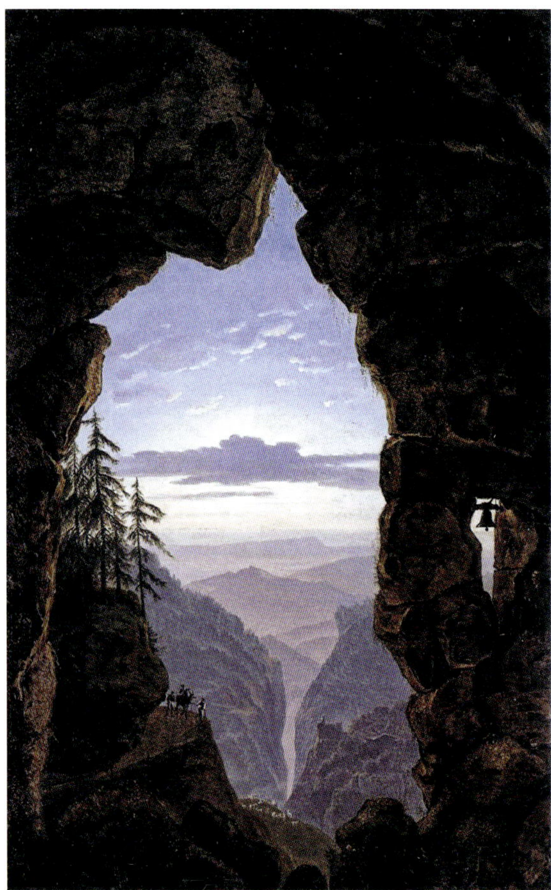

8 Karl Friedrich Schinkel, *Felsentor*, also known as *The Gate in the Rocks*, 1818, oil on canvas, 74 × 48 cm, Alte Nationalgalerie, Berlin.

[. . .] forced into regulation boots, while their bodies were squeezed into tight uniforms.'[29] During a house-hunting expedition in Vienna, North's parents found themselves caught up in a disturbance at the city's cathedral when a 'mob broke in to fetch out seats and other movables to make a barricade'. There were shots fired, with armed men 'pointing their guns at a door behind the pulpit'. No one was harmed during the incident, but later that night '[Theodor Franz, Count Baillet von] Latour, the Minister of war, was hanged on a lamp-post and shot at by students'.[30] North's father enquired if they could leave the city but was told it was too dangerous to do so. Frederick nevertheless secured 'two good porters with wheelbarrows' and took the family to Vienna's railway station, from where they caught a train to the city of Baden in Switzerland, north-west of Zurich.[31]

Despite these continual relocations, North was able to amass significant knowledge of European art and music during the family's travels. Journeying through conflict-torn Germany, North began 'to know the famous pictures by heart – all that is too well known to need description'.[32] The Norths met with artists, including one referred to by North simply as 'Dahl' and another as 'Vogelstein'. The former is likely to have been the so-called 'father' of Norwegian landscape painting, Johan Christian Dahl (1788–1857), who was in Dresden at the same time as the Norths, and the latter the German painter, Christian Vogel von Vogelstein (1788–1868). Vogelstein gave North's mother a study 'for his large painting of a martyr taking leave of her child through prison bars, as he said the face resembled hers'.[33] North also writes of meeting the German painter, etcher and draughtsman 'Old [Friedrich August] Moritz Retsch' (1779–1857), who lived 5 miles from Dresden, noting that the artist had 'won many honours by his genius for illustration' and that Retsch's 'drawings were done with pencil, shaded with the greatest fineness'.[34] North enthuses about going to 'all Mozart's operas and masses' while in Gratz, and of 'singing and translating all the solos and duets' as well as passing the time by playing the piano. Upon arriving in the Swiss municipality of Mur, North was provided with a 'delightful old singing mistress' who had 'been famous in her youth'.[35]

The family's travels may also have introduced North to the works of Caspar David Friedrich (1774–1840), a member of the German Romantic movement whose paintings depict sublime German landscapes. The subject matter and composition of Friedrich's painting *Der Watzmann* (1824–5; fig.6) are strikingly akin to those of mountain landscapes painted by North years later while travelling (fig.7). There are, moreover,

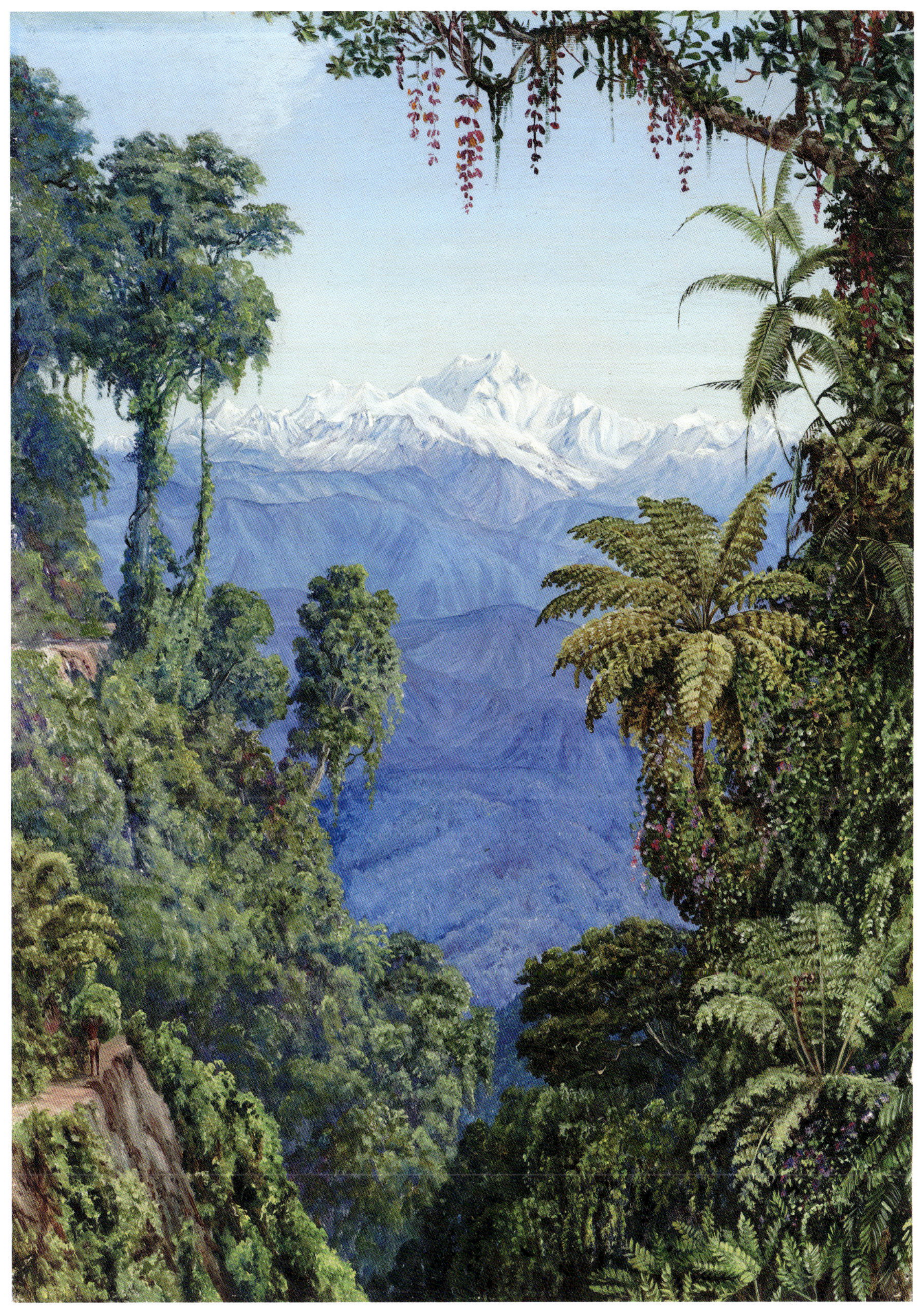

9 Marianne North, 270, *A Distant View of Kinchinjunga from Darjeeling*, oil on board, 47 × 34 cm, Royal Botanic Gardens, Kew.

compositional similarities between North's landscapes and those by the German painter Karl Friedrich Schinkel (1781–1841). The composition of Schinkel's painting, *Felsentor* or *The Gate in the Rocks* (1818; fig.8), which frames a mountain view in portrait rather than landscape format, is echoed by North's painting 270, *A Distant View of Kinchinjunga from Darjeeling* (fig.9). The same compositional device was applied by North to paintings of landscapes in Tenerife, the Himalayas and the Sierra Nevada. North's leanings towards the picturesque are clearly combined in those paintings with elements of the Romantic sublime (fig.10).

On returning to England in 1850, North took part in numerous musical events following incessant practising under a Herr Kufferath; most likely the German pianist and composer Louis Kufferath (1811–82), one of three musical brothers. As North indicates, Kufferath had been a pupil of the now much better-known German composer Jakob Ludwig Felix Mendelssohn (1809–47). North writes of attending performances by the internationally renowned Swedish opera singer Jenny Lind (1820–87), and becoming awe-struck by the performances of German-born opera singer Madame Sontag (1806–54).[36] North took singing lessons with the singer, teacher and composer, Charlotte Sainton-Dolby (1821–85) and writes of learning to admire Dolby 'more and more, till both our days for singing were over. I loved her for herself, as well as for her voice, and I believe she liked my singing, as she used to make me take the contralto solos in the concerts.' North adds that 'I never did well on those occasions, having a [...] habit of nervousness; when told to stand up and show off.'[37]

While at Rougham, North passed the 'hours of everyday on horseback, painting and singing' but did not take regular part in social events such as the balls or parties widely enjoyed by others of the same class, stating that 'we were not what is called a sociable family'.[38] A reluctance to participate in social events was not entirely unusual amongst middle- and upper-class women of Victorian Britain. May Lyttelton, daughter of the George William Lyttelton, 4th Baron Lyttleton, commented on the dreariness of upper- and middle-class Victorian life. The historian Sheila Fletcher describes May's feelings, stating that 'by the time she had arranged her books and taken a pleasant ride in the hills she felt [...] restless beyond measure!' Croquet at the house of a favourite neighbour left May 'very actively bored'. As Fletcher indicates, May's 'diary shows her greatly afflicted with inferior dinner partners, the maddening click of billiard balls and the deathly tedium of archery meetings'.[39] Any boredom that North might have experienced in relation to day-to-day life was doubtless alleviated by the family's travels, including a visit to the opening of the Great Exhibition of 1851 in London, the world's first industrial fair.[40]

North took 'lessons in flower-painting from a Dutch lady, Miss van [*sic*] Fowinkel', Magdalena von Fowinkel (1785–1875), from whom North acquired 'the few ideas I posses [*sic*] of arrangement of colour and of grouping'.[41] Fowinkel exhibited paintings at the Royal Academy in London between 1831 and 1846.[42] North also writes of having 'a few lessons in water-colour flower-painting' from English flower painter Valentine Bartholomew (1799–1879), a Painter in Ordinary to Queen Victoria.[43] As the cultural historian Suzanne Le-May Sheffield indicates,

> Such lessons were usually nothing more than money-making ventures for the artist who gave them and were intended to refine a young lady's talent but were not supposed to encourage her to aspire to the dizzying heights of the professional, artistic world [...] women's art while often considered [...] skilful, was very rarely praised as the work of genius. Such talent was equated with masculinity.[44]

North complains that 'the only master I longed for would not teach, i.e. old William Hunt whose work will live for ever, as it is absolutely true to nature'.[45] William Henry Hunt (1790–1864), an eminent and widely admired painter of naturalistic still-lifes and genre pieces of children, spent winters at Hastings. North was clearly piqued by this refusal and writes somewhat waspishly of another who attracted Hunt's attention as '"That Boy" [...] whom Hunt taught to be anything he chose as model, blowing the hot pudding, fighting the wasp, or taking the physic'.[46] Hunt did agree to teach the educationalist, early feminist, women's rights activist and painter Barbara Leigh Smith (1827–91), later known as Barbara Leigh Smith Bodichon, who established a professional career as a painter and whose signature technique of painting with a 'mixture of transparent and body colour over a ground of Chinese white to give luminosity' was almost certainly learned from Hunt.[47] Like North, Leigh Smith Bodichon is known to have visited the pharmacist John Hornby Maw's (1800–1885) house in Hastings with its collection of watercolours by Turner (fig.11).[48] North notes that Hunt's studio in Hastings belonged to Maw.[49] During the first half of the 19th century, many artists, both amateur and professional, painted the ruins on Castle Hill at Hastings.[50] Among them, in addition to Hunt and Turner, were the English landscape painter David Cox (1783–1859), a leading member of the Birmingham School of landscape painting, John Linnell (1792–1882) and English architectural and landscape watercolourist Samuel Prout (1783–1852). As the art historian Pamela Hirsch indicates, the Leigh Smiths were friendly with people who 'were Liberal in politics and intellectual and artistic in their interests', adding that North was to become one of Leigh Smith's 'closest friends in later years'.[51]

Hunt's depictions of nature are highly detailed, so much so that they sometimes approach the photographic. Ruskin describes Hunt as having given 'bench-marks at which to aim as an artist' and developed 'a remarkable facility for handling the watercolour medium' (fig.12). According to Ruskin, 'No one has ever excelled him [Hunt] in painting geological specimens and rocks.'[52] North's painting 015, *Armed Bird's Nest in Acacia Bush, Chili* (fig.13), may well be a homage to Hunt. North's painting depicts a bird guarding its nest with surrounding flora and a mountain landscape in the background. The depiction of the nest and flora are strikingly like works by Hunt. Other paintings by North, such as 440, *Earth-Nut and a Prickly Gourd, St John's Kaffraria* (fig.14), and 057, *Wild Flowers of Brazil* (fig.15), replicate Hunt's naturalistic depictions of hedgerows. Hunt's choice of working on a small scale was something that North, as an amateur painter, could replicate with relative ease. North tells us that 'apple-blossoms and birds'-nests, with their exquisite mosses and ivy-leaved backgrounds' depicted by Hunt 'were to be found in the hedges and gardens of Hastings'.[53]

The ornithological illustrator, topographical painter, writer of nonsense poems, musician, traveller and travel writer Edward Lear (1812–88) was a major influence on North's work as a botanical and landscape painter. Lear visited the North family at Hastings when North was a young girl, settling 'himself as a lodger' because of the fig trees in the Norths' garden, representations of which were added to landscape paintings Lear worked on in Hastings. North writes that Lear 'was most good natured in letting us watch him at work, and used to wander into our sitting-room through the windows at dusk when his work was over, sit down to the piano, and sing Tennyson's songs for hours, composing as he went on'; performances that North found highly amusing.[54] The Tennyson to which North refers is Alfred, Lord Tennyson (1809–92), 1st Baron Tennyson and Poet Laureate to Queen Victoria, who, amongst other things, wrote the still well-known verse 'The Charge of the Light Brigade' (1854). While lodging with the Norths at Hastings, Lear 'painted a great view from Windsor' for a former Prime Minister of Britain, Lord Derby (1799–1869), which Frederick North bought when Derby rejected the painting, keeping it 'within sight of his room' – a kindness that Lear 'never forgot'.[55] In the winter of 1868, Lear wrote the nonsense poem 'The Owl and The Pussy-Cat' for North's niece Janet Addington Symonds and gave North 'great encouragement in her painting'.[56] Around this time, North was taught to paint in oils by the Tasmanian painter Robert Hawker Dowling (1827–86), who spent a Christmas with the North family. Dowling was a portraitist and painter of religious and oriental subjects who exhibited at the Royal Academy

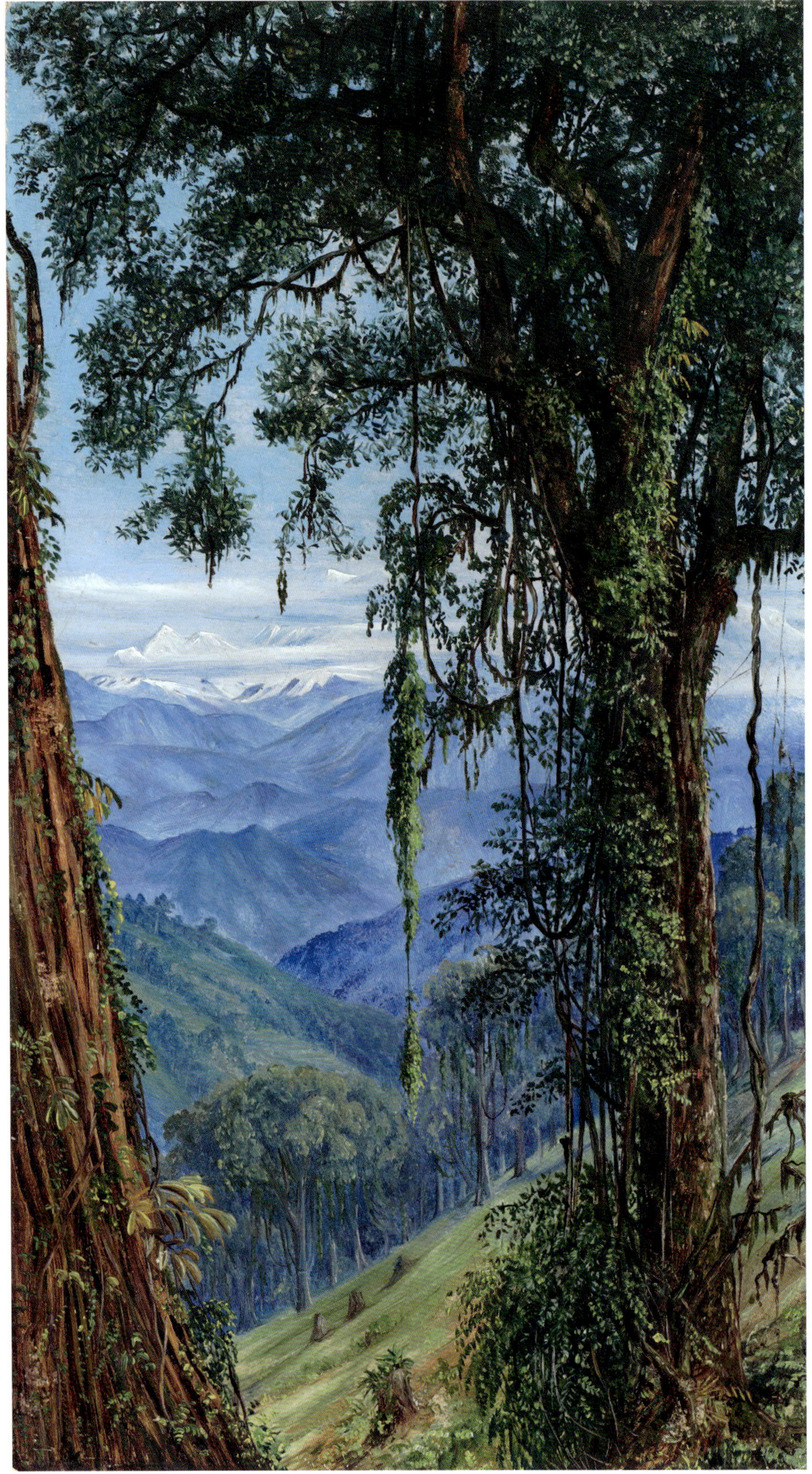

10 Marianne North, 230, *View from Rungaroon, near Darjeeling, India*, oil on board, 50.7 × 28.6 cm, Royal Botanic Gardens, Kew. This painting shows aspects of both Caspar David Friedrich and Friedrich Schinkel.

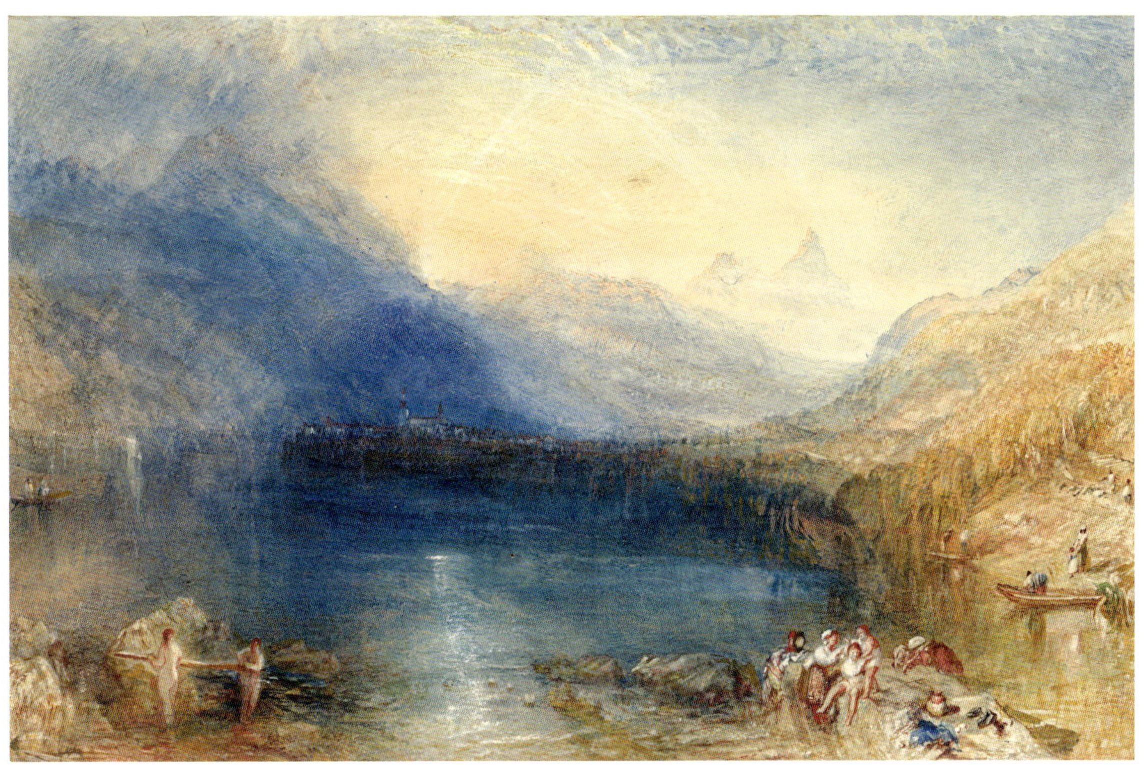

11 Joseph Mallord William Turner, *The Lake of Zug*, 1843, watercolour over graphite, 29.8 × 46.6 cm, The Metropolitan Museum of Modern Art, New York.

in London between 1859 and 1882. Before these lessons, North had always painted with watercolours but, as a result of Dowling's teaching, developed a passion for oil painting, describing it as 'a vice like dram-drinking, almost impossible to leave off once it gets possession of one'.[57] Hunt's technique of building up layers in watercolour to give a dense colouration and luminosity was readily transferable to oils.

In May 1854, Frederick was once again elected to parliament. This success was marred shortly afterwards by the death of North's mother Janet on 17 January 1855. North writes that, before dying, Janet 'made me promise never to leave my father', adding that Frederick 'missed her [Janet] much when she was gone'.[58] A grief-stricken Frederick left Hastings for London accompanied by North, taking an apartment in Victoria Street, Westminster, near the soon-to-be site of Victoria railway station (opened 1860). During this stay in London, North writes of driving with Frederick to Chiswick Gardens for 'specimen flowers to paint' as well as visits together to the Royal Botanic Gardens at Kew in Surrey, just outside London. At Kew, North was introduced by Frederick to the then director of the Gardens, Sir William Hooker (1785–1865), who presented 'a hanging bunch of the *Amherstia noblis*' that made North 'long more and more to see the tropics'.[59] North writes that 'London was full of delights for me, though I never went through much of the treadmill routine called "Society"'. Frederick would later give the house at Rougham to North's brother Charles when the latter married Augusta Keppel in 1859, the eldest daughter of a neighbour, the Reverend Thomas Keppel, rector of North Creake.[60]

During parliamentary recesses, North and Frederick

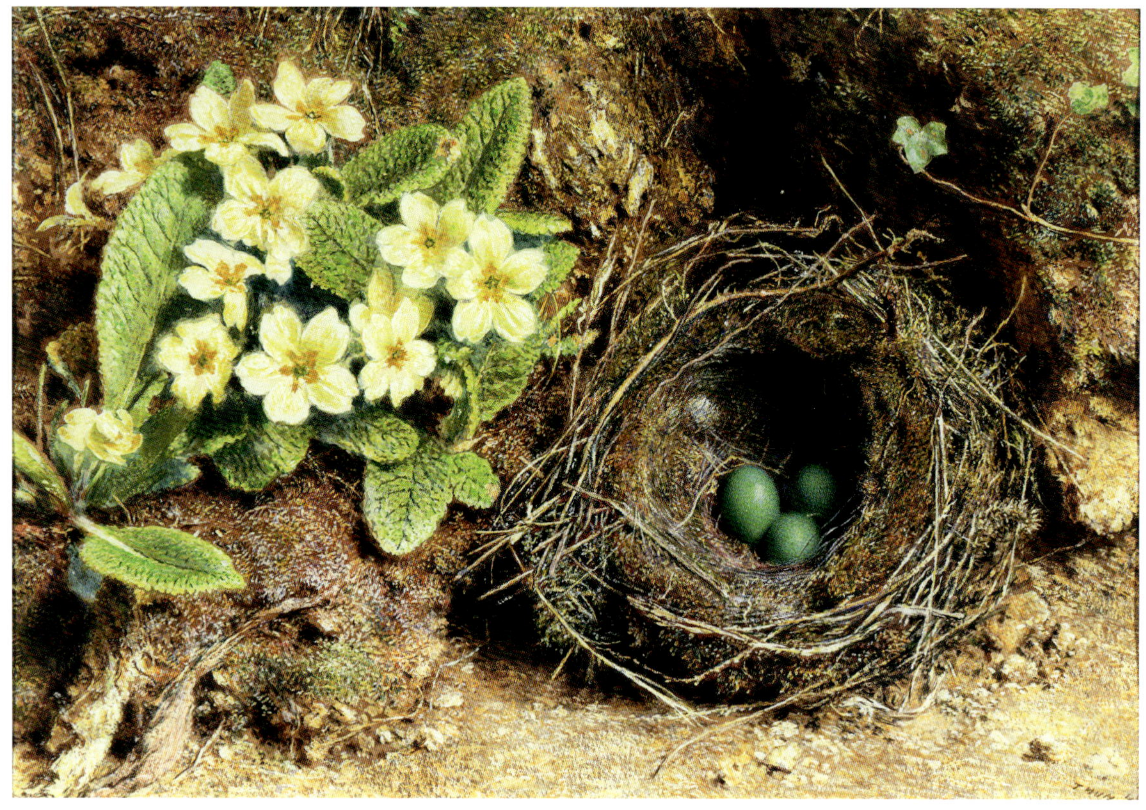

12 William Henry Hunt, *Primroses and Bird's Nest*, 1830, watercolour on paper, 18.4 × 27.3 cm, Tate Collection.

travelled in Europe, journeying on the continent's railways and visiting such places as Mont Blanc and Monte Rosa on the French-Swiss-Italian border.[61] In 1861, their travels took them to Constantinople in Turkey and Athens in Greece. After Janet's death, North 'was eager to arrange his [Frederick's] quarters to his liking and was willing to undertake any and all domestic chores necessary while they were travelling'. North was not simply a handmaiden to Frederick's wishes, however, and shared fully in 'his love for natural history, for antiquities, for painting, for foreign customs and for travel'.[62] On a trip to Switzerland in 1864, North and Frederick met the English novelist and social commentator Elizabeth Gaskell (1810–65) at Pontresina near St Moritz. The English poet, literary critic and cultural historian John Addington Symonds (1840–93) was also present. Symonds had been introduced to the North family the previous summer and would go on to marry the youngest daughter Catherine in 1865.[63]

Frederick lost the election to the Hastings parliamentary seat in the same year as Catherine married. North and Frederick ventured abroad once more, this time travelling across eastern Europe, through the Adriatic and on to Damascus in Syria, where they spent the winter on a 'Nile boat' and did not return to England until 1866.[64] Sheffield writes that North's 'travels with her father opened to her new vistas and allowed plenty of time to sketch and paint – ancient ruins, thronging markets, majestic mountains' and to try 'different techniques'. North's 'views of landscapes around her provided natural history as well as art studies, and she discussed geology with her father in Egypt and collected sea shells at Suez. Meeting up with the Francis Galtons in Switzerland afforded discussions of the glaciers.'

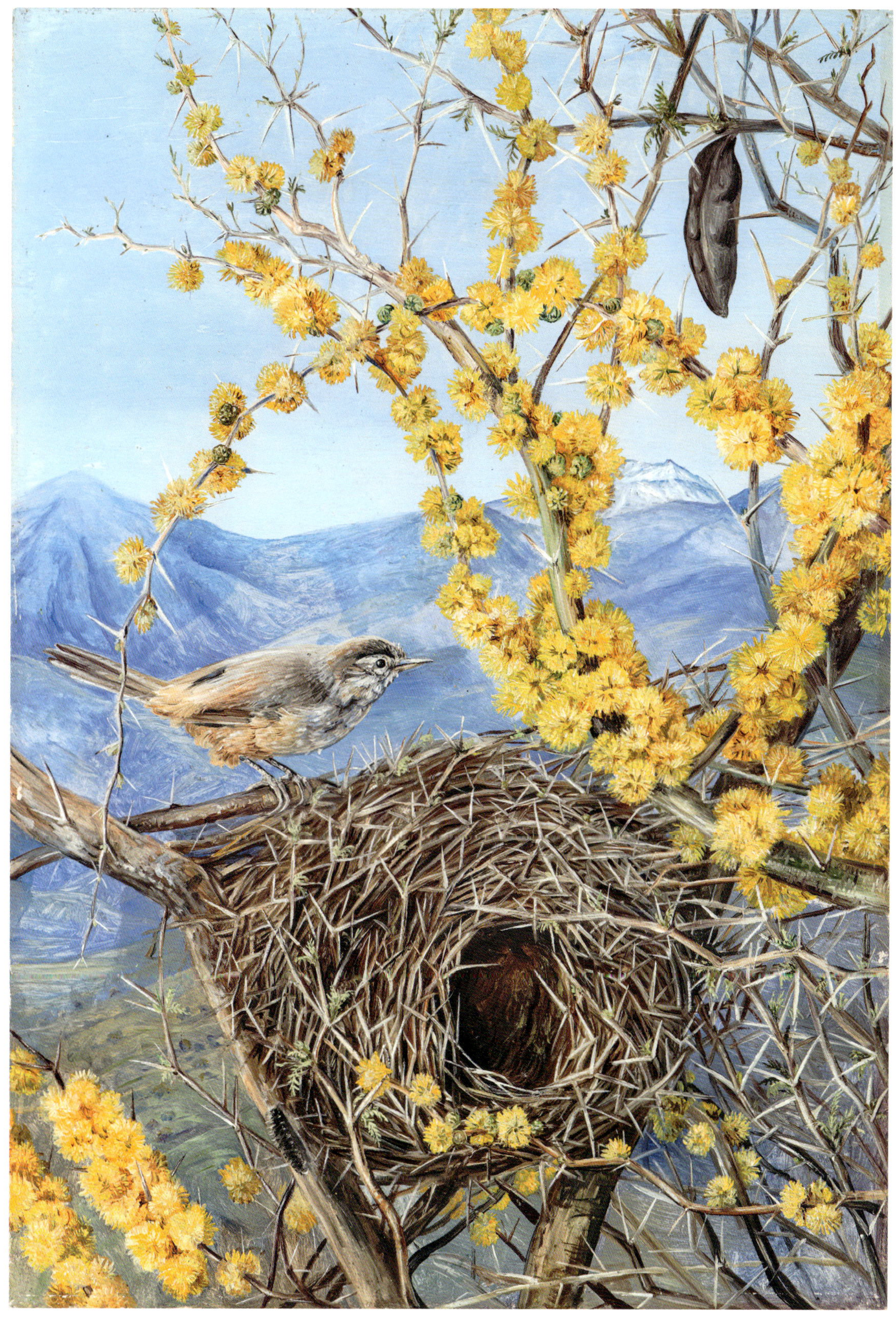

13 Marianne North, 015, *Armed Bird's Nest in Acacia Bush, Chili*, oil on board, 51 × 35 cm, Royal Botanic Gardens, Kew.

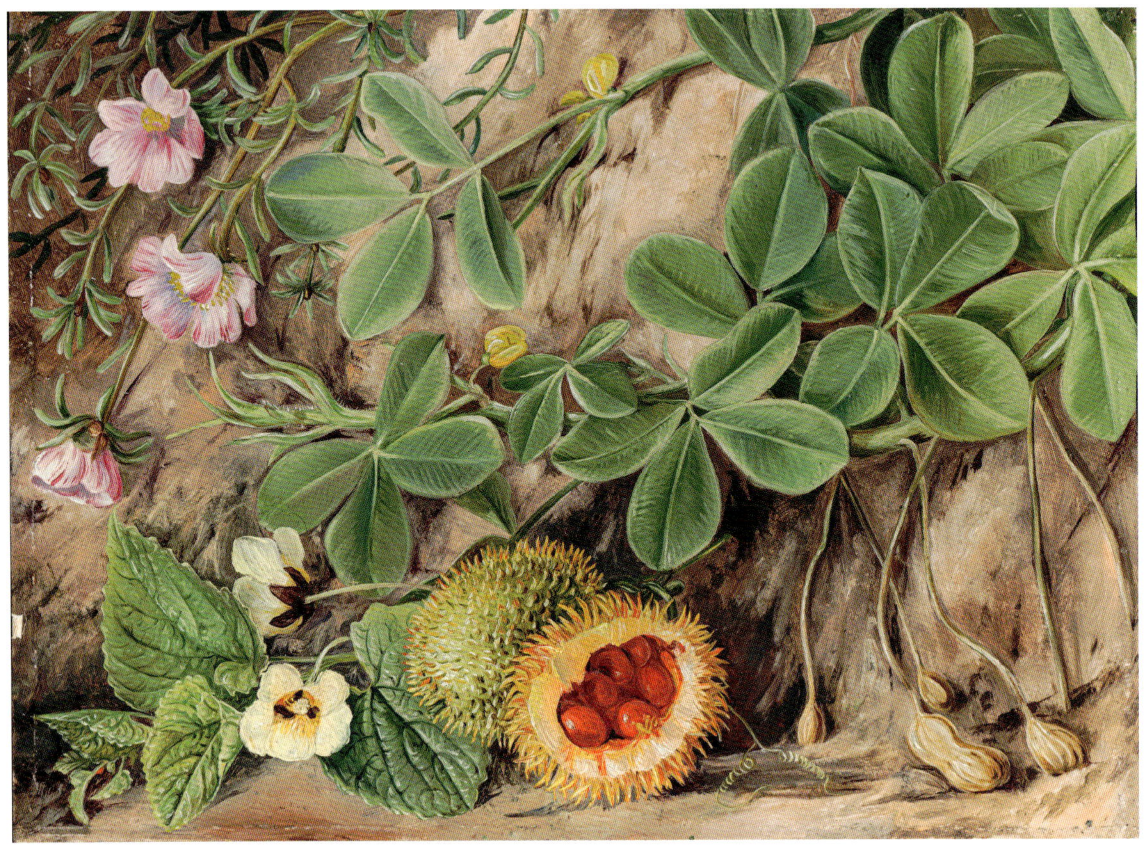

14 Marianne North, 440, *Earth-Nut and a Prickly Gourd, St John's Kaffraria*, oil on board, 25.4 × 35.4 cm, Royal Botanic Gardens, Kew.

North's paintings were also arguably 'informed by visits to view the art treasures of Florence and Rome.'[65]

Back in London, North became reacquainted with Edward Lear, who visited the Norths at Christmas while Frederick was sick in bed suffering with congestion of the lung.[66] In 1867, Frederick decided to move with North back to Hastings, away from the polluted air of London. North writes that once there Frederick saw to the construction of 'three glass-houses: one for orchids, another for temperate plants, and another quite cool for vines',[67] most likely influenced by visits to the glasshouses at Kew Gardens. The following year, Frederick was accused of bribery, but vehemently denied it, as did North.[68]

By 1869 Frederick's health had declined once again, perhaps in part because of the bribery accusations, and so travelled with North to the spa town of Gastein, south of Salzburg in Austria. On arriving, Frederick grew stronger for a time, and, according to North, after two weeks 'planned walking over the hills to Heiligenblut – eighteen hours!' The pair 'went up an Alp 3000 feet above Gastein', with Frederick feeling so well that 'he went up another hill the next day [. . .] but it was too much; his old disease returned'. Frederick was advised by a doctor to return to England, and died on 29 October 1869, three days after arriving in Hastings.[69] North recalls that

> The last words in his mouth were, 'come and give me a kiss, Pop, I am only going to sleep'. He never woke again, and left me alone. I wished to be so; I could not

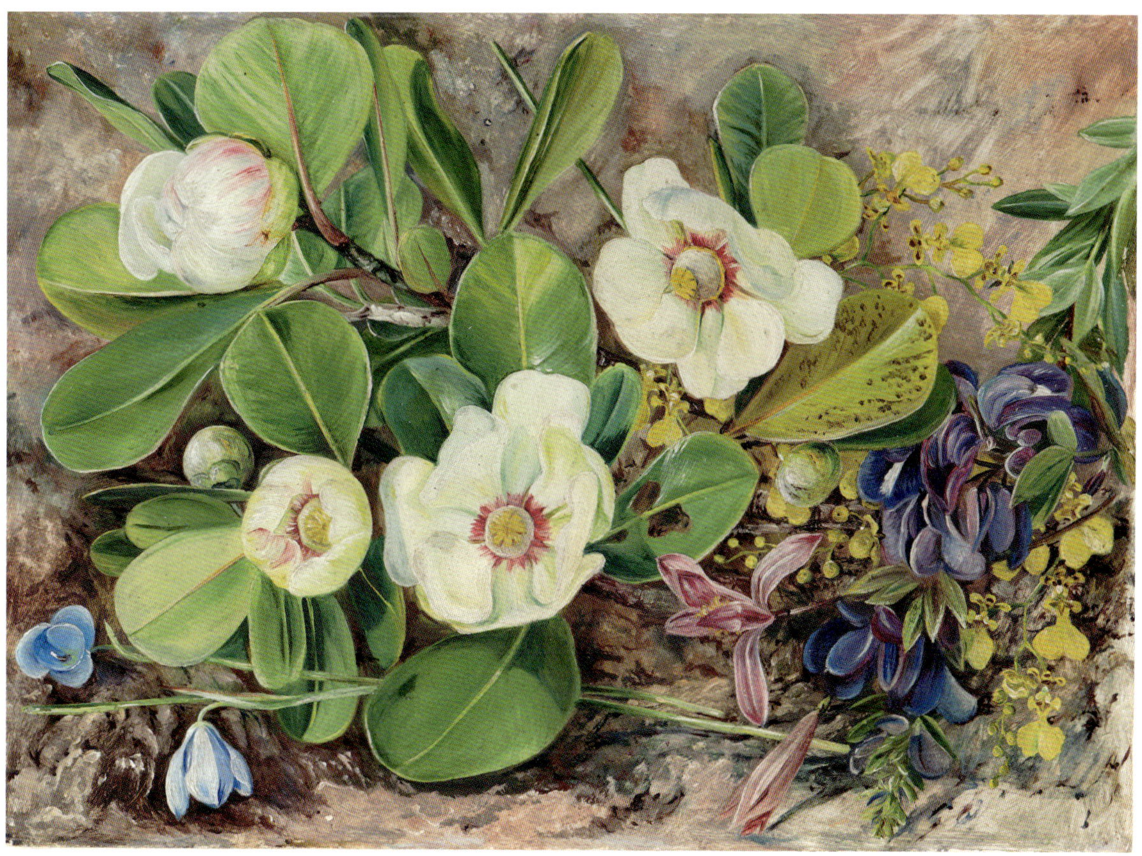

15 Marianne North, 057, *Wild Flowers of Brazil*, oil on board, 25 × 35 cm, Royal Botanic Gardens, Kew.

> bear to talk of him or of anything else, and resolved to keep out of the way of all friends and relations till I had schooled myself into that cheerfulness which makes life pleasant to those around us.[70]

After Frederick's death, North left the house at Hastings 'for ever, and my affairs in the hands of our kind friend Mr. Hunt of Lewes'.[71] North writes that 'For nearly forty years he [Frederick] had been my one friend and companion and now I had to learn to live without him, and to fill my life with other interests as I best might', adding, 'As soon as the household at Hastings was broken up, I went straight to Mentone to devote myself to painting from nature, and try to learn from the lovely world which surrounded me there how to make that work hence-forth the master of my life.'[72] North left England with the family servant, Elizabeth, for Mentone and the Sicilian Riviera, later returning to the Victoria Street apartment in London.[73] North inherited a significant sum of money from Frederick which, together with the family's social connections, assured continuing financial independence and the opportunity to travel and develop a career as a botanical and landscape artist. Without this inheritance North may well have remained an obscure figure. On 12 July 1871, North embarked on a major trip, first to Canada and the United States and then on to South America, asking Charles Kingsley and others to provide letters of introduction to people in Brazil and the West Indies.[74]

2

Social, Scientific and Artistic Connections

Society in 19th-century Britain was for the most part both rigidly hierarchical and patriarchal. Movement between social classes was restricted by expectations of marriage between individuals of comparable status in terms of their wealth and/or existing positions in society. At the same time, women of all classes were expected to marry and to be subordinate to men. Marianne North's behaviour and attitudes in this respect were complex and contradictory. North conformed in many ways to the established mores of leisured upper-middle-class life in Britain during the 19th century but never married. After the death of Frederick, North was financially independent and able to live and travel freely – an unusual combination for a woman in Victorian Britain. North's niece Margaret Addington Symonds 'thought that many people must have wished to marry her' but that North had rejected several suitors, among them one who was asked 'to leave the room and then shut the door behind him'.[1]

North's life up to the death of Frederick was lived before the passing into English law of the reforming Married Women's Property Act (1870), which gave women the legal right to their own earnings and to inherit property. Prior to the Act, men took over ownership of their wife's assets on marriage. Financially, North had little incentive to marry, and after Frederick's death was well past the usual age in Victorian Britain for doing so. While unusual, it was not entirely unheard of in Victorian society to live as a financially independent single woman. North was friendly with notable independent women who never married, such as the English Egyptologist, traveller and author Amelia B. Edwards (1831–92). North met Edwards while travelling shortly after Frederick's death, and remarked that Edwards's 'bright companionship and varied interests did me the world of good', describing the author as being able to write 'without fear of interruption' in a 'luxurious library'.[2]

North was highly affectionate towards Dr Arthur Coke Burnell (1840–82), a British civil servant in Madras, India, as well as a scholar of Dravidian languages (the four major languages of south Indian culture: Telugu, Tamil, Kannada and Malayalam) and Sanskrit. Through Edward Lear, North was commissioned to illustrate what would eventually be an unpublished book by Burnell on Hindu sacred plants (figs 16 and 17). While travelling

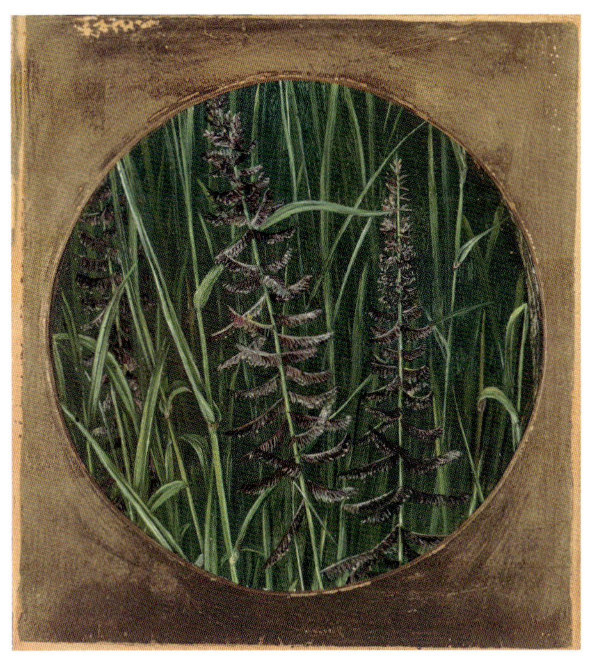

16 Marianne North, 320, *A Sacred Grass*, oil on board, 30.1 × 27.3 cm, Royal Botanic Gardens, Kew.

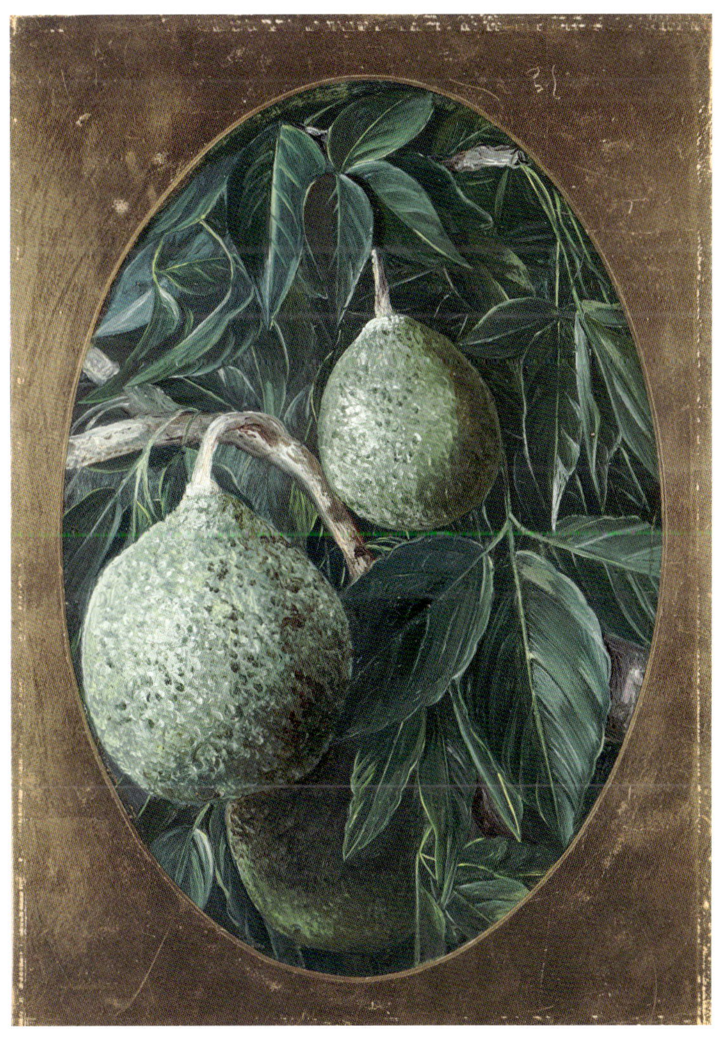

17 Marianne North, 299, *The Bael Fruit*, oil on board, 36.9 × 26.3 cm, Royal Botanic Gardens, Kew.

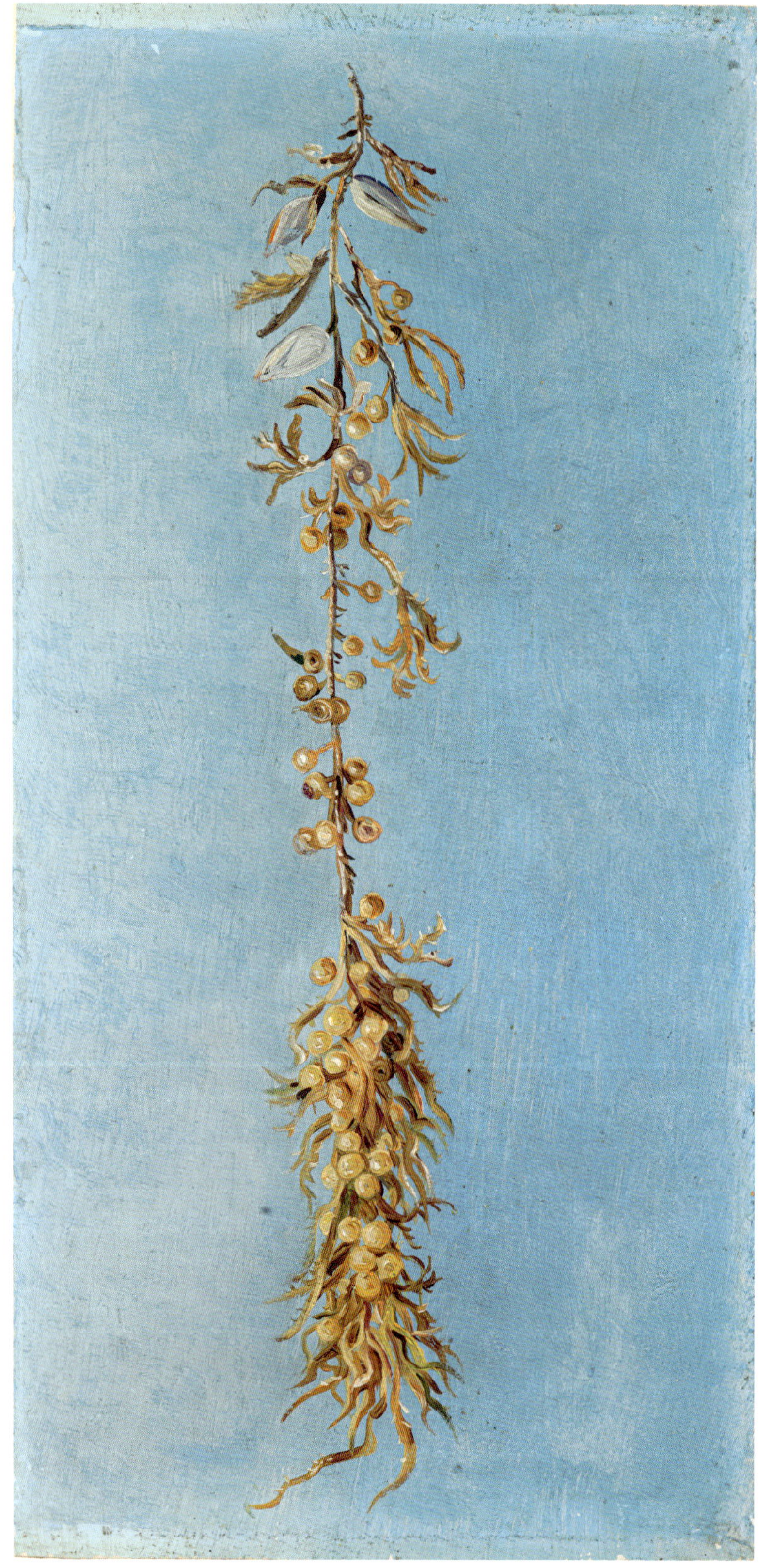

18 Marianne North, 163, *Study of Gulf Weed*, oil on board, 26 × 12 cm, Royal Botanic Gardens, Kew.

in India in 1878, North writes to Burnell, 'I have found no one yet in India who talks as you do & seldom meet anyone who takes interest in anything here', remarking further, 'when you are on the move, can't you get a new photograph done of yourself I want one very much as you really are, with long hair below your ears & deep sunken eyes no beauty, but something different from others.'[3] Letters to Burnell also give indications of North's views on marriage:

> Never fear, you will fall a victim to some clever mother-in-law in time! And be tied to a croquet-badminton young person in high heeled boots and no end of nervous gentility – it is a terrible experiment matrimony for a man especially, as a woman is something like your cat and gets to like the person who feeds her and the house she lives in – but men if they have brains have a romantic idea of companionship in their wife and then discover they have no two ideas in common – after the first prettiness [*sic*] have lost their charm – I pity you in advance when that stage comes! And I pity the poor wife too when she finds herself snubbed, and only a sort of upper servant to be scolded if the pickles are not right – and then she will have to amuse herself by flirting with the most brainless of the male croquet-badmingtons [*sic*] – and then you will lock yourself up and sulk and think it isn't your fault, and wish yourself free again.[4]

North adds, 'you must not think because I abuse womankind of the C B [croquet and badminton] family I do not love many others. I have rare friends in England but nearly all married – so you need not fear my designs on your freedom.'[5]

North lived at a time of precipitous social, cultural, political and scientific change and was aware of the radical movements of the 19th century, including feminism, revolutionary socialism and anti-creationist science. North did not identify explicitly as a feminist nor as a radical social reformer, but was connected, either directly or by one or two degrees of separation, to some of the most prominent forward-thinking figures of the 19th century. North's brother-in-law, John Addington Symonds, describes the artist as 'good humoured' and 'a little satirical', but also as 'bored and irritated by conventional "society people"'; longing 'for stimulating conversation with intelligent and interesting scholars or Bohemians.'[6] North was immersed in an upper-middle-class Victorian society that was concerned with and constantly debated radical ideas,[7] although the extent to which the artist was influenced by the radical movements of the 19th century is unclear.

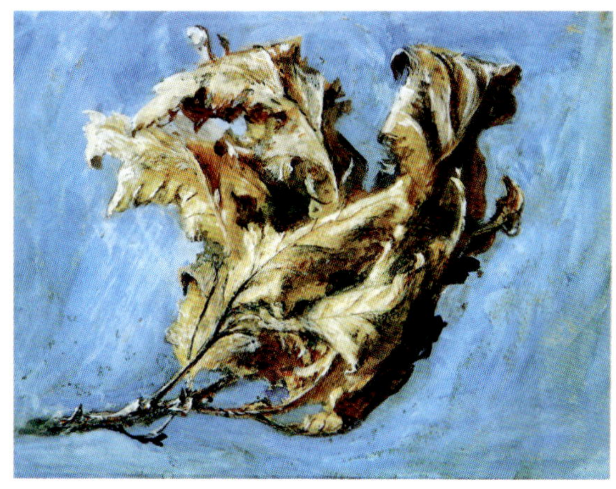

19 John Ruskin, *Spray of Dead Leaves*, also known as *Fast Sketch of Withered Oak*, 1879, watercolour and body colour on paper, mount 29.5 × 41.8 cm, support 14.4 × 18.8 cm, Collection of the Guild of St George, Sheffield Museums Trust.

One of North's closest long-term friends was the social reformer, pamphleteer, journalist, co-founder of Girton College, prolific traveller and flower painter Barbara Leigh Smith Bodichon, who had been taught by William Henry Hunt. Leigh Smith Bodichon was the first cousin of the English health reformer Florence Nightingale (1820–1910), and a close friend to the English writer George Eliot (Mary Ann Evans; 1819–80).[8] Leigh Smith Bodichon was also associated with members of the Pre-Raphaelite Brotherhood and their circle, including the painter, spiritualist and feminist Anna Mary Howitt (1824–84), whose history painting of Boudica (d.*c.*60–61) – the woman leader of a rebellion against Roman rule in Britain during the mid-1st century CE – included Leigh Smith Bodichon as a model. John Ruskin was publicly critical of Howitt's painting and wrote privately to ask 'What do you know about Boadicea [*sic*]? Leave such subjects alone and paint a pheasant's wing.'[9] Despite this, Ruskin's paintings and ideas influenced the work of several Victorian women artists.[10] North's painting 163, *Study of Gulf Weed* (fig.18), with its depiction of the plant against a plain bright blue background, is compositionally like Ruskin's painting *Spray of Dead Leaves* or *Fast Sketch of Withered Oak* (1879; fig.19).

The Pre-Raphaelite Brotherhood was founded in London in 1848. Its members, who included the artists Dante Gabriel Rossetti (1828–82), William Holman Hunt (1827–1910), John Everett Millais (1829–96) and James Collinson (1825–81), as well as the art critic Frederic George Stephens (1827–1907), were opposed to the prevailing artistic conventions of mid-19th-century Victorian Britain, in addition to the teaching methods of the Royal Academy of Arts, London, which favoured the style and techniques of European academic painting from the time of the Italian Renaissance painter Raphael (Raffaello Sanzio da Urbino; 1483–1520) onwards. The Pre-Raphaelite Brotherhood used painterly techniques involving the application of bright colours over a white ground – an approach later adopted by European Impressionists – in contrast to the building up of deep contrasts between light and dark paint over a toned ground characteristic of academic painting. This was coupled with painting directly onto canvas in front of the subject without extensive use of preparatory sketches and studies.[11] Members of the Pre-Raphaelite Brotherhood also adopted an exhaustive approach to the representation of nature, whereby 'No detail [was] too trivial to be recorded'[12] – as exemplified by Millais's painting *Ophelia* (1851–2).

The Pre-Raphaelite Brotherhood had a significant impact on European, American, Russian, Australian and Japanese painting throughout the latter half of the 19th century, before its work became unfashionable among cultural elites during the early 20th century, in the face of European and American avant-garde modernism.[13] Artists associated with Pre-Raphaelitism would go on to develop a scientific approach towards representation. Scientists in turn looked to Pre-Raphaelitism as a model way of communicating ideas about nature and science. North adopted the Pre-Raphaelite Brotherhood's technique of painting directly onto canvas in front of the subject and using bright colours over a white ground, and also drew directly upon similar techniques to those used by William Henry Hunt. Sheffield writes that North 'sought not only the challenge of painting out-of-doors, which in itself was full of pitfalls and difficulties' but also 'set herself tasks which challenged her artistic ability'.[14] The Pre-Raphaelite Brotherhood's painstaking attention to detail and building up of saturated colour coincides with that of 19th-century flower and botanical painting more generally (fig.20).

In a letter to Burnell, North writes of hosting a dinner party that included the Holman Hunts as guests.[15] North befriended a cousin of Millais while painting in Sarawak, referred to only as 'Mr. E.', whose own 'sketches and illustrations of [. . .] different adventures in pen and ink were most excellent'.[16] In another letter to Burnell, North refers to Julia Jackson, an associate of the Pre-Raphaelite movement, stating, 'she was the great Pre-Raphaelite ideal [. . .] and is a very beautiful creature'.[17] North was a friend of the British photographer, and aunt to Julia Jackson, Julia Margaret Cameron (1815–79). Cameron appears to have started taking photographs as early as 1839, assembling albums of prints and presenting them to family members before 1864.[18] Cameron developed a 'distinctive idiom in dialogue with Rossetti's work', often using 'a single female sitter'.[19] Holman Hunt 'led the Pre-Raphaelite revolution in depicting effects of light in nature, and [. . .] introduced the practice of painting in the open from the motif like a camera'.[20] The invention of photography was testing to Victorian aesthetic sensibilities, not least those of the Pre-Raphaelite

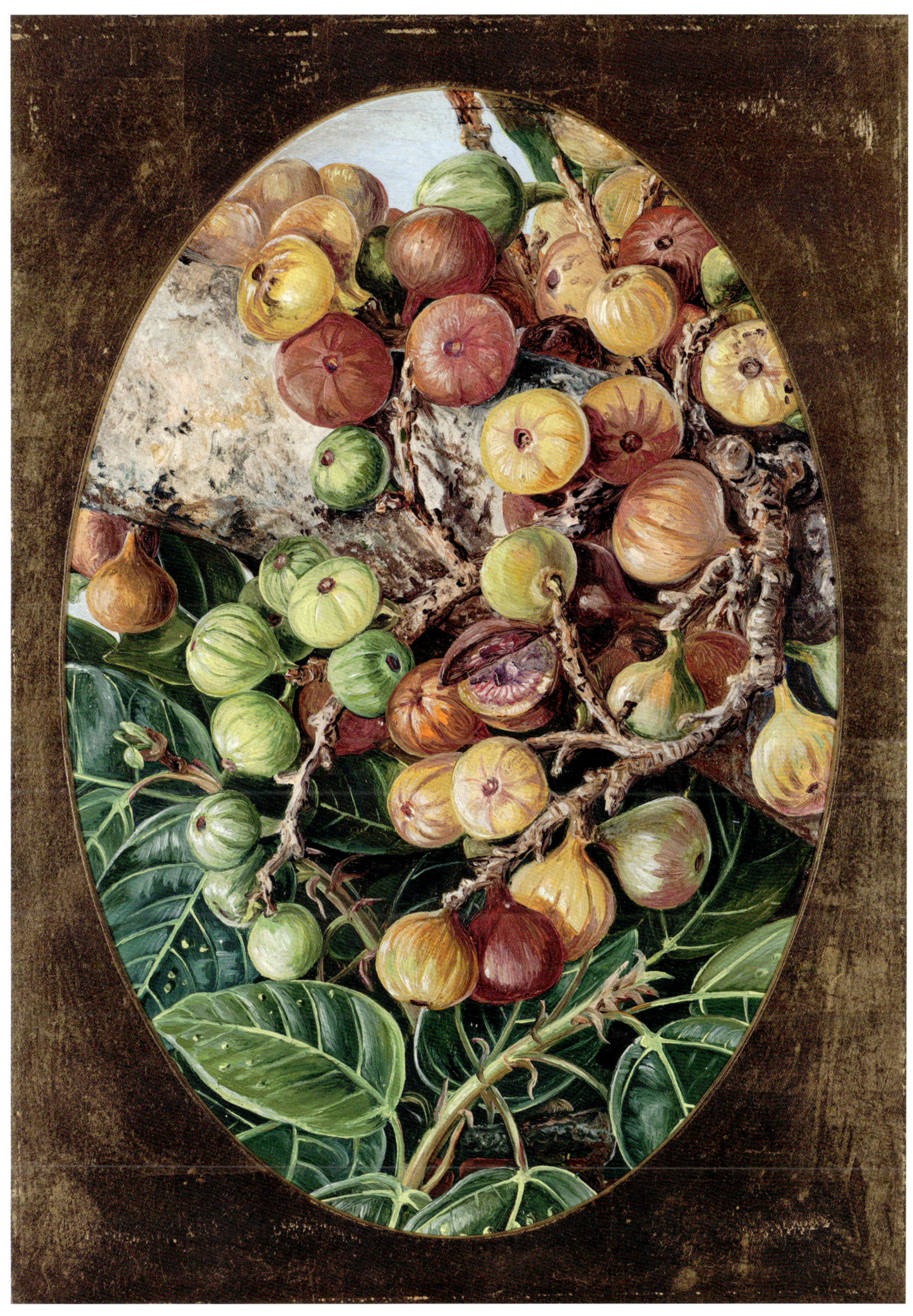

20 Marianne North, 306, *Foliage and Fruit of Fig Tree held Sacred by the Hindoos*, oil on board, 37 × 27.1 cm, Royal Botanic Gardens, Kew.

Brotherhood, provoking debates about the necessary individual characteristics of photographs and paintings.[21] Writing in *The New Path* (1863), the American journalist, diplomat and photographer William James Stillman (1828–1901) states that with the invention of photography the 'direct copying of nature could not be carried further' since 'every irregular split and crack and broken surface [...] [can be] given with faultless mirror-like accuracy'.[22]

The Aesthetic movement in England was made up chiefly of a small, loosely associated group of poets, thinkers, craftspeople and artists living in the Holland Park and Chelsea areas of London. As the art historian Stephen Calloway indicates, the aesthetic movement was, like the Pre-Raphaelite Brotherhood, united in its 'opposition to prevailing orthodoxies concerning art and design' but did not have 'any comfortably shared vision or precise definition of the beautiful'.[23] One of the key artists associated with the aesthetic movement is the English painter Frederic Leighton (1830–96), whose studio house is still situated with its original interior largely intact at Holland Park Road, London. Leighton's house, which was designed by the architect George Aitchison (1825–1910), incorporates a picture gallery and a painting studio, as well as spaces for everyday living. Receiving areas on the ground floor are decorated with tiles from the Islamic Near East in keeping with fashionable orientalising stylings of the late 19th century. The construction of the house was completed in 1866, with fresh decorative schemes added until Leighton's death.[24] The exterior of the house is plain brick. Leighton held Sunday salons where callers 'had the freedom to explore the interiors and collections'.[25] Leighton's house, along with the painter Frederic Edwin Church's (1826–1900) similarly decorated house, Olana, may have influenced the design of the North Gallery at Kew. Julia Margaret Cameron was another Holland Park-based associate of the aesthetic movement, as was the poet Charles Algernon Swinburne (1837–1909).[26] Swinburne was a friend of Lear and an admirer of North's paintings.[27]

After the publication of Darwin's *On the Origin of Species*, the Pre-Raphaelite movement became divided between Darwinians and those of more conventional religious beliefs.[28] North appears not to have been concerned with the difficulties posed to conventional religiosity by Darwin's theories, unlike Holman Hunt and Ruskin who 'held firmly by their belief in natural theology'.[29] Swinburne was a fellow of the Anthropological Society of London and inclined towards science rather than creationism.[30] As the art historian John Holmes indicates, Swinburne's nature poems, 'though actively enchanting, are not personifications that intimate that flowers or rivers have purposes or feelings'.[31]

North knew Charles Darwin and may have been part of the worldwide network of individuals who collected data in support of the naturalist's research. In correspondence with Burnell, North writes about an expedition to 'Narkunda' (Narkanda, a high-altitude part of the Shimla district in the Indian state of Himachal Pradesh) in search of botanical subjects to paint. North refers to specific plants including several unnamed varieties, adding, 'the seeds ripen then leaves grow up and hide them from the eyes of the hungry birds (fact for Darwin!)'.[32] In further correspondence with Burnell, North describes Darwin as 'the greatest man living, the most truthful, as well as the most unselfish and modest always trying to give others rather than himself the credit of his own great thoughts and work'.[33] In a letter to North, Darwin writes, 'I am glad that I have seen your Australian pictures, and it was extremely kind of you to bring them here', continuing in the same letter, 'I am often able to call up with considerable vividness scenes in various countries which I have seen [but they] must be a mere barren waste compared with your mind'.[34] Darwin had previously advised North to visit Australia, emphasising that one 'ought not to attempt any representation of the vegetation of the world' until after visiting the continent, since its plant life was 'unlike that of any other country'.[35] North describes a visit to see Darwin towards the end of the scientist's life, writing, 'We sat on the grass under a shady tree, and talked deliciously on every subject [...] for hours', including the paintings North had made in Australia.[36]

Correspondence between North and Darwin extends to detailed scientific discussion. In the letter praising North's Australian paintings Darwin makes specific reference to the plant '*Raoulia eximia*, a native of the middle Island of New Zealand, and allied to the *Gnaphaliums*', adding that it might be of the 'genus Porites'.[37]

North also knew the British naturalist Alfred Russel Wallace (1823–1913), who developed a version of evolutionary theory in parallel to Darwin's. The uniformitarian geologist Charles Lyell and biologist Joseph Dalton Hooker (1817–1911) arranged for Wallace and Darwin to present their thoughts on evolution at a specially arranged meeting of the Linnean Society in London in 1858. Darwin agreed to speak after the publication of Wallace's article 'On the Law which has Regulated the Introduction of New Species' (1855). Darwin had been reluctant to publish, but did so at length, and in greater scientific detail than Wallace, in *On the Origin of Species* a year after the meeting at the Linnean Society.[38] North invited Wallace to the opening of the North Gallery at Kew. Wallace, who admired North's paintings of South Africa, responded by apologising for not being able to attend the event because of a prior engagement outside London.[39]

Darwin's theory of evolution presented a radical challenge to religious notions of an unchanging, divinely created nature by identifying inheritable variations of biological traits among animal and plant populations, and how some of these biological variants are better adapted to survival and reproduction under local conditions, leading some species to survive through such natural selection while others go extinct. Many within Britain's scientific community disagreed, including the botanist and director of Kew Gardens, Joseph Hooker, who despite being a friend of Darwin's was reluctant to accept the full, anti-creationist, implications of the theory, upholding instead the opinion of established natural theology that species were 'definite creations' and seeing variation within species as a part of a divinely inspired natural order.[40] North appears to have had a more Darwinian way of thinking than Hooker and was certainly sceptical of established religion, often avoiding attendance at church services. Like Darwin, North may have had leanings towards atheism.[41]

While travelling during the 1870s and 1880s, North received assistance from local British authorities and expatriates as well as others in finding transport and accommodation, and in making useful social connections.[42] In 1871, the artist visited the United States for the first time and was introduced to many prominent politicians, scientists and artists there. North received a letter of introduction to visit the then President of the United States, Ulysses S. Grant (1822–85), at the White House. During the visit, the First Lady, Julia Boggs Grant (1826–1902), 'hunted up a German book full of dried grasses' to show to North.[43] While in the United States, North was befriended by the Swiss-American biologist and geologist Louis Agassiz (1807–73) who had procured a grant from the Prussian government in 1846 to explore America with the support of the eminent German scientist and early ecologist Alexander von Humboldt (1769–1859). The British geologist Charles Lyell secured Agassiz a position at the Lowell Institute in Boston, where Agassiz gave a series of lectures.[44] Agassiz was a member of the Saturday Club, an informal monthly gathering established in Boston in 1855 by 11 men whose interests spanned poetry, scholarship, science, art, law, medicine, business and good citizenship.[45]

The scholar, poet and abolitionist Ralph Waldo Emerson (1803–82) was also a member of the Saturday Club. Emerson was a noted exponent of Transcendentalism, arguably the first significant intellectual movement developed by a European American. Transcendentalism held two seemingly contradictory views: first, a belief, distilled from English and German Romanticism, in personal freedom and self-expression outside the control of established society and its institutions – such as organised religion and politics – as a force for progressive change; and second, that every individual is both an index of and has partial insights into a unifying being or 'over soul' present

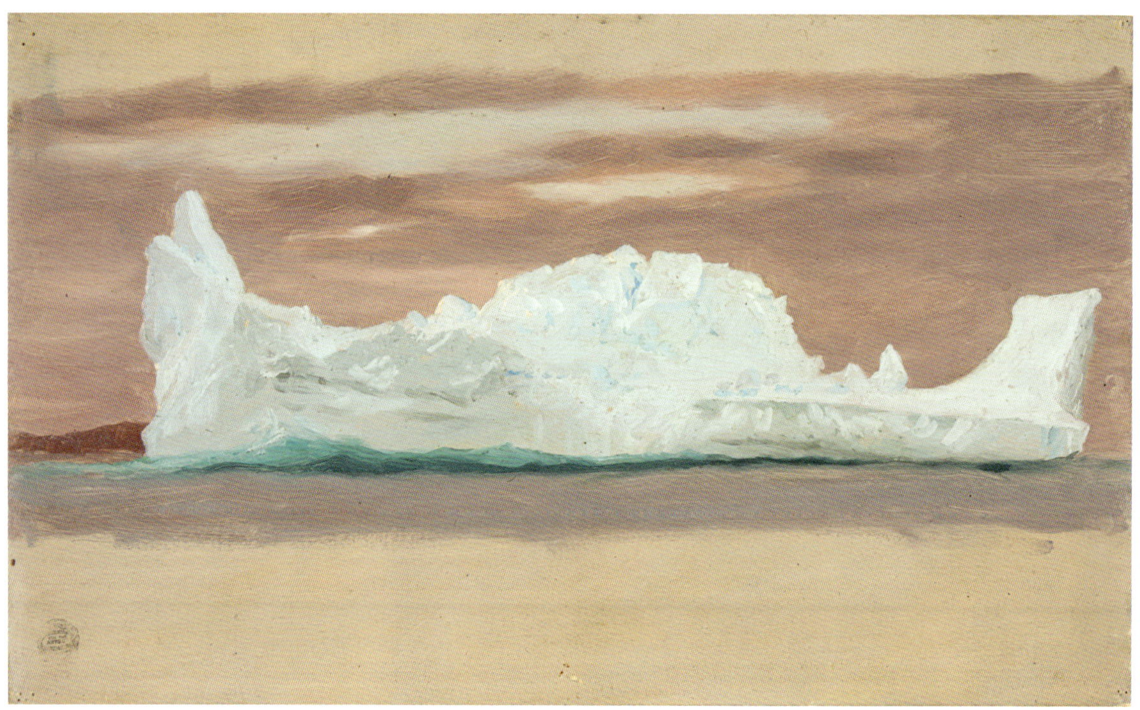

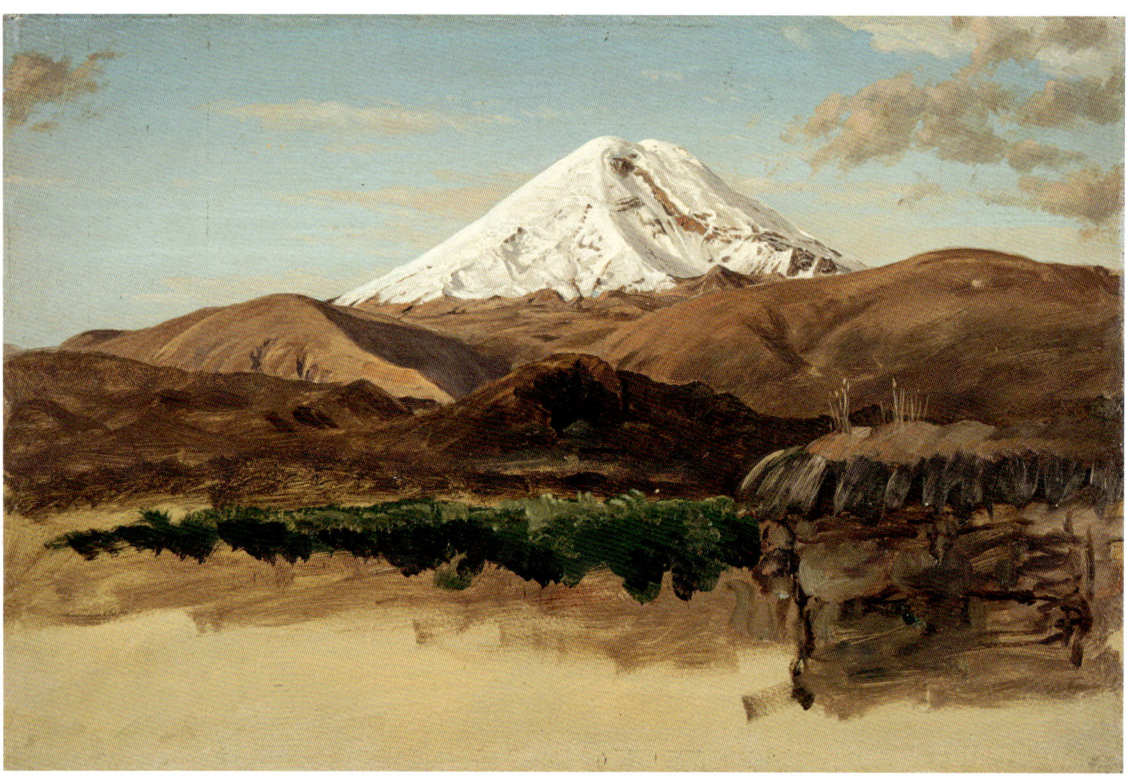

21 (top) Frederic Edwin Church, *Floating Iceberg under Cloudy Skies, Newfoundland*, July 1859, brush and oil paint, graphite on cardboard, 30.4 × 50.9 cm, Cooper Hewitt, Smithsonian Design Museum.

22 (below) Frederic Edwin Church, *Mount Chimborazo*, 1857, brush and oil paint, traces of graphite on paperboard, 34.2 × 52.2 cm, Cooper Hewitt, Smithsonian Design Museum.

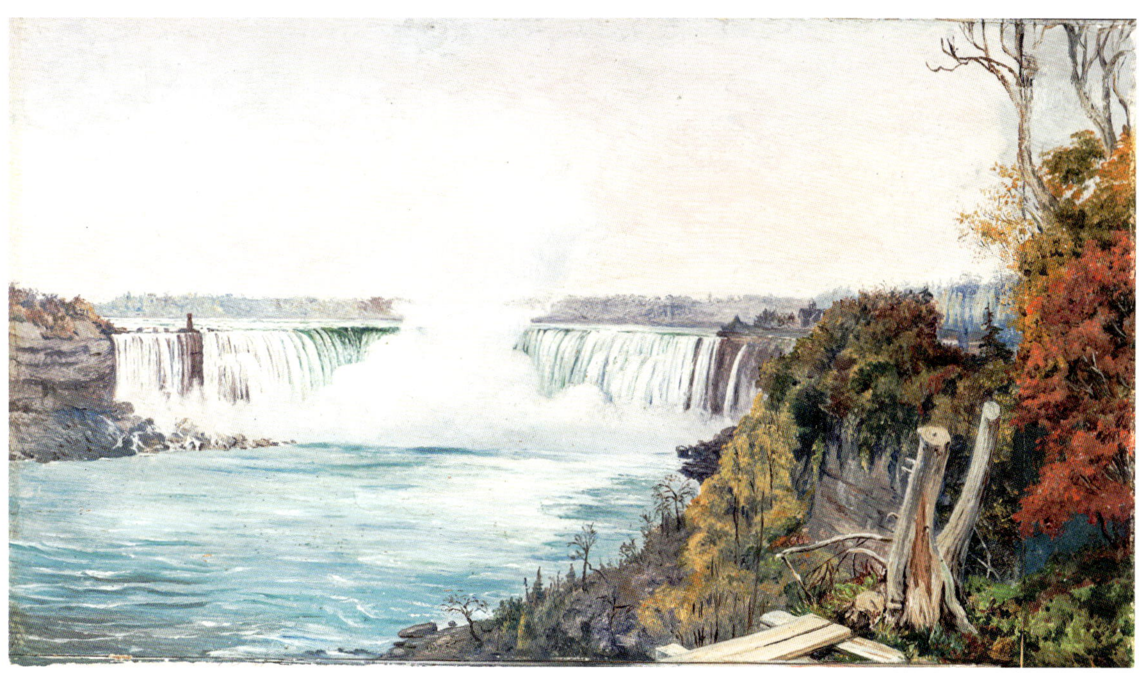

23 Marianne North, 187, *View of Both Falls of Niagara*, oil on board, 28 × 49 cm, Royal Botanic Gardens, Kew.

in all things. In Emerson's view, community can only be achieved through the insights and actions of truly self-reliant individuals. American Transcendentalism maintained a deep reverence for nature and desire to preserve the natural world in its pristine state against purely material progress. Nature was conceived of as a place of heightened aesthetic experience in which individual insights into a transcendent divinity could be intuitively glimpsed. Such thinking echoes that of Thomas Carlyle, Charles Kingsley and John Ruskin in Britain. Transcendentalism was formative on a specifically American cultural outlook, not least in relation to the arts.

During the mid- to late 19th century, Transcendentalist ideas were espoused by artists belonging to the Hudson River School of painters and the related artistic movement known as Luminism. The Hudson River School was the United States' first home-grown art movement. The English-born painter Thomas Cole (1801–48) initiated the school with a series of landscape paintings of the Hudson River Valley and surrounding locations, completed after an expedition along the river and into the Catskill Mountains in 1825. Cole's paintings of the Hudson River Valley, which were strongly influenced by the work of the French neoclassical painter Claude Lorrain and the English Romantic painter J.M.W. Turner,[46] depict the American landscape as both sublimely vast and pristine. Other prominent members of the school were Cole's friend Asher Brown Durand (1796–1886), Frederic Church and John Frederick Kensett (1816–72). Women painters linked to the Hudson River School include Susie M. Barstow (1836–1923) and Julie Hart Beers (1835–1918). In June 1859, Church accompanied Agassiz on an expedition to Newfoundland and Southern Labrador, making sketches there for paintings of icebergs (fig.21).[47] Church's enormous panoramic paintings of the American landscape, among them depictions of Niagara Falls and the icy seas off the United States' north-eastern coast, drew huge paying crowds during the mid-19th century. Landscape paintings associated with the Luminist movement are characterised by their modest scale, atmospheric stillness and subtle, often crepuscular, lighting effects – traits influenced by Dutch landscape painting of the 17th century.[48] Some artists of the Hudson River School, such as Church and Kensett, also produced paintings in a Luminist style.

Both the Hudson River School and Luminism can be understood to embody the principles of Transcendentalism through their expressive depictions of natural wilderness and symbolic representations of America as a new Eden away from Europe. As the art historian Barbara Novak indicates, American artists of the 19th century projected 'religious, moral, philosophical and social ideas [...] [onto] the American landscape', thereby developing a nationalistic iconography that placed the 'face of God in the landscape'.[49] The landscape artist and member of the Hudson River School J.F. Cropsey (1823–1900) writes of the 'axe of civilization' that 'is busy with our old forests' and 'fast seeping away the relics of our national infancy'. Cropsey also comments that

> What were once the wild and picturesque haunts of the Red Man, and where the wild deer roamed in freedom, are becoming the abodes of commerce and the seats of manufactures [...] Yankee enterprise has little sympathy with the picturesque, and it behooves our artists to rescue from its grasp the little that is left before it is too late.[50]

North saw paintings by the Hudson River School at the Johnson Gallery while visiting New York in 1871, describing the gallery as 'a most exquisite collection of pictures. The great Niagara, and a beautiful sunset scene in a swamp by Church were there. The latter is a wonderful picture. The Four ages of life by Coles, and splendid Mullers and Cromes were there too. Every picture was a gem.'[51] North was invited by Church to visit the family farm on the Hudson. At the time, the Churches were living in an old cottage farmhouse while a larger house was being constructed for them nearby. North describes the house, known as Olana, as having been designed by Church,

> after the pattern of a Damascus house, with a court in its middle paved with marble, having a splashing fountain in its centre. He had also had bricks and tiles made of different oriental patterns and ornamented the outside with them, but the floors were not yet laid down. The view from the arched entrance was fine, of the Catskill Mountains [...] and the winding River Hudson.'[52] North likened the Hudson to 'a very mild Rhine minus the castles'[53]

North writes of Church's studio on the Hudson as 'a detached building, with a picture in progress of Chimborazo, which seemed to me perfection in point of truth and workmanship' (fig.22). Church showed North 'other tropical studies which made me more than ever anxious to go and see those countries', describing 'three pictures in oils – one of the Horse-shoe Falls of Niagara, a study of Magnolia flowers, and one of some tropical tree covered with parasites' which were hung in North's tiny bedroom.[54] Church had developed a 'deep interest in botany and horticulture' that found 'lasting expression' in the gardens at Olana.[55] North's landscape and botanical paintings after 1871 owe a clear debt to Church in their attention to naturalistic detail, Luminist-style lighting and evocations of Hudson River-style sublimity (fig.23). North's rugged independence as a woman painter also echoes the Transcendentalist outlook embodied by the Hudson River School. Church's designs for Olana, which echo those for Leighton's house at Holland Park in London, may have influenced the design of the interior of the North Gallery at Kew.

Church was an admirer of the writings of the scientist and traveller Alexander von Humboldt, who wrote numerous scientific and popular books on a myriad of subjects including botany, travel, geographical surveying, plant geography, vulcanology and zoology.[56]

Central to Humboldt's thinking was the idea that the natural world is divided into differing regions, each with its own empirically observable localised climate and geology as well as interrelated species of animals and plants.[57] Humboldt's monumental five-volume work *Cosmos: A Sketch of a Physical Description of the Universe* (1845–62) extends this mapping of the world's natural economy to natural phenomena throughout the universe as well as relationships between the earthly and the cosmic.[58] Humboldt contended that art, and in particular landscape painting, could be used experimentally to express the regional qualities of, and complex interrelationships between, things in nature in addition to their wider place in the universe.[59] In Humboldt's view, panoramic paintings which represent landscapes through widened, sometimes 360°, fields of vision would be most effective in this respect. Like many others in Europe and America during the mid-19th century, Church was hugely impressed by Humboldt's far-reaching vision and produced sketches directly from nature in response. Church writes that sketches directly from nature 'are the only means by which the artist, on his return, may reproduce the character of distant regions in more elaborately finished pictures.'[60] Philosophical ideas on science and art were for many American painters a route to God, and, as Novak indicates, it was 'hoped that art's interpretive capacities would reconcile the contradictions science was forcing on the nineteenth century.'[61]

North, too, was aware of Humboldt, writing during a visit to the Laguna Islands of 'the famous view of the peak, described so exquisitely by Humboldt', and of a hotel garden containing 'The famous Dragon Tree, which Humboldt said was 4000 years old.'[62] Humboldt's ideas may not only have shaped North's practice of painting in situ, but also the laying out of the North Gallery at Kew as a globally panoramic and regionally differentiated representation of nature. Humboldt's writing was certainly formative on Darwin's career and early travels as a biologist.[63] As the historian Iain McCalman indicates, Darwin wanted to match Humboldt's 'rare union of poetry with science', believing that 'the naturalist's task was to discover both the diversity and the underlying unity and harmony of nature. Like a poet, he would work to penetrate the mystery behind the veil of reason, but he would do so in the service of science.'[64]

The Hudson River School and the Luminists were, like the Pre-Raphaelites, divided on Darwin's ideas of evolution. Church was an 'ardent proponent of a creationist protestant universe, a universe that had become threatened by the revolutionary concepts advanced by Charles Darwin and his many followers.'[65] The views of Martin Johnson Heade (1819–1904), a friend of Church and a fellow member of the Hudson River School, on Darwinian evolutionary theory are not known. Heade's paintings nevertheless influenced Darwin's understanding of dynamic evolutionary relationships between animals and their natural surroundings,[66] characteristically combining separate composite studies of flora and/or fauna and landscape settings to produce single, seemingly coherent, images. Many of North's paintings depart from orthodox scientific botanical illustrations of single plants on an otherwise blank background by using a combinatory technique akin to Heade's compositional layout. North's painting 096, *Orchid and Humming Birds, Brazil* (fig.25), for example, is very close in its composition and subject matter to Heade's painting, *Hummingbird and Passionflowers* (*c*.1875–85; fig.24). Other pertinent examples include North's paintings 097, *Foliage and Flowers of a Coral Tree and Double-Crested Humming Bird, Brazil*, and 415, *Honeyflowers and Honeysuckers, South Africa.* The art historian Katherine E. Manthorne comments that Heade and North both made images of 'vegetal chaos'[67] rather than pared-down strictly scientific representations of natural order (fig.26).

North travelled to Australia in 1880, arriving in Brisbane on 8 August. The visit was in response to Darwin's suggestion of painting Australian plants in their natural environment as well as an invitation to meet with the female botanical painter Ellis Rowan

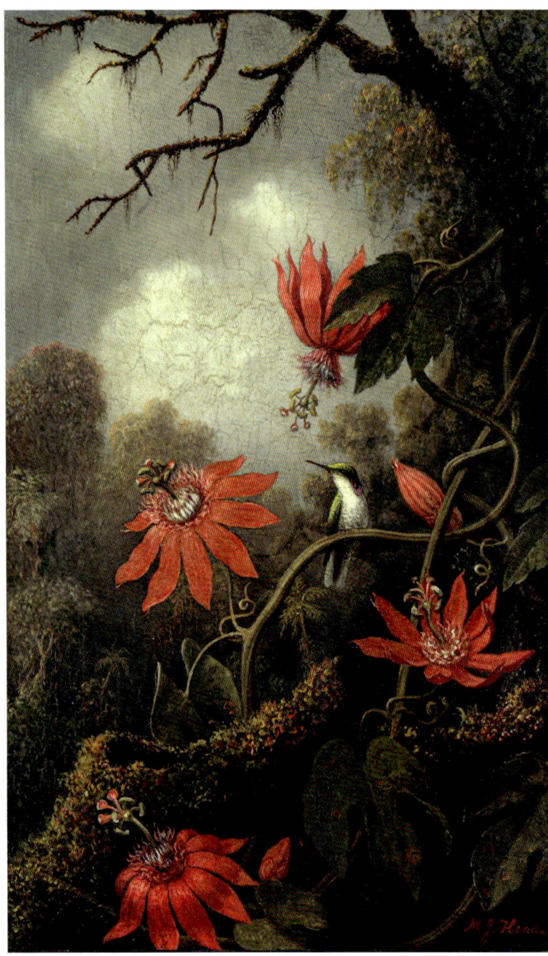

24 Martin Johnson Heade, *Hummingbird and Passionflowers*, *c.*1875–85, oil on canvas, 50.8 × 30.5 cm, The Metropolitan Museum of Art, New York.

(1848–1922), who lived in Albany, Western Australia. North and Rowan met for the first time in England, after which North encouraged botanists at Kew to look at Rowan's paintings. North writes to Kew botanist and entomologist William B. Hemsley (1843–1924) of being fortunate in buying several of Rowan's paintings, 'so you shall have them to show your friends as soon as I have put them into a book', adding, 'I admire them exceedingly.'[68] In a letter to the director of Kew Gardens, Joseph Hooker, North describes Rowan's paintings as 'very beautiful and worth your attention.'[69] Rowan's paintings were, according to North, exquisitely done 'in a peculiar way of her own on gray paper'.[70] In turn, Rowan may have been influenced by North not only in the use of oils on canvas, but also in depicting flowers in their natural settings,[71] as well as the inclusion of Hudson River- and Luminist-style atmospheric lighting. Rowan writes of North, 'I became her devoted admirer and she became the pioneer of my ambition.'[72] Inspired by North, Rowan embarked on a series of painting expeditions outside Australia, and North's visit may also have resulted in Rowan writing about those expeditions as a record for posterity.[73] During the visit to Albany, Rowan introduced North to 'quantities of the most lovely flowers – flowers such as I had never seen or dreamed of before.' North describes Rowan's garden as leading 'right on to the hillside at the back, and the abundance of different species in a small space was quite marvellous.'[74]

Like North's, Rowan's paintings cross the boundary between science and art and are of only limited value to scientific classification. As the art historian Judith McKay indicates, not only do 'they lack critical detail that is necessary and fundamental in so-called "true" botanical illustrations', but also 'artistic licence has been taken [. . .] to produce aesthetically pleasing depictions [. . .] Rather than recording all details of her subjects, background plants and plant associations or landscapes have been rendered anonymous.' McKay also explains that Rowan 'joined parts of different species on the one stem to produce a pleasing arrangement', citing Rowan's painting of 'small tubular flowers [. . .] mounted atop a twig of *Lysiphyllum hookeri*' and another where 'the stem of *Hoya nicolsoniae* has been made to emerge from the stem of *Niemeyera prunifera* [. . .] an entirely unrelated species' (fig.27).[75] McKay concludes that while the scientific value of Rowan's paintings is 'limited', they are nevertheless 'an outstanding historical record of some of Queensland's flora painted by a botanically aware artist in search of the picturesque.'[76] Rowan upheld 'North's dictum that flowers should be recorded on the spot in their native habitats',

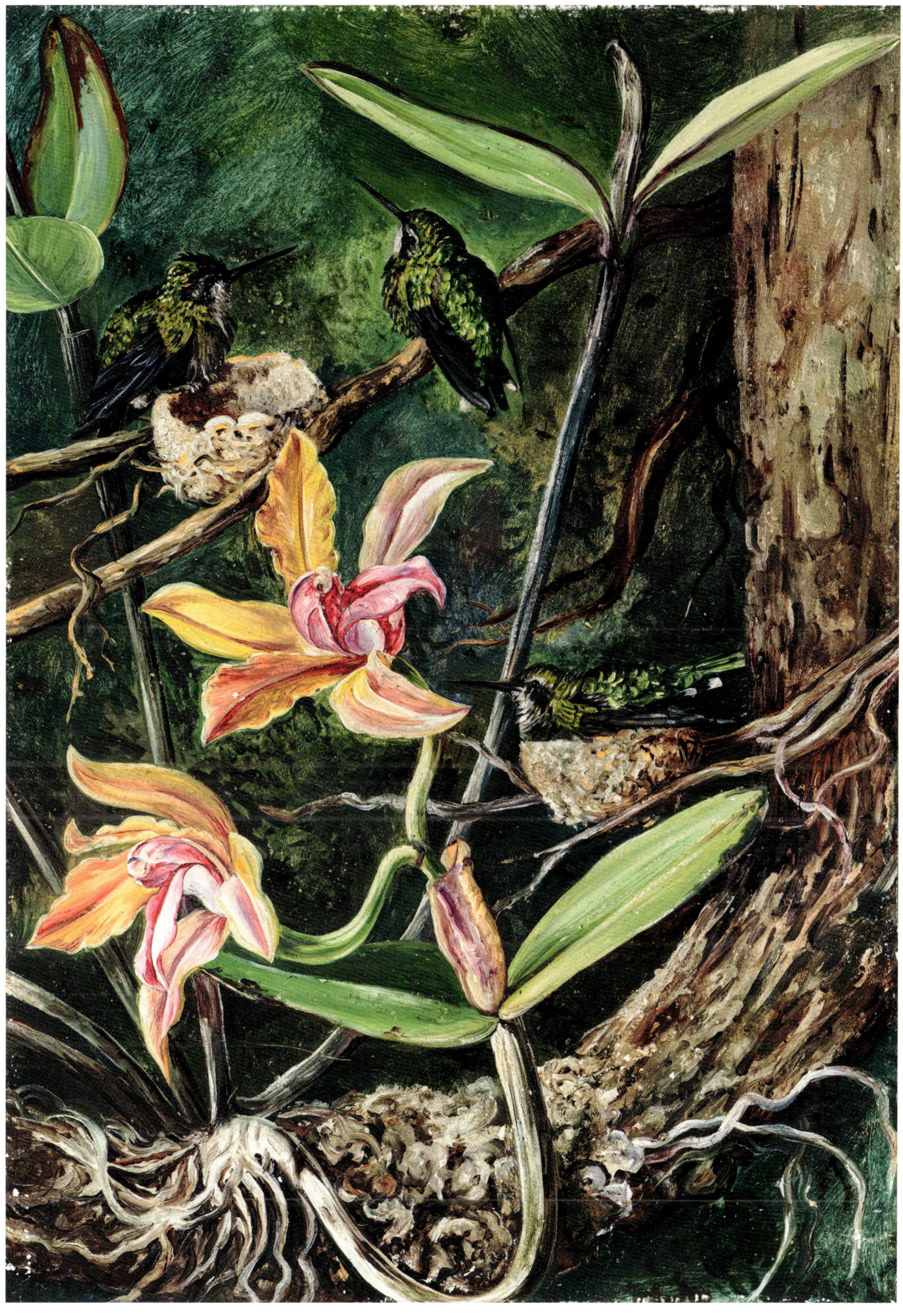

25 Marianne North, 096, *Orchid and Humming Birds, Brazil*, oil on board, 35 × 25 cm, Royal Botanic Gardens, Kew.

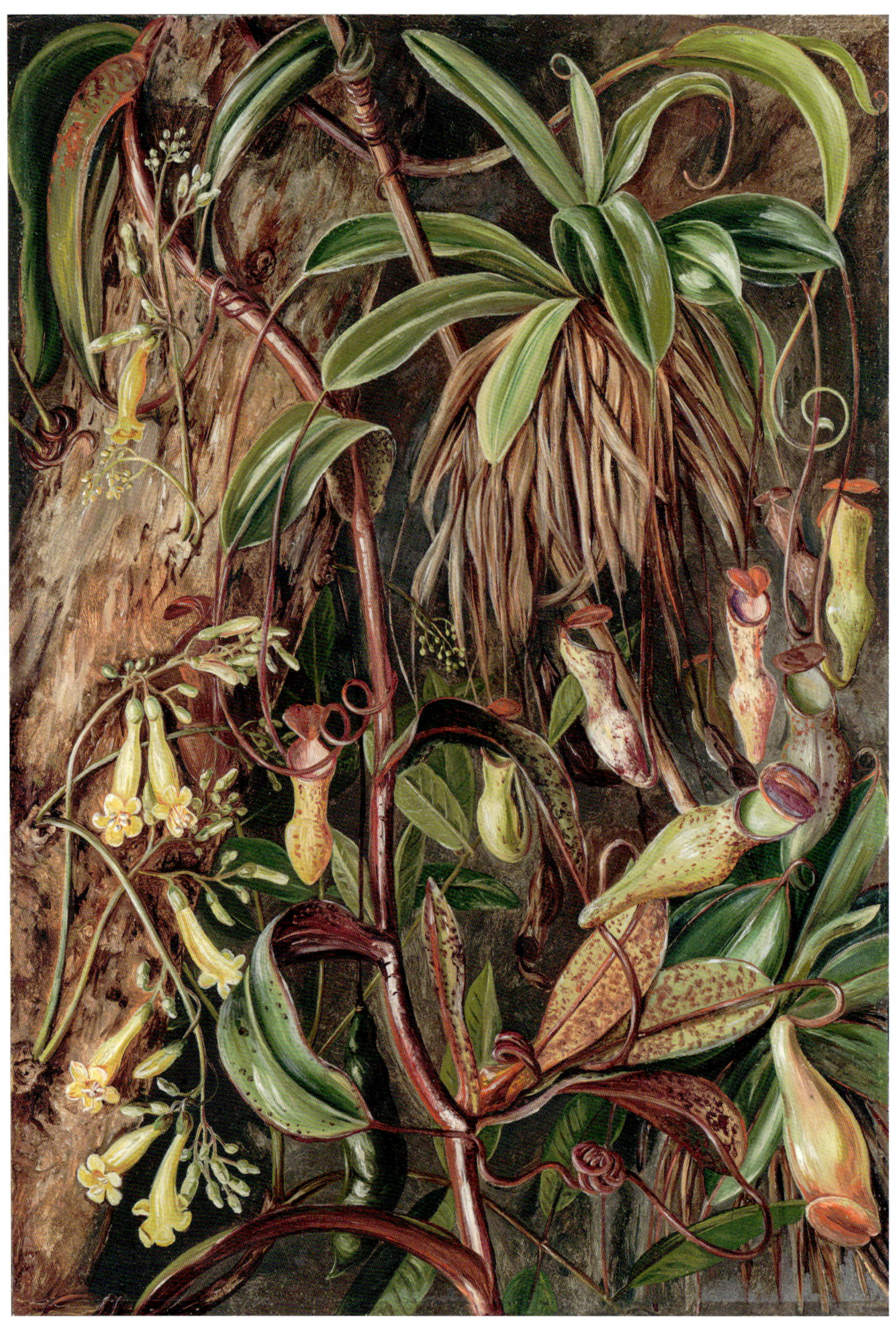

26 Marianne North, 468, *Seychelles Pitcher Plant and Bilimb Marron*, oil on board, 50.5 × 35.3 cm, Royal Botanic Gardens, Kew.

but 'in fact did most of her Queensland paintings in [...] a nearby hotel or homestead'.[77]

The botanical historian Anthony Huxley indicates that North's paintings while in Australia became noticeably more 'impressionistic' in style,[78] perhaps under the influence of Rowan whose application of paint is generally looser than North's. The tonal range of North's Australian paintings made outdoors is considerably lighter than the artist's usual painting style, such as in painting 745, *Evening Glow over The Range*, where pale pinks, greens and blues have been applied. North was clearly responding to the localised effects of Australia's strong sunlight (fig.28). In painting 752, *View near Brighton, Victoria*, the brightness of the Australian sun has bleached out the colour of the grasses and vegetation in the background, and in painting 792, *Plant and Animal Life at Mudgee, New South Wales*, there is very little in the way of dark shadow.

During the 19th century, Australia was highly susceptible to the spreading of non-native plants and animals brought into the continent from around the British Empire and the rest of the world. North comments on seeing 'miles of pasture' in Australia punctuated by the yellow, dandelion-like flowers of the '*Cryptostemma calendulacean* [*sic*; *Arctotheca calendula*]' plant. The plant's seed had apparently come from 'the Cape [of South Africa] only a few years before and now grew everywhere'.[79] The rapid spread of 'usurping' northern hemisphere plants in Australia and New Zealand during the 1840s led many to fear that the smaller local genera there would eventually be wiped out.[80] North writes of the introduction of non-native plants to New Zealand, describing the air as 'thick with thistledown' and the 'native weeds [...] being stifled by Scotland's royal flower'.[81] In Australia, the artist stayed at a house where 'The garden was full of imported bushes and plants.'[82] While visiting the wife of the Australian Prime Minister in Camden, New South Wales, North found 'twenty-five different species of wildflowers in ten minutes, close to the house, and painted them. The garden was cut in terraces,

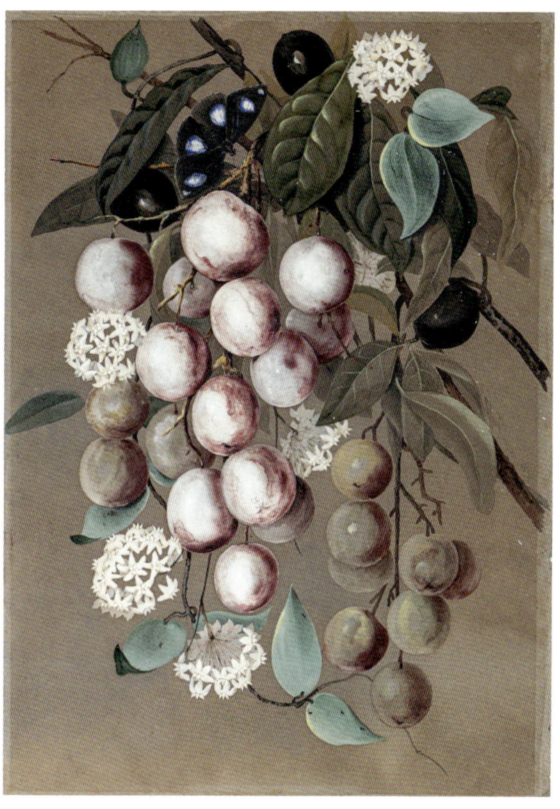

27 Ellis Rowan, *Nicholson's Wax Vine (Hoya nicholsoniae)*, n.d., watercolour and gouache on toned wove paper (grey), 54.6 × 37.9 cm, Queensland Museum Collection.

descending into real virgin forest, with fine gums and banksias left standing amongst the imported flowers.' North declares that 'One could hardly see where the wild and the tame joined.'[83]

Australia's European settlers wanted to be surrounded by plants, as well as animals, that were familiar to them. Such animals and plants were a source of food as well as a visual reminder of the settlers' previous homes. North writes of the flora of Deloraine, Tasmania, as being 'far too English' since it contained 'hedges of sweet-brier, hawthorn, and blackberry, nettles, docks, thistles, dandelions' and that 'It is curious how we have introduced all our weeds, vices and

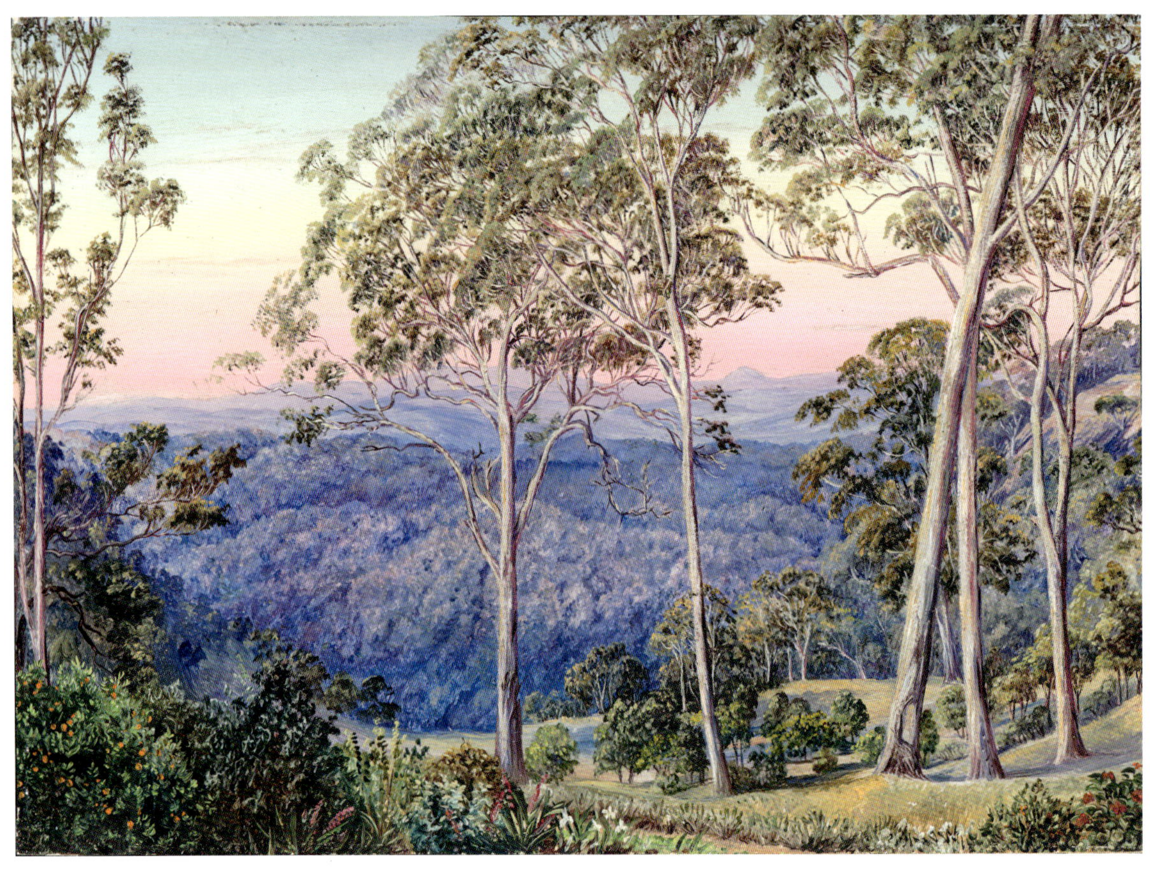

28 Marianne North, 745, *Evening Glow over The Range*, oil on board, 34.4 × 47.7 cm, Royal Botanic Gardens, Kew.

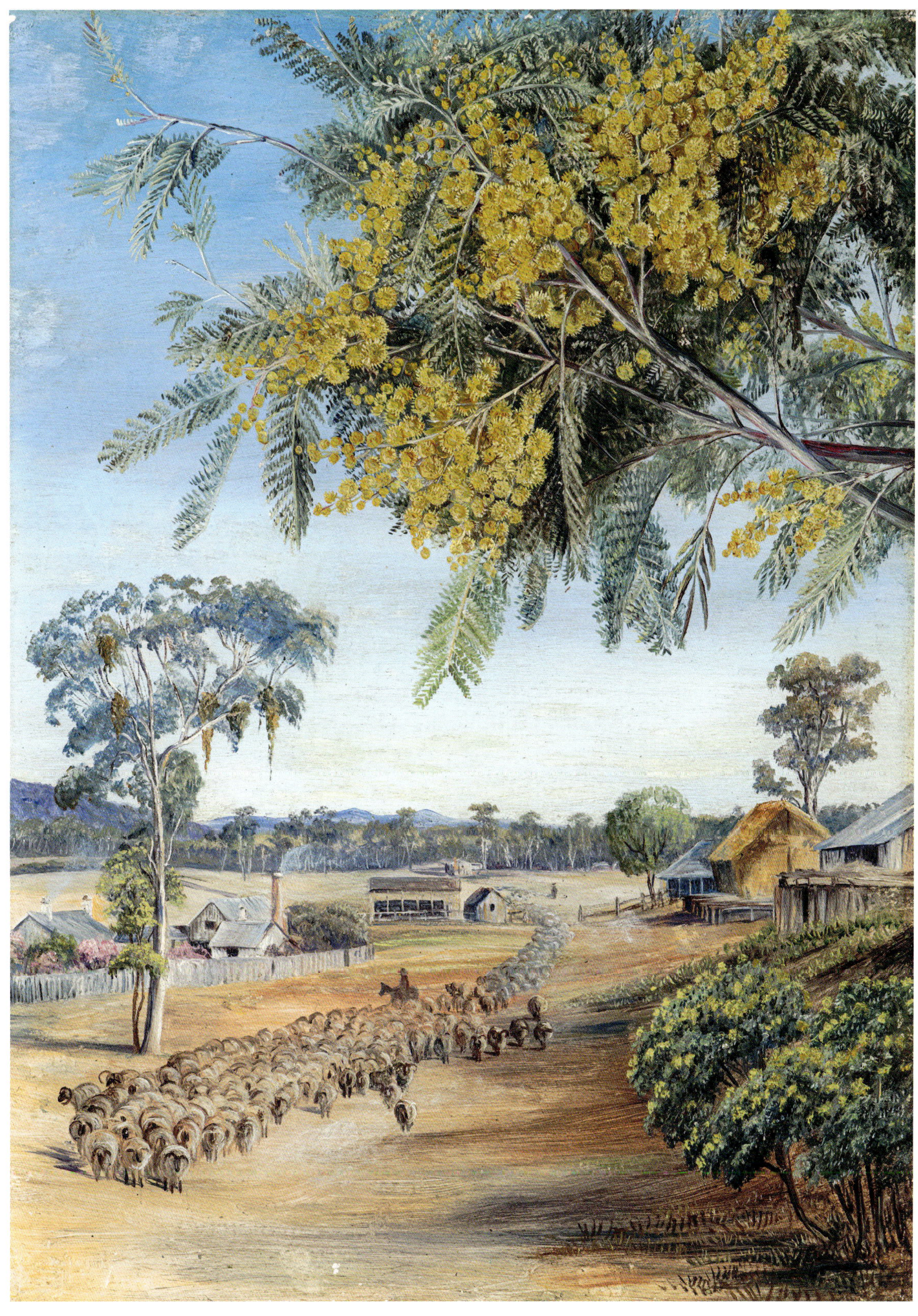

29 Marianne North, 726, *Flowers and Foliage of the Silver Wattle, Queensland*, oil on board, 47.2 × 34 cm, Royal Botanic Gardens, Kew.

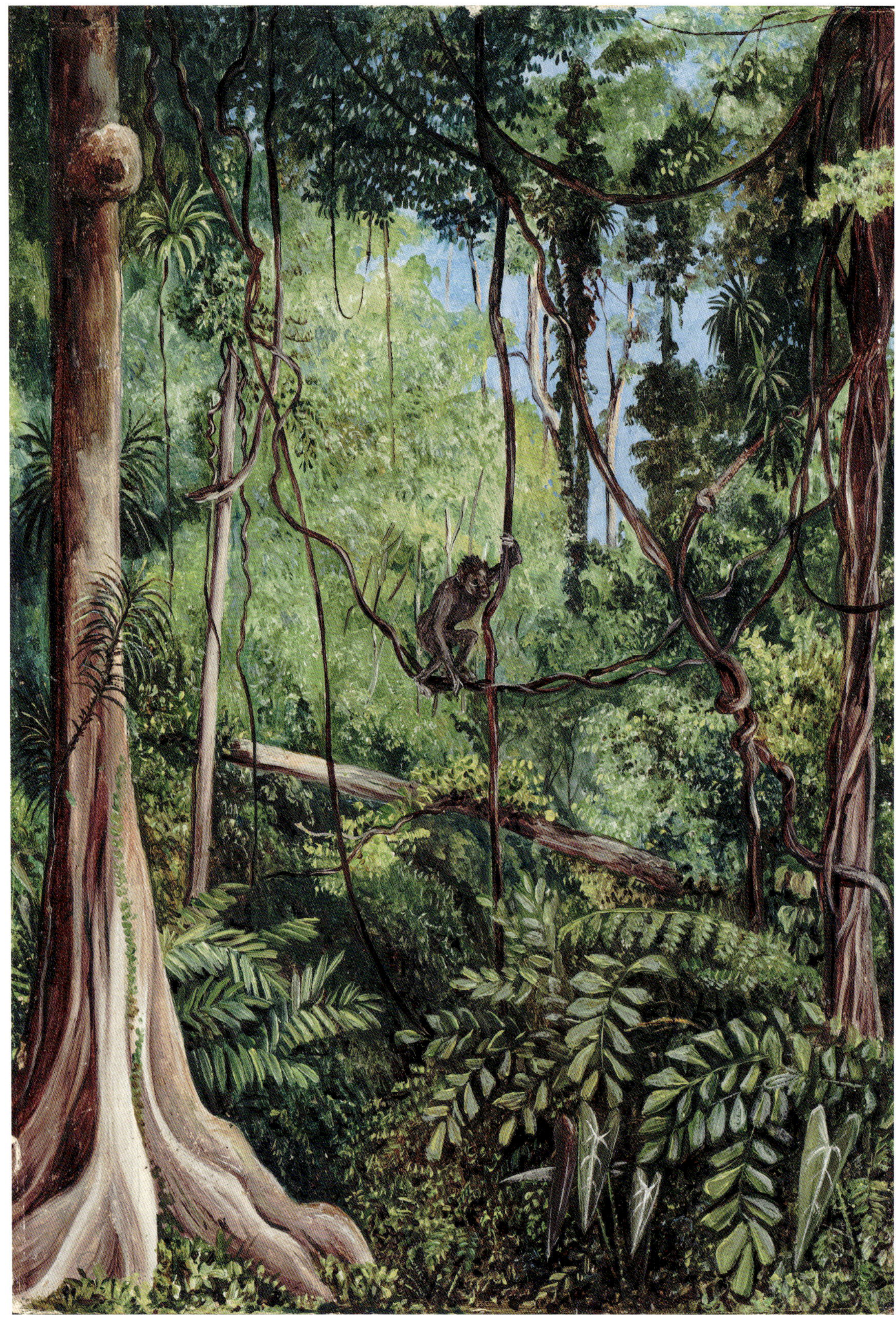

30 Marianne North, 545, *Forest Scene, Matang, Sarawak, Borneo*, oil on board, 35.3 × 25 cm, Royal Botanic Gardens, Kew.

prejudices into Australia, and turned the natives (even the fish) out of it [. . .] all the native plants (if there are any) were burnt up.'[84] The practice of introducing European plants into the Australian landscape as part of continuity farming methods and the secure provision of food sources was accompanied by the introduction of European animals, especially sheep. As the historian Alfred Crosby indicates, by clearing woodland and growing crops, settlers 'saved newly bared topsoil from water and wind erosion and from baking in the sun', enabling it to be used as a source of 'essential feed for exotic stock' (fig.29).[85]

North appears to have been in two minds about the environmental changes wrought on Australia by Europeans, often decrying and accepting aspects of those changes in the same piece of writing. On a visit to Perth in Western Australia, the artist was informed that a small tree, '*Eucalyptus marcrocorpa* [*sic*; *marcrocapa*]', was about to flower. North writes that 'the tree had been common [. . .] in old days' but 'the sheep had taken a fancy to it and had gradually eaten it all up', and that the locals 'were carefully saving the seeds of this one that they might sow them and raise up more food for the sheep!'[86] While visiting the 'Bunga [*sic*; Bunya]' mountains in Queensland, North comments on the industrial exploitation of the landscape and its consequences, writing, 'I went rather out of my mind' at the sight of 'The ruthless killing of miles of noble trees.'[87] Writing while travelling in South Africa, North describes 'Wynberg, seven and a half miles round the western side of Table Mountain', where 'groves of European fir-trees, oaks, and fruit orchids grow' with the 'ground under them' covered with white gums, Australian gums, wattles and casuarinas that were 'in full bloom and perfectly at home there.'[88] And in Arlington in the United States, near to the home of General Lee, North writes of seeing 'little houses built for the accommodation of sparrows; the birds had been imported from England to get rid of a caterpillar which had been infesting trees and eating up everything.'[89]

North also witnessed examples of rare and anomalous plants while on an expedition to Brazil in 1872–3, while visiting the home of Danish palaeontologist, zoologist and archaeologist Dr Peter Wilhelm Lund (1801–80), who was a long-term resident of Brazil and is considered the 'father' of Brazilian palaeontology and archaeology. North writes of how Lund 'made several collections of natural curiosities and plants' which were sent on to Copenhagen for further study and classification. Lund corresponded with many scientists in Europe but lived alone.[90] According to North, Lund's garden was 'full of rare plants and curiosities collected and planted by himself'. North painted some of them, including 'a rare blue potederia' that 'the doctor had persuaded with considerable difficulty to grow on the lake' and which delighted Lund.[91] The artist also travelled 'along the high banks overlooking the Rio das Velhas, which eventually runs into the Rio San Francesco, and enters the sea above Bahia', where, North writes, 'In the fresh clearings I saw many new gorgeous flowers, as well as some old friends, including the graceful amaranth plant of North Italy.' This prompted North to ask the question: 'How did it get to the two places so far apart? I longed more and more for some intelligent botanical companion to answer my many questions.'[92] North appears to have been very well informed about botany and the geographical locations of plants. According to Lys de Bray, North commented that 'she saw but no two flowers, orchids, that were truly native to the Seychelles, everything else being from Madagascar, or the East or West Indies.'[93]

Concerns among Europeans about the impact of colonialisation on the environment were expressed as early as the 17th century. British natural philosopher John Woodward (1665–1728) began a series of experiments on plant nutrition in 1696 and published the first significant writings on plant transpiration in 1699. Woodward demonstrated that 'the greater part of the water absorbed by a growing plant is exhaled through its pores into the atmosphere', and was also 'intimately concerned with rates of environmental changes over time and environmental influences on disease and extinctions', developing a 'global approach to the gathering of data and the construction of theory' concerning 'relations among plants, atmosphere and climate'. Woodward's systematic global approach, which prefigures that of Humboldt, is set out in the treatise *Brief Instructions for Making Observations in All Parts of the World, as also for Collecting* (1696).[94] Another British natural philosopher and early scientist, Stephen Hales (1677–1761), sought to measure the impact of deforestation on the natural environment as part of emerging ecological concerns during the 17th century.[95] The work initiated by Woodward and Hales underpinned the development during the 18th and into the 19th century of Edenic Romantic and physiocratic interests in environmentalism. Such interests were bolstered after 1820 by the writings of, amongst others, Humboldt and the French naturalist Pierre Poivre (1719–86), the latter being 'persuaded of the value of tree planting and protection of the environment' through 'observations of Indian and Chinese forestry and horticultural methods'.[96] What is now referred to as ecology was identified as a scientific discipline in the mid-1860s by the German biologist Ernst Haeckel (1834–1919). Haeckel coined the term 'Oecologie' to signify 'the investigating of the total relations of the animal both to its inorganic and to its organic environment' in what the historian John Holmes describes as amounting to 'the study of all those complex interrelations referred to by Darwin as the conditions of the struggle for existence' (fig.30).[97]

North's exposure to the ideas of Humboldt, Emerson and Darwin, brought into sharper focus perhaps by the work and intellectual interests of Church and the Hudson River School, as well as North's personal observations of environmental change, came about in the context of continuing scientific concerns with the natural environment initiated nearly two centuries earlier. In the preface to the original catalogue of the North Gallery at Kew, director Joseph Hooker writes of 'how many of the habitat's [*sic*] are already disappearing or are doomed shortly to disappear before the axe and the forest fires, the plough and the flock, of the ever advancing settler or colonist' and that 'Such scenes can never be renewed by nature, nor when once effaced can they be pictured to the mind's eye, except by records such as this lady has presented to us, and to posterity.' Hooker adds, there is thus 'even more reason than we have to be grateful for her fortitude as a traveller, her talent and industry as an artist, and her liberality and public spirit'.[98]

3

Paintings, Styles and Influences

Visual representations of plants have been produced since prehistoric times. The earliest existing images include highly stylised cave paintings at Altamira and Lascaux as well as bas-reliefs from ancient Egypt. The first-known dedicated botanical illustrations are in a treatise on medical botany by the Syriac Christian physician, Yahya ibn Sarafyun (Serapion the Elder) published in the 9th century. Early Christian and Islamic botanical illustrations were highly influential on the medical study of plants in Europe, leading to the establishment of various schools of plant and flower painting.[1] During the Renaissance, European artists made significant contributions to the development of botanical illustration. Leonardo da Vinci (1452–1519) and Albrecht Dürer (1471–1528), though very different in their approaches, both applied geometry to the representation of natural forms. Da Vinci also depicted plants in their natural settings rather than simply as decorative or allegorical embellishments to larger painterly compositions.[2] A possible example of the use of an optical device to assist with the depiction of plants in nature is Dürer's *Large Turf* (1503), which depicts a patch of grass against a white background and is so exceptionally detailed that it is likely to have been produced using a lens rather than the naked eye.[3]

In the 17th and 18th centuries, Dutch artists produced highly realistic representations of flowers. Examples include illustrations by the artist Jacob Van Huysum (1687/9–1740) who in 1730 was commissioned by the English Parliamentarian Hugh Walpole to produce a *Catalogue Plantarum*. Flower paintings by Dutch artists are usually composites that bring together representations of individual blooms produced separately over time, often across seasons, to create an aesthetically pleasing compositional whole. The depiction of flowers in containers on tabletops or plinths adds to the sense of compositional integrity by providing viewers with a visual frame of reference for judging where individual blooms are in spatial relation to one another.[4] Dutch flower painters used optical devices that helped to produce highly detailed representations of nature[5] – as exemplified by the artist Jacob Vosmaer's painting, *A Vase with Flowers* (probably 1613; fig.31). This conjunction of art and technology was readily accepted in Holland at the time as part of a culture celebratory of artistic and scientific endeavour.[6]

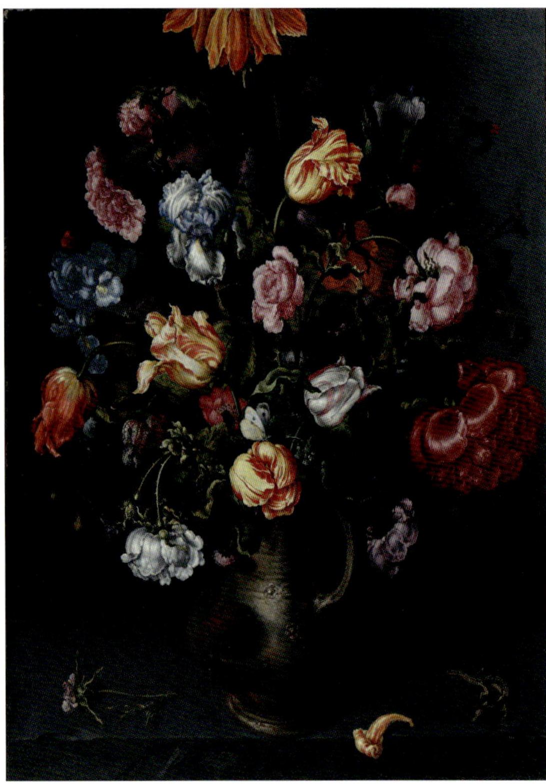

31 Jacob Vosmaer, *A Vase with Flowers*, probably 1613, oil on wood, 85.1 × 62.5 cm, The Metropolitan Museum of Art, New York.

Illustrations used specifically to support botanical taxonomy were first developed in the 16th century by the German physician and botanist Leonhard Fuchs (1501–66).[7] The 18th-century German botanical painter Georg Dionysius Ehret (1708–70) produced illustrations that combine Fuchs's emphasis on topological detail with the system of plant classification developed by the Swedish botanist Carl (Carolus) Linnaeus (1707–78; fig.32). Ehret's systematic representation of plants and their various parts is still used by scientific botanical illustrators today. Linnaeus established an ordered taxonomical approach to planting at the Uppsala University Botanical Garden which placed plant species together in groups according to the structure of their reproductive parts.[8] Linnaeus's *The Species Plantarum* (1753) is an illustrated survey of all the then-known plant species organised according to this approach. Linnaeus was assisted in this project by numerous fellow botanists who were asked to send plant specimens, complete with flowers, to Uppsala.[9] Among them was the American botanist John Bartram (1699–1777) who collected plants from across the Americas. Scientific botanical illustration was further developed during the 18th and 19th centuries by the Austrian brothers Ferdinand (1760–1826) and Franz Bauer (1758–1840). Ferdinand was an illustrator on Matthew Flinders's expedition to Australia at the request of the British botanist Joseph Banks (1743–1810). Franz eventually settled in England and worked at Kew Gardens.[10] Illustrations by the Bauers firmly established the scientific convention of representing the structure of plants to best advantage from multiple viewpoints in flattened form without the inclusion of shadow; the artistic convention of describing form using *chiaroscuro* obscures both structural detail and local colour.[11]

According to the conventions established by Ehret and the Bauers, botanical illustrators are tasked with providing botanists with clear, taxonomically ordered representations of individual plant species. Following Ehret, depictions of plants are accompanied on the same page by schematic renderings of the plant's constituent parts. Instead of capturing the whole at one sitting, botanical illustrators concentrate on cumulatively representing one small part of the plant at a time. They also use the technique of topological drawing that pictorially flattens the image, making the plant and its parts easily readable to science. Botanical illustrations are generally treated as technical working documents. The illustrator may, however, add a degree of personal style and even project additional meaning onto the illustration, if this does not interfere with the scientific requirements of the work. Despite these specialist requirements, botanical illustrations are nevertheless open to aesthetic appreciation outside science. The botanical historian Marion Arnold broaches the technical difficulties that can compel botanical illustrators to make aesthetic judgements, stating that a plant specimen may be 'damaged or ravaged by insects or in bud' and therefore require imaginative reconstruction.[12]

In 19th-century Britain, a sharp modernising distinction began to develop between artistic and scientific approaches to visual representation. Artists and scientists both maintained the importance of truth to nature. Artists did so, for the most part, by continuing to uphold classical notions of ideal beauty as ultimate truth, while scientists aspired to unmediated forms of objective topological representation. This distinction placed scientific illustration, like photography, in a culturally subordinate position in relation to high art. John Ruskin very much admired the work of natural history illustrators because of its fidelity to nature but 'resisted the rise of scientific naturalism' and the emphasis among botanists on 'dissection and classification'.[13] Ruskin's high-cultural views, which continued to hold sway for the 19th and much of the 20th centuries, account for the work of botanical illustrators being almost wholly absent from art-historical discussion. As Arnold attests, even now 'the greatest natural history artists [...] are not usually considered alongside the watercolourists of mainstream [art] history'. Despite botanical illustrators producing works of undeniable aesthetic beauty, their work cannot be easily disentangled from its perceived role as primarily a means of representing/elucidating scientific knowledge.[14]

Nearly all the paintings upon which North's reputation as a botanical illustrator are founded were produced during a remarkably short period, between 1871 and 1885. They include studies of individual and related groups of plants, as well as topographical landscapes prominently featuring plant specimens, in a variety of media, including oils and watercolours. North's productivity during that short period is astounding given that many of the paintings were produced, or initiated at least, during the artist's extensive worldwide travels. There is no evidence that North set out initially to produce a systematic global representation of plant life in its natural regional settings. Such an outcome was nevertheless realised by the display at the North Gallery at Kew, with many of the paintings being produced specifically to fulfil the gallery's panoramic vision of nature. North's botanical paintings were intended principally as objective records of nature rather than idealising works of art.

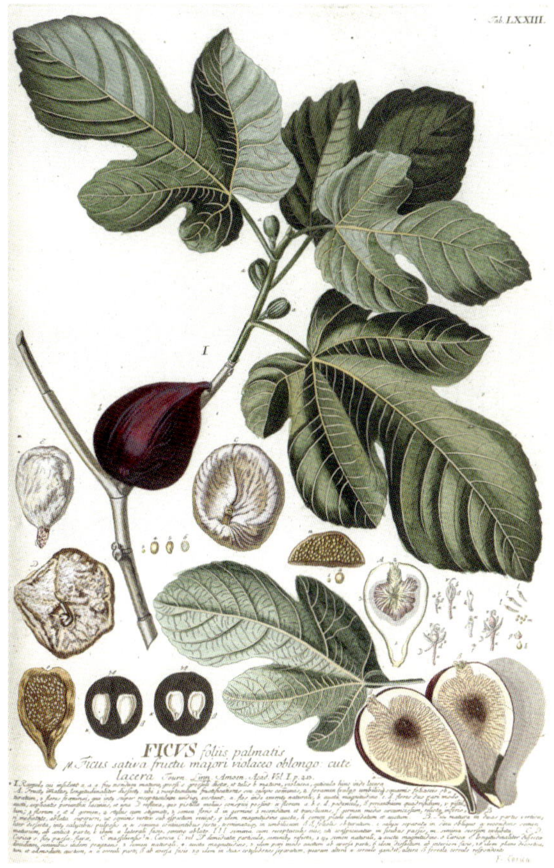

32 Georg Dionysius Ehret, *Ficus carica*, from *Plantae Selectae*, illustrations by G.D. Ehret and engravings by J.J. Haid, 1750, mezzotint, 43 × 26.5 cm, Royal Botanic Gardens, Kew.

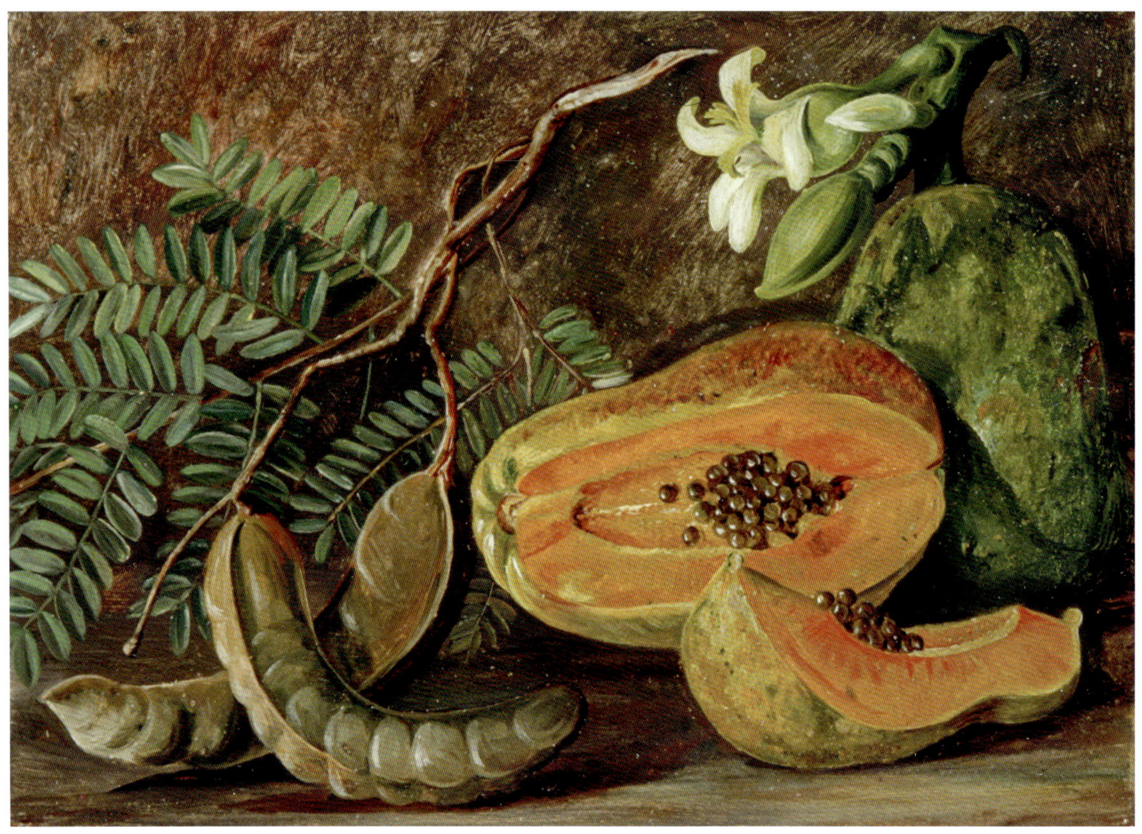

33 Marianne North, 700, *Foliage and Fruit of the Tamarind and Flowers and Fruit of the Paw Paw in Java*, oil on board, 25.2 × 35.4 cm, Royal Botanic Gardens, Kew.

They are relatively flatly lit (without deep shadow) which indicates a willingness to conform somewhat to the established conventions of botanical painting. North's paintings are, however, far from being in exact accordance with the conventions laid down by Ehret and further developed by the Bauers. North often represents all the constituent parts of a plant together as a structural whole as they appear in nature – for example, in painting 700, *Foliage and Fruit of the Tamarind and Flowers and Fruit of the Paw Paw in Java* (fig.33) – rather than separately according to scientific expectations. North's habit of depicting plants in their natural settings rather than against plain backgrounds is also unusual to science, utilising techniques that are generally closer to those of European still-life flower paintings of the 19th century – as exemplified by paintings 504, *Group of Flowers, Painted in Teneriffe* (fig.34), and 615, *Collection of Fruits, Painted at Lisbon* (fig.35). In some of North's paintings – for example, 266, *Loose-skinned Orange of Colombo, Ceylon* (Sri Lanka; fig.36) – fruits and flowers are placed on plinths or ledges in a manner akin to 17th- and 18th-century still-life paintings such as the German artist Georg Flegel's (1566–1638) *Still Life* (probably *c.*1625–30; fig.37). In many of North's paintings scientific accuracy is subordinated to overall pictorial composition and aesthetic affect.

North also appears to have combined separate representations of differing plant parts produced over time, with some based on secondary sources rather

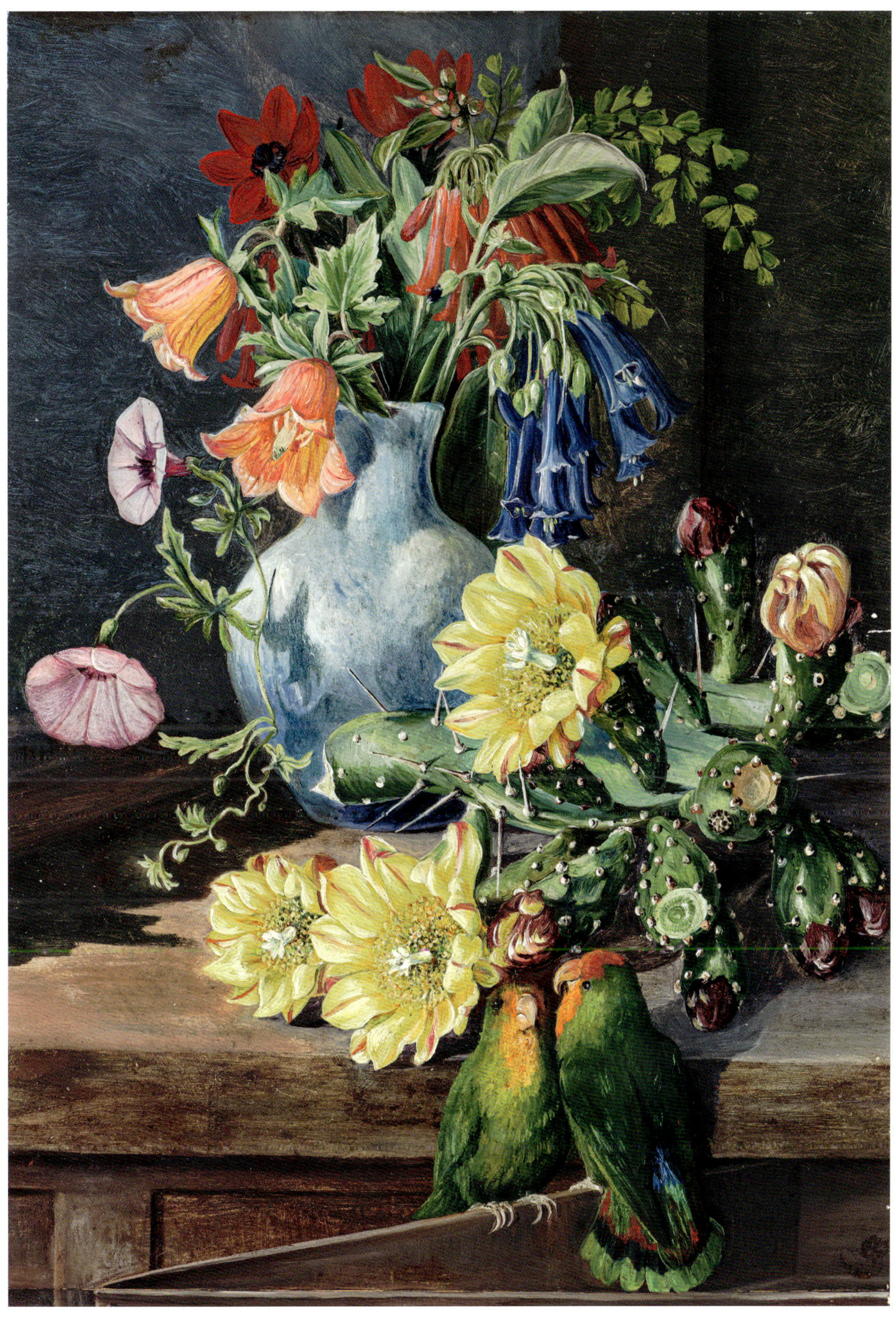

34 Marianne North, 504, *Group of Flower, Painted in Teneriffe*, oil on board, 47 × 34.2 cm, Royal Botanic Gardens, Kew.

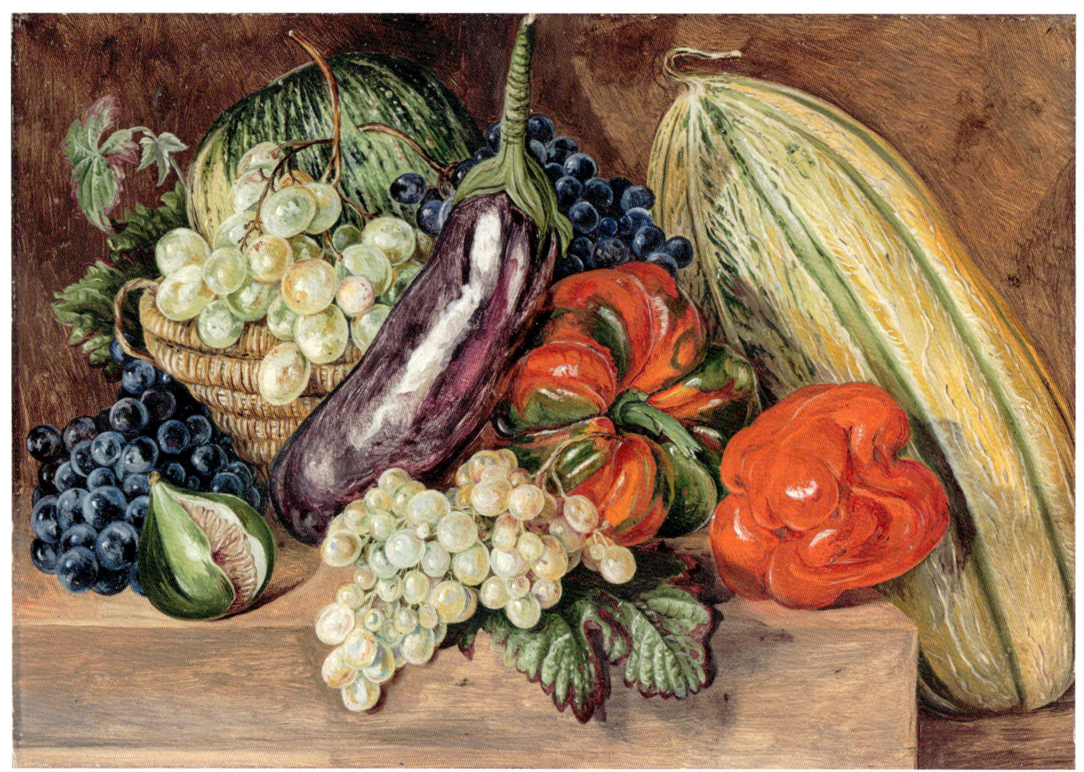

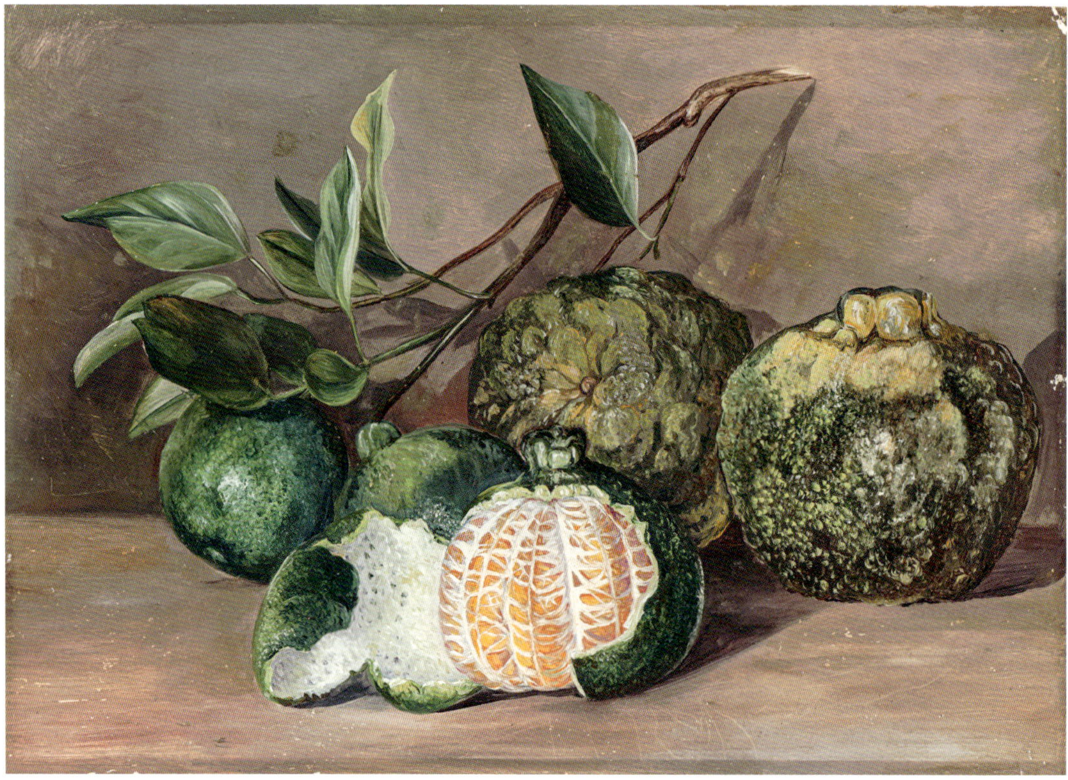

35 (top) Marianne North, 615, *Collection of Fruits Painted at Lisbon*, oil on board, 33.1 × 47.2 cm, Royal Botanic Gardens, Kew.

36 (below) Marianne North, 266, *Loose-skinned Orange of Colombo, Ceylon*, oil on board, 23.7 × 34 cm, Royal Botanic Gardens, Kew

than on direct observation from nature, to produce seemingly integrated pictorial compositions. While thanking William Hemsley for sending drawings of a *Datura* plant 'to copy', North adds, 'you need not trouble about that [drawing of a potato flower] I can copy out of Gerrards [*sic*] Herbal.'[15] In a following letter North asks of 'that gorgeous large white lilac clematis one sees in shows of American or Japanese origins often tipped with pink & as big as a saucer', admitting 'It is a shame to take up your time with such questions but I cannot find these new things in books.'[16] In another letter to Hemsley concerning the decoration of the North Gallery, the artist writes, 'I am working hard at my door frame' and 'illustrating the most gorgeous flowers of the old world & the new' and that 'they are all painted from old studies of my own or different illustrations of bot [botanical] magazines illustrations & publications', ending the letter, 'I do not want to be accused of stealing them.'[17] North also writes to J.D. Duthie of wanting a fresh flower to paint, 'as it will not keep & the first you gave me fell all to pieces before I could paint them.'[18] The unorthodoxy of North's painting coincides with evident aspirations towards their showing in artistic contexts. Writing to Arthur Burnell in 1878, North describes 'taking a Gallery [at] 9 Conduit Street for my Indian sketches', asking if Burnell 'could write a line to the [Royal] academy', adding, 'I am ignorant about advertising – but it must be done to pay the rent!'[19] Writing to Burnell two years later, North states: 'I have just finished a large picture of Kinchinjinga to try its fate at the R.A. [Royal Academy of Arts, London] and hope to paint a companion picture of a South country swamp to match it before April.'[20]

Writing in the 1950s, the historian of botanical illustration William T. Stearn indicates that botanists at that time regarded North 'primarily as an artist, although she discovered and portrayed species new to science'. Stearn also asserts that 'artists will hardly agree, for her painting is almost wholly lacking in sensibility'. Stearn suggests that a 'disagreeable impression' is made by North's paintings, arguing that this is 'enhanced through her determination to display 832 paintings in a gallery [the North Gallery at Kew] barely capable of showing fifty to advantage', adding that North's work, 'being painted in oils, is almost unaffected by light and remains perennially gaudy'. In Stearn's view, North should be acknowledged chiefly for travelling the world in search of spectacular plants which 'she painstakingly and accurately recorded in oils in their natural surroundings'.[21] This identification of North's paintings as falling unsatisfactorily somewhere between art and science reflects rationalising mid-20th-century high-modernist concerns with the categorical limits of differing specialisms. High modernism of that time was critical of uncertain specialist boundaries between science, art and popular culture. It also regarded a great deal of Victorian painting as unduly historicising. As the art historian Hope Kingsley indicates, historicism 'is usually understood as the antithesis of Modernism, whose ethos has a break with precedent and whose motivation was a search for new modes of expression.'[22] North's allegiance to the accepted conventions of 19th-century painting and their continuing validation of classical representation and aesthetics – as exemplified by French artist Henri Fantin-Latour's (1836–1904)

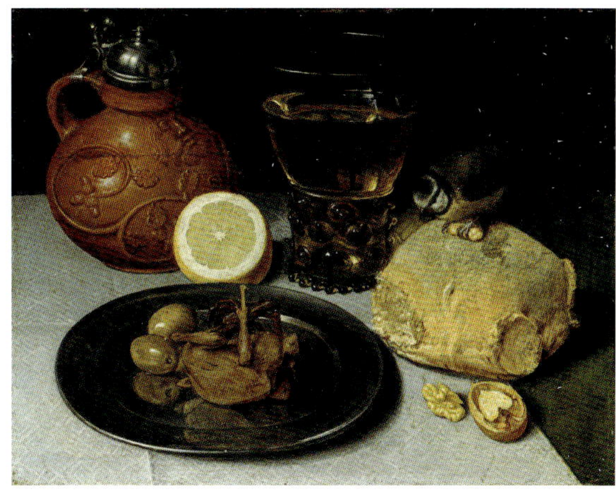

37 Georg Flegel, *Still Life*, probably *c.*1625–30, oil on wood, 27 × 34 cm, The Metropolitan Museum of Art, New York.

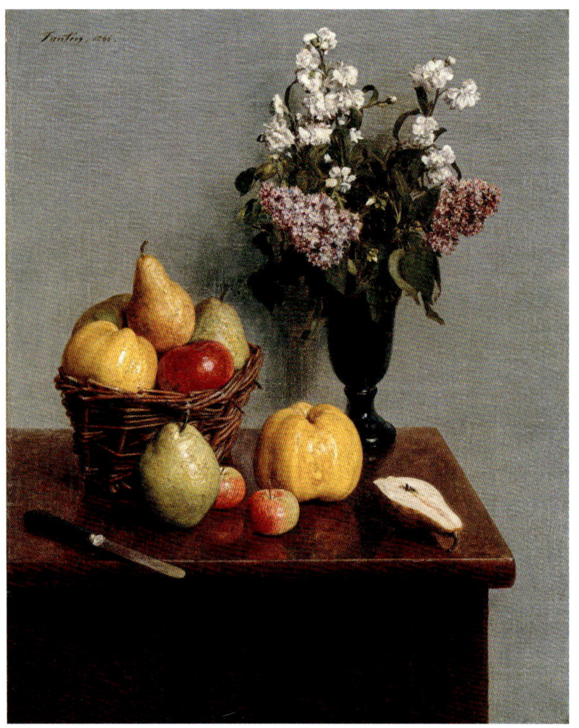

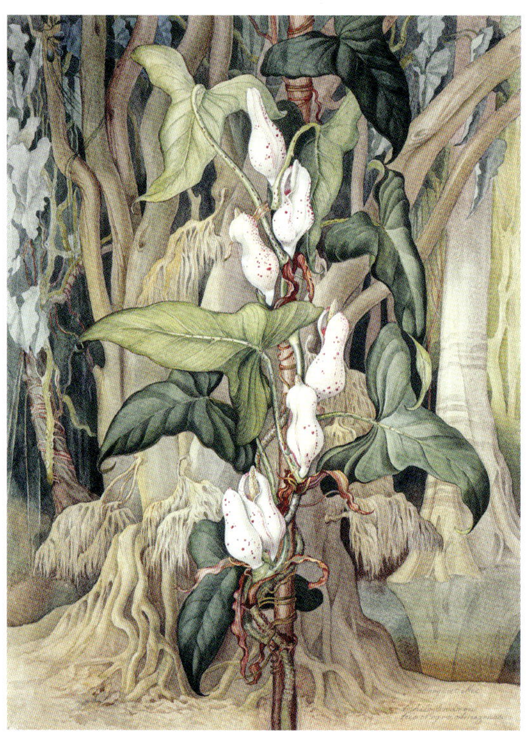

38 (left) Henri Fantin-Latour, *Still Life with Flowers and Fruit*, 1866, oil on canvas, 73 × 60 cm, The Metropolitan Museum of Art, New York.

39 (right) Margaret Mee, *Philodendron sp. Rio Negro, Amazonas*, 1992, pencil and gouache on paper, 64 × 47 cm, The Shirley Sherwood Collection.

Still Life with Flowers and Fruit (1866; fig.38) – is anathema to modernist ideas of cultural progress.

North's paintings were not received so disparagingly during the 19th century. At the time, they were regarded, despite their technical unorthodoxy, as innovations valuable to science. In a letter to Burnell, North writes of having produced '240 oil studies' that 'Dr. Hooker and Dr. Allman both say a selection ought to be published as the plants (the mangrove for instance) have never been truly painted before'. In the same letter North acknowledges the wide appeal of botanical painting to 19th-century audiences, asserting that 'one half of the people who look over my work do it because it is the fashion to do so'.[23] Kingsley states that, in the Victorian era, 'history was what made art new, as a greater professionalism in archaeology and anthropology gave artists a more accurate understanding of the past'.[24] North's work is thoroughly modern in the context of 19th-century Britain. For many artists in 19th-century Europe there was an imperative to adapt scientific innovation and related philosophical discourses to aesthetics. Edward Lear regarded North as a 'great draughtswoman and botanist'.[25] As the cultural historian Suzanne Le-May Sheffield indicates, North was 'by no means content to have her work construed simply as the product of a [...] female pastime [...] within the framework of the "feminine" occupations of botany and botanical art'.[26]

A more fitting assessment of North's painting than that given by Stearn is possible in relation to postmodernism's return to historicism and the mixing of high and popular culture as well as art and science.

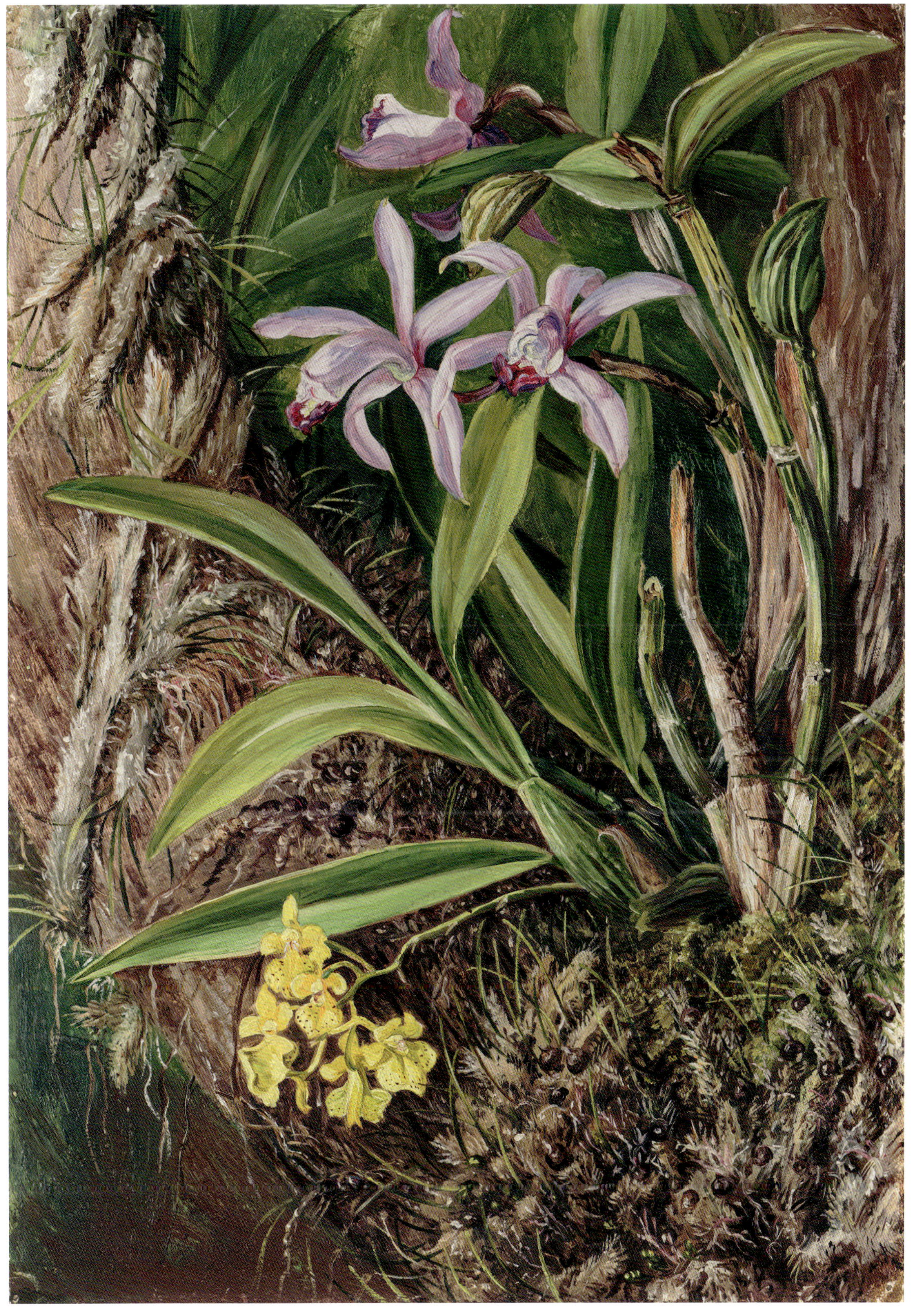

40 Marianne North, 093, *Brazilian Orchids and other Epiphytes*, oil on board, 35 × 25 cm, Royal Botanic Gardens, Kew.

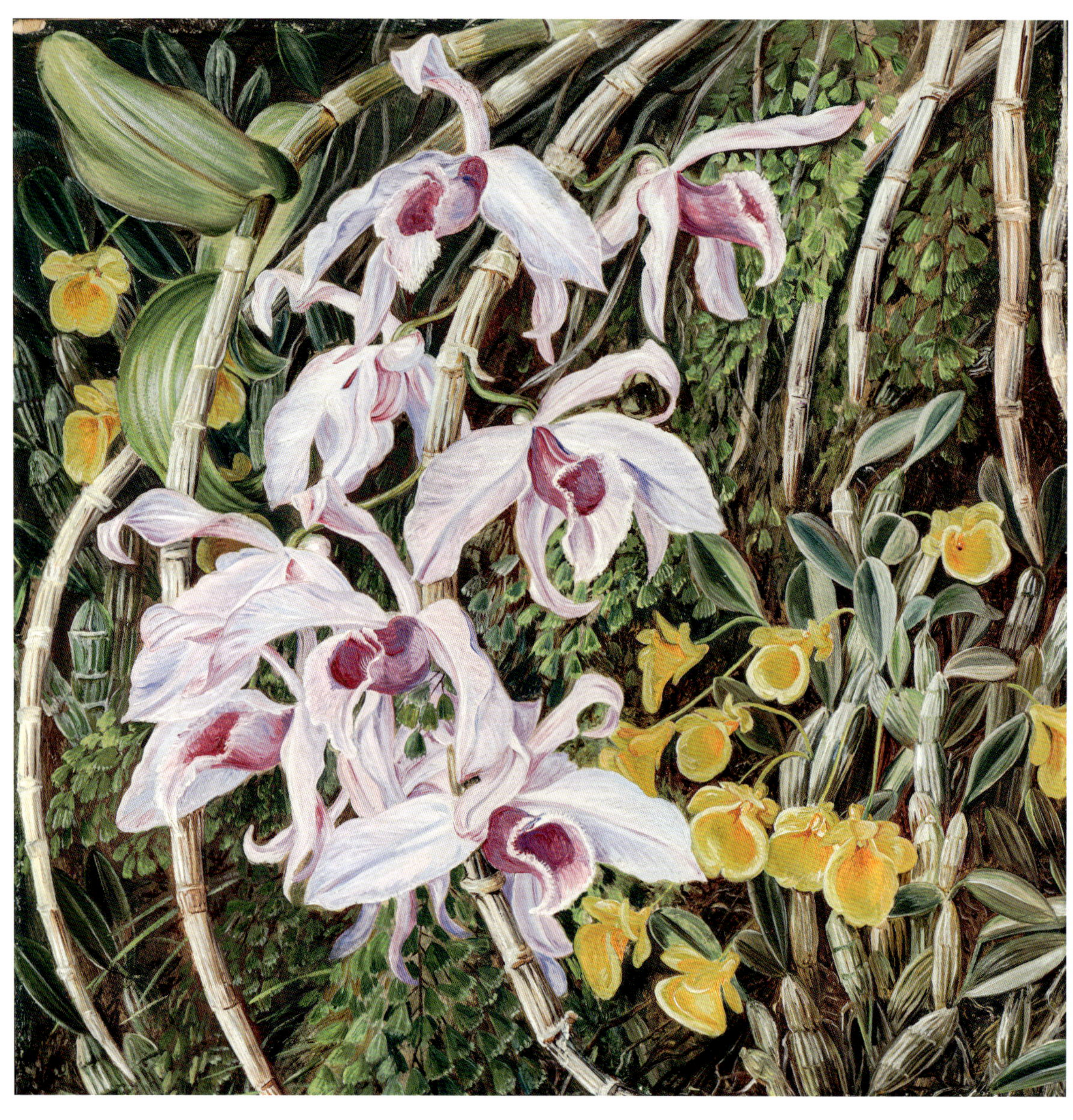

41 Marianne North, 287, *Orchids of Tropical Asia*, oil on board, 32.4 × 32.2 cm, Royal Botanic Gardens, Kew.

This is not to say that North's paintings should be considered anachronistically as postmodernist, but rather that the historical context of their making in 19th-century Britain did not yet fully uphold the starkly rationalising high-modernist categorisations criticised by postmodernism. In many ways, cultural perspectives after high modernism have involved a return to past uncertainties straddling what might be seen as historically aberrant modernist sensibilities. Writing in the early 2000s, Marion Arnold describes North's painting as meeting 'the primary requirements of botanists – she provides a recognizable likeness – but she also celebrates nature's lush growth, rhythms, forms and strong colours. By creating habitat studies, she articulates a concept of interconnectedness.' Arnold goes on to state that North conveys 'her perceptions of natural space rather than designing conceptual arrangements of plant fragments' and that this signifies that North's 'focus is more that of an ecologist than a taxonomist, and her eye is that of the artist not the specialist illustrator'.[27] As Sheffield indicates, North embarked upon a 'scientific endeavour that was to link art and science, bringing new perspectives to both. Her work thus rested on the margins of art and science.'[28]

North's blurring of the boundary between art and science is in many respects prescient of more recent, arguably postmodernist, developments in botanical illustration. Botanical illustrators/painters such as Pandora Sellars (1936–2017) and Margaret Mee (1909–88) have combined the conventions of scientific recording with a strong sense of pictorial aesthetics derived from their initial art school training. Illustrations by Mee such as *Philodendron* (1992; fig.39) incorporate graphically decorative presentations of flora and fauna as backgrounds to depictions of individual plants. This is similar to some of North's paintings, including 093, *Brazilian Orchids and other Epiphytes* (fig.40). Sellars's illustrations also involve a strong sense of pattern and compositional organisation. Mee's work and that of Sellars is, though, in much greater conformity to the established expectations of science. Sellars's illustrations integrate Ehret's schematic depiction of plant parts into overall pictorial designs, as opposed to depictions separate from the main illustration. This integration resonates with many of North's paintings, of which 287, *Orchids of Tropical Asia* (fig.41), is, for example, strikingly similar to Sellars's *Laelia tenebrosa* (1989; fig.42). It should also be said that botanical illustrations by the likes of Ehret and the Bauers are often taken out of context and admired for their aesthetic qualities rather than their scientific rigour.

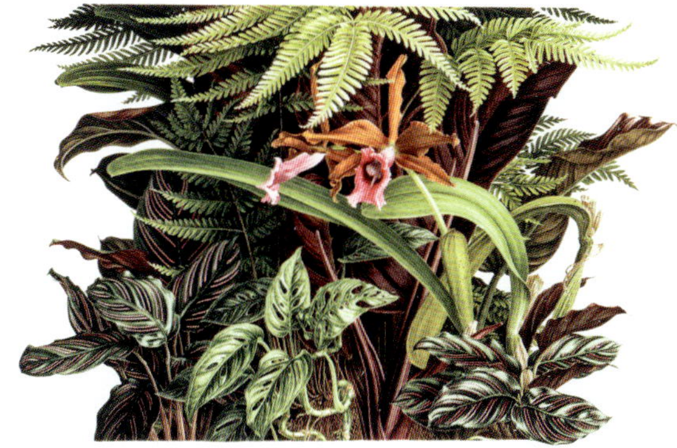

42 Pandora Sellars, *Laelia tenebrosa*, 1989, watercolour on paper, 41 × 60 cm, The Shirley Sherwood Collection.

Further formal resonances can be discerned between North's paintings and those of the 20th-century Mexican artist Frida Kahlo (1907–54). Kahlo produced still-life paintings that drew upon the work of the 19th-century Mexican botanical artist José Hermenegildo de la Luz Bustos (1832–1907), as well as on Mexico's folk-art traditions. Kahlo was, like North, largely self-taught and chose to depart from the conventions of Euro-American classical painting in favour of a sometimes ostensibly primitive personal style. Although there is no direct connection between Kahlo's work and North's, there are nevertheless striking formal similarities between the former's *Still Life with Parrot and Flag* (1951) and the latter's 490, *Fruit Grown in the Seychelles* (fig.43).

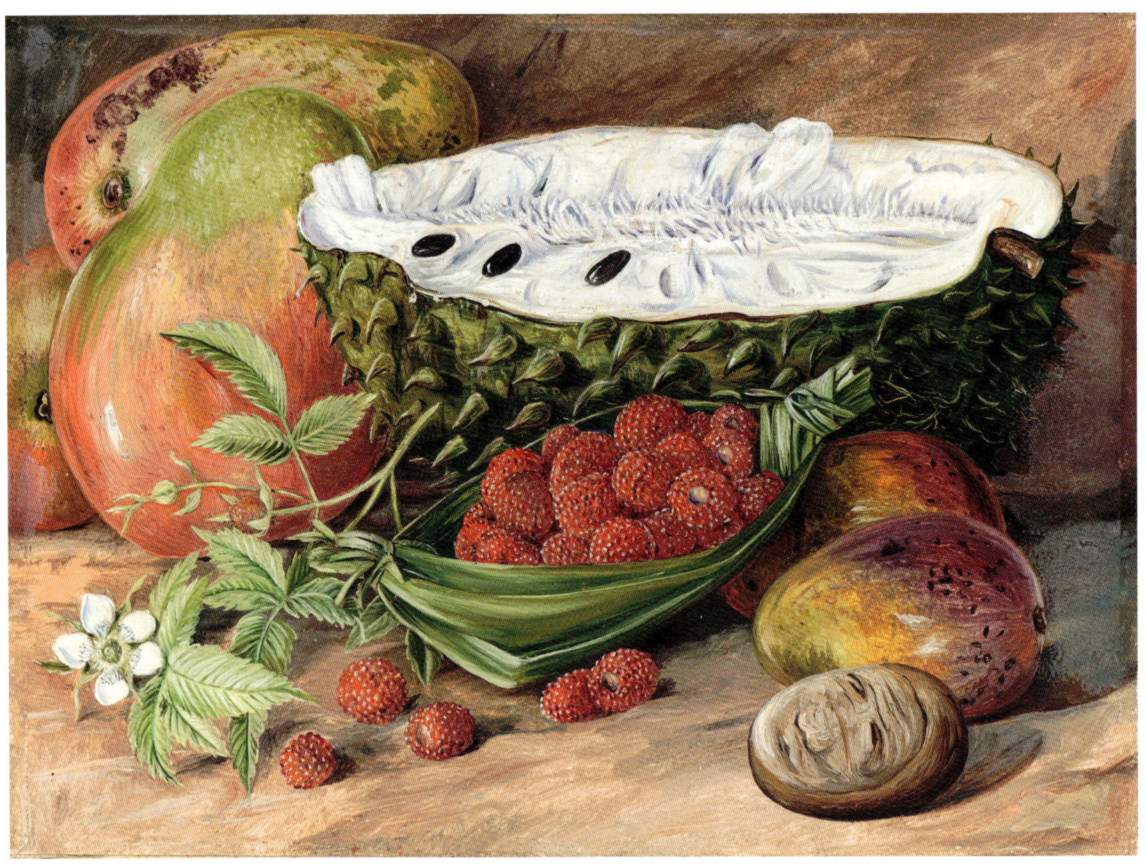

43 Marianne North, 490, *Fruit Grown in the Seychelles*, oil on board, 25.6 × 35.2 cm, Royal Botanic Gardens, Kew.

Kahlo's painting *Still Life with Hummingbird*, also known as *The Flower Basket* (1941), is, moreover, similar in style to North's 027, *Chilian Lilies and other Flowers in Black Jug and Ornamented Gourd for Maté*, 012, *Some Wild Flowers of Quilpué Chili*, and 375, *Flowers of St John's in Pondo Basket* (fig.44). In the context of 20th-century high art, Kahlo is now thought of as a genius. North most decidedly is not, almost certainly because of the uncertain relationship of the artist's paintings to both art and science.

The combination of art and science in North's paintings was not, it seems, intended as unsettling. North attempted to complete paintings using as much scientific rigour as possible. A measured 1:1 scale life-size correspondence between plant and image are requirements of botanical illustration. Botanical illustrators typically use dividers to attain that correspondence. Within the sphere of artistic practice, makers would normally expect to scale a given subject up or down through the application of middle-distance measurement using a pencil or another straight object held at arm's length in front of the subject with one eye closed; or, if not those things, an imaginative unmeasured approach to depiction. North was tutored by several professional artists and would have acquired a basic knowledge of compositional geometry and middle-distance measuring techniques, developing a semi-artistic approach to botanical painting that indicates a striving for scientific 1:1 correspondence without the strict use of dividers.

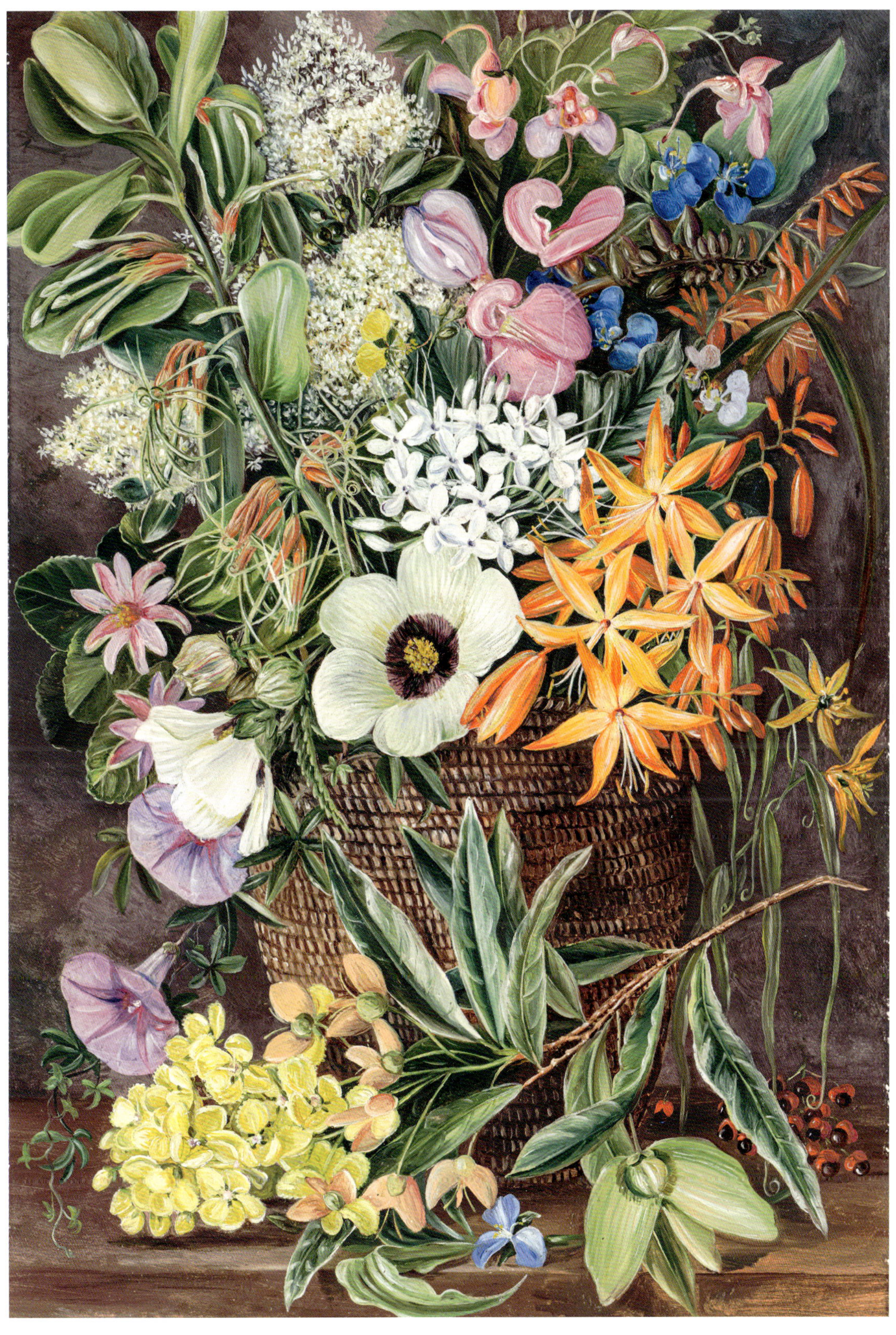

44 Marianne North, 375, *Flowers of St John's in Pondo Basket*, oil on board, 50.8 × 35.4 cm, Royal Botanic Gardens, Kew.

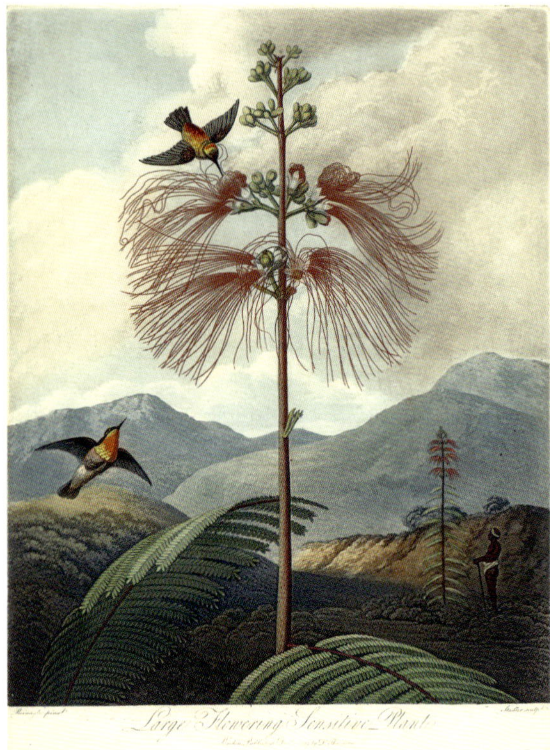

45 Philip Reinagle, *Large Flowering Sensitive Plant*, in Robert Thornton, *The Temple of Flora*, 1812, mezzotint, 53.4 × 43 cm, Royal Botanic Gardens, Kew.

Differences between high art and botanical illustration also occur in relation to the use of colour. Representation of colour in artistic painting is affected by perceptions related to distance (aerial perspective) – with colours becoming less saturated and tending towards neutral or bluish tones as the distance increases – as well as those chosen through an artist's aesthetic intentions or predilections. Early scientific colour theory is aimed at systematically clarifying the inherent structure of colour in the natural world rather than its subjective perception. Linnaeus's categorisation of species provided the initial stimulus to the development of colour systems of this sort related to botany during the 18th and 19th centuries.[29] This scientific understanding of colour was resisted by artists. The 19th-century French painter Eugène Delacroix (1798–1863), for example, felt compelled to devise a more subjective artist-friendly approach.[30]

North's intentions in this regard were, it appears, principally scientific, writing in a letter to Burnell of a plant encountered in the Himalayas that 'I wrote the colours down and their proportions and mean to paint it.'[31] North also writes to Hemsley of painting from blooms and the preparations required for painting. North asks if Hemsley knows 'anyone who would send me a simple bloom of *augroerum Aesquilpedale* [*sic*; *Angraecum sequipedale*]', adding, 'will you tell them I want it' and that 'I drew a lovely one in the house [at Kew] [. . .] but it is too precious to pick & it would make such a picture with that gorgeous *dhadegasta* [?] moth'.[32] Writing again to Hemsley, North states that 'Veitch [a seed provider] has sent a gorgeous spray [. . .] with 2 spurs all curled & 3rd flower an exquisite fellow with long straight spur too long to get on to my sheet of paper! So I must get a canvas', adding that another painting will be produced the next day, 'which one intends to give to Veitch'. North thanks Hemsley for procuring a moth, writing, 'it is such a joy to look at his [Veitch's] flowers & the gorgeous moth I hope to colour it with – thank you for getting it for me'.[33]

North writes of problems with composition and depicting objects life size on a single canvas or sheet of paper. One account concerns the artist's first attempts at painting outdoors in the Pyrenees and Spain, stating 'I had an idea till then [of only drawing] near objects the size of life', but the temptation of depicting a wider landscape of poplar trees, a river and the vision of fresh snow on the mountains was too great.[34] North writes of a huge lily in Borneo, 'with white face and pink stalks and backs, resting its heavy head on the ground', describing how the flower 'grew from a single-stemmed plant, with grand curved leaves above the flower'. North comments further that the flower head was 'two feet across' and complains of the technical difficulty of

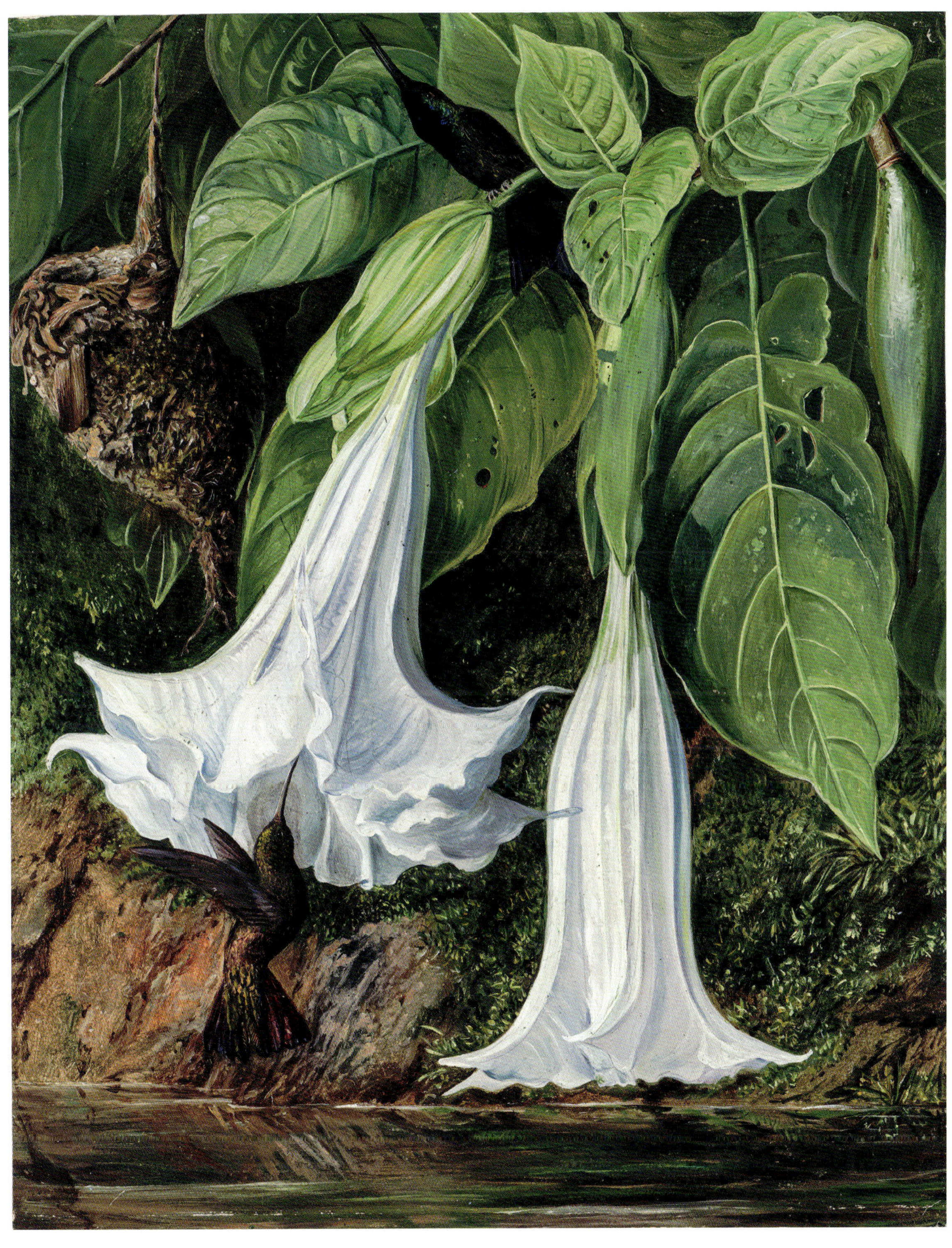

46 Marianne North, 047, *Flowers of Datura and Humming Birds, Brazil*, oil on board, 50.8 × 35.4 cm, Royal Botanic Gardens, Kew.

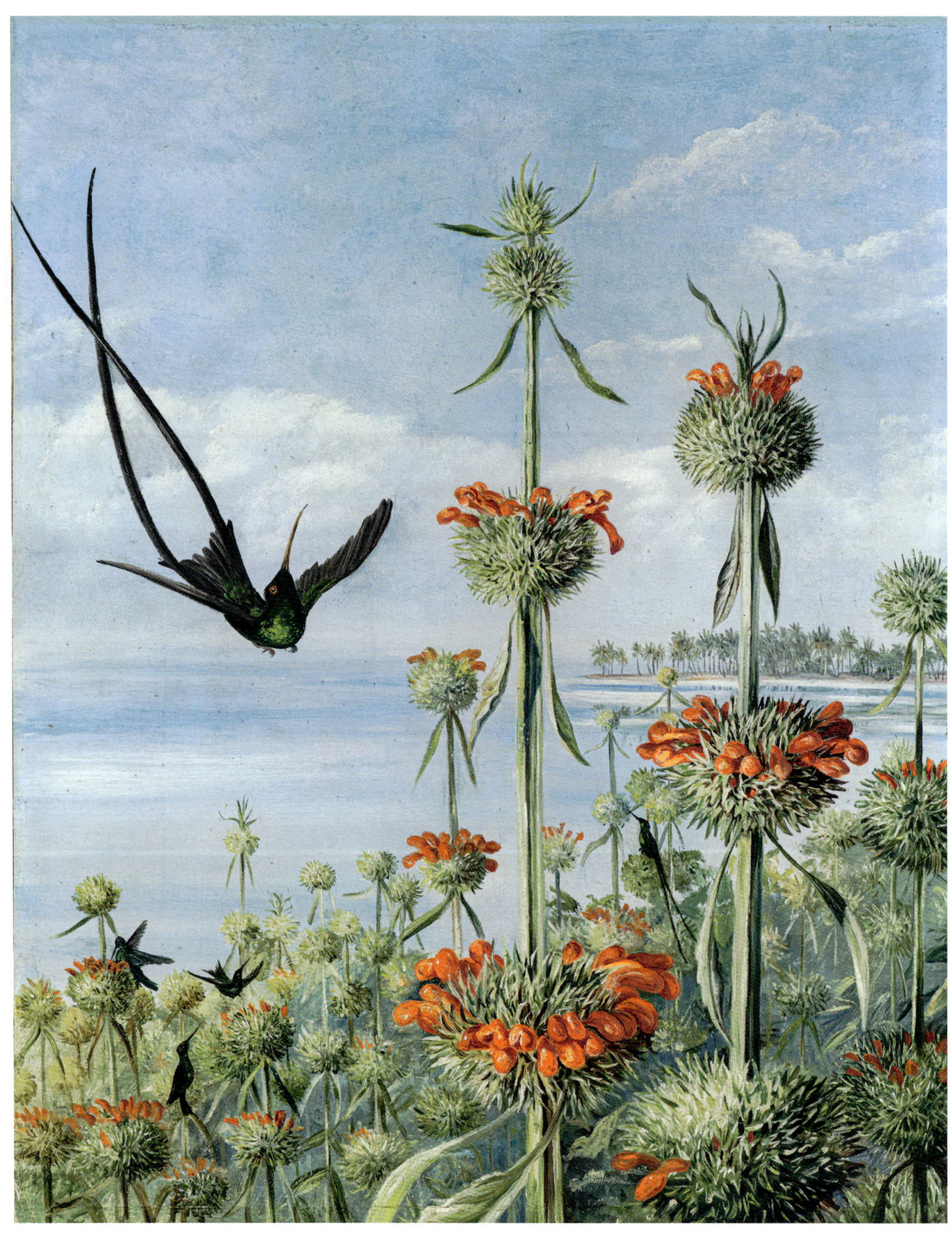

47 Marianne North, 124, *Leonotis nepetaefolia and Doctor Humming Birds, Jamaica,* oil on board, 44 × 35 cm, Royal Botanic Gardens, Kew.

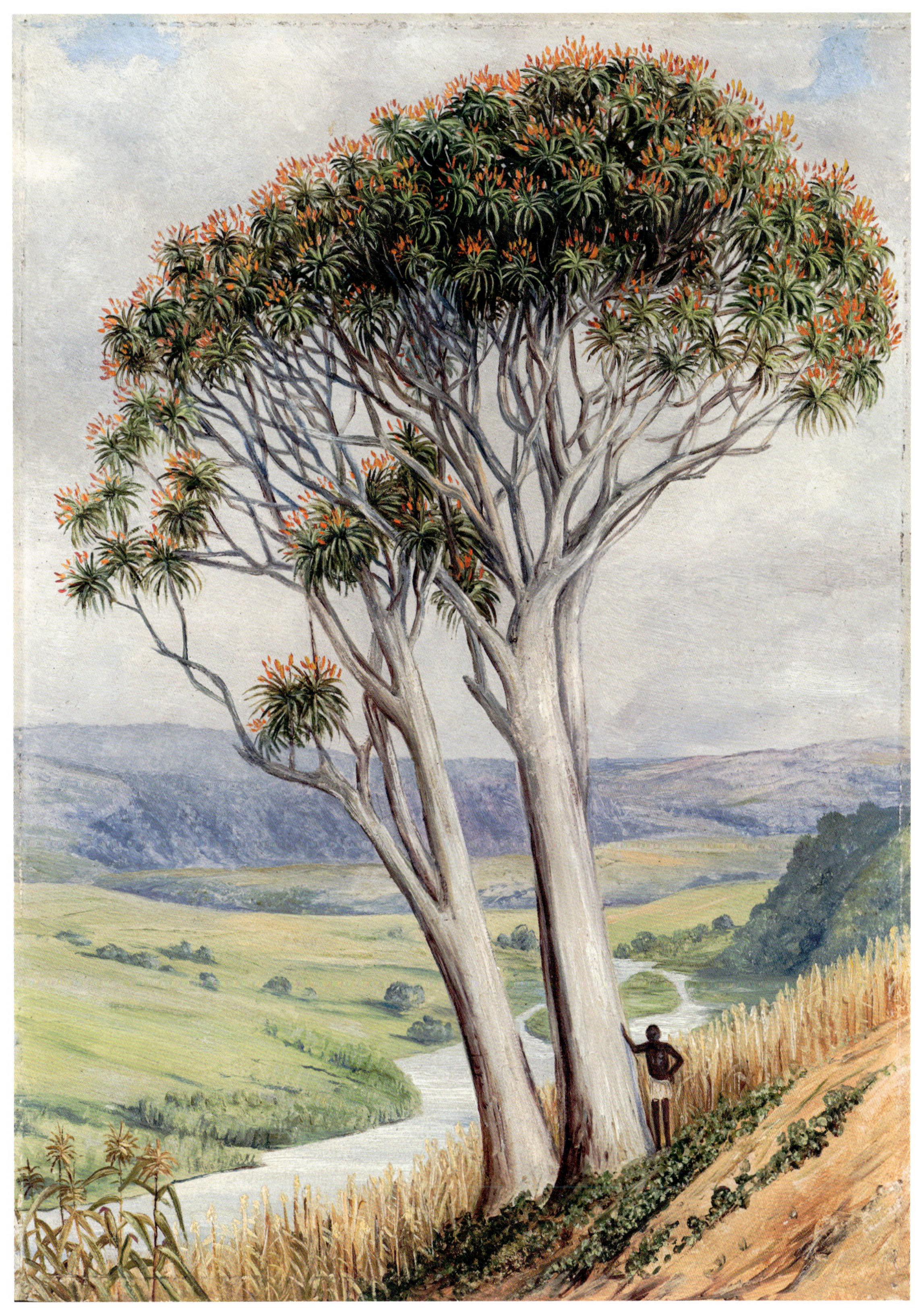

48 Marianne North, 383, *A Remnant of the Past near Verulam, Natal,* oil on board, 35.3 × 25.3 cm, Royal Botanic Gardens, Kew.

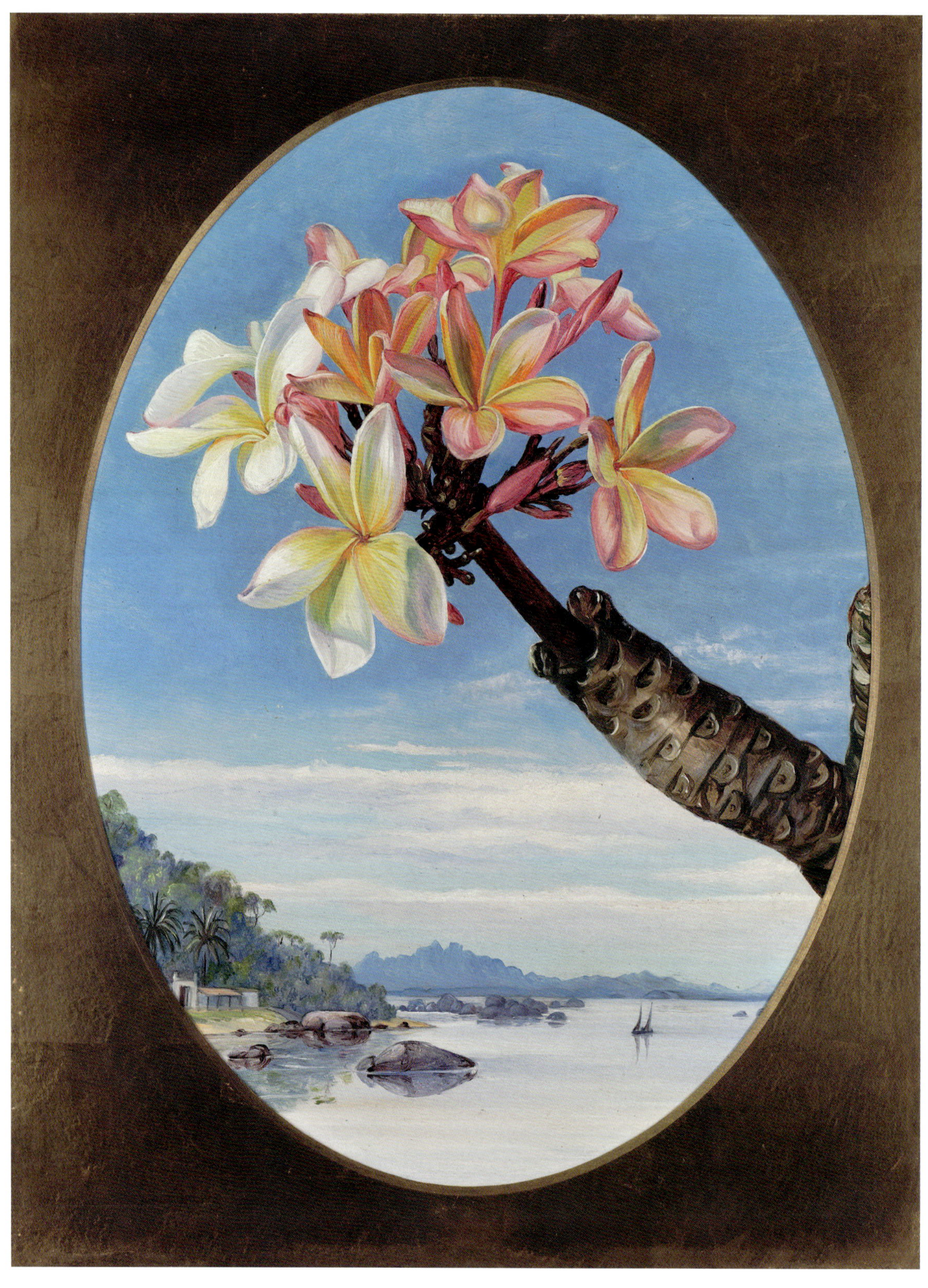

49 Marianne North, 170, *Flowers of Jasmine Mango or Frangipani, Brazil*, oil on board, 45 × 35 cm, Royal Botanic Gardens, Kew.

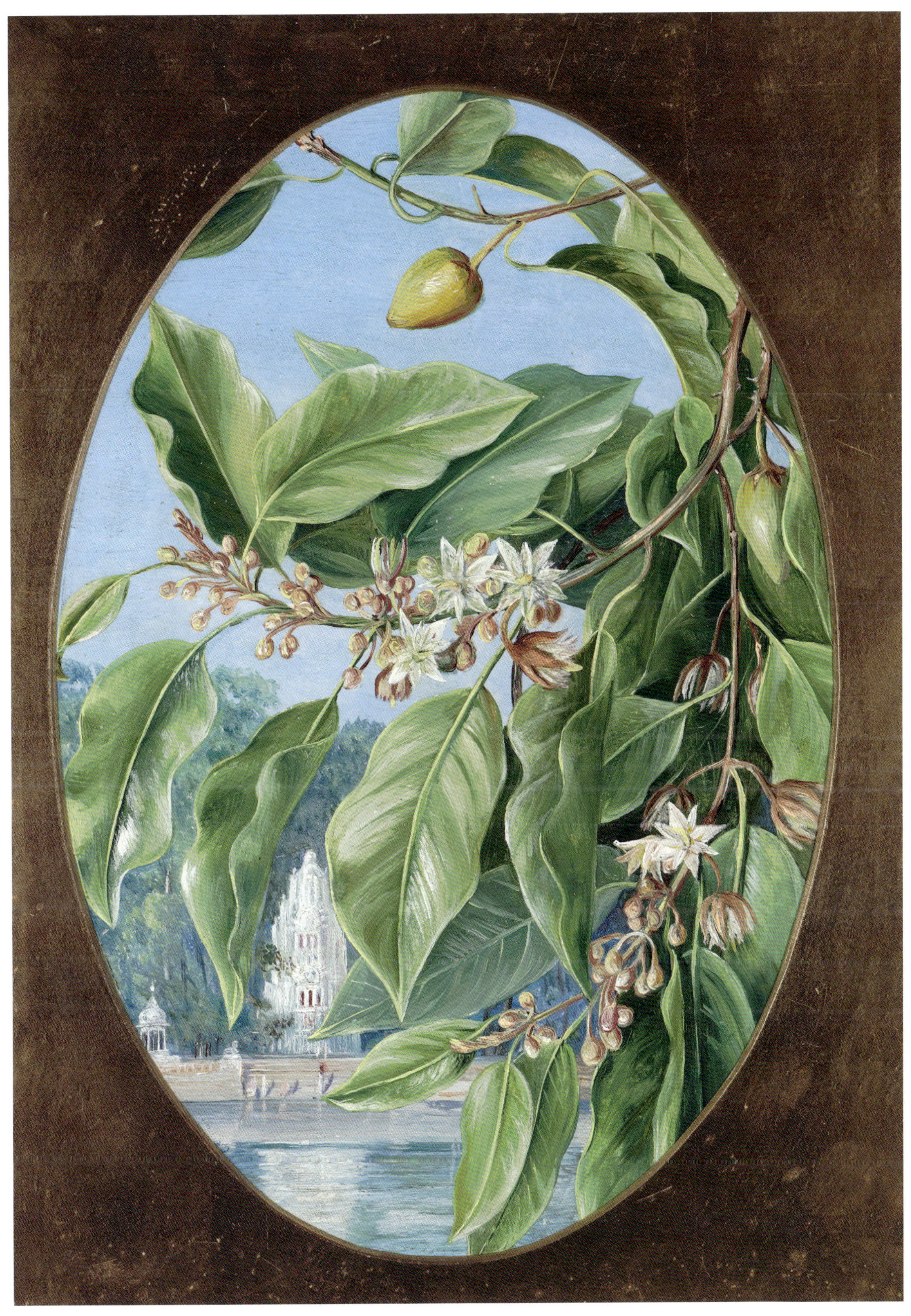

50 Marianne North, 301, *Foliage, Flowers, and Fruit of a Tree Sacred to Krishna*, oil on board, 37 × 25.9 cm, Royal Botanic Gardens, Kew.

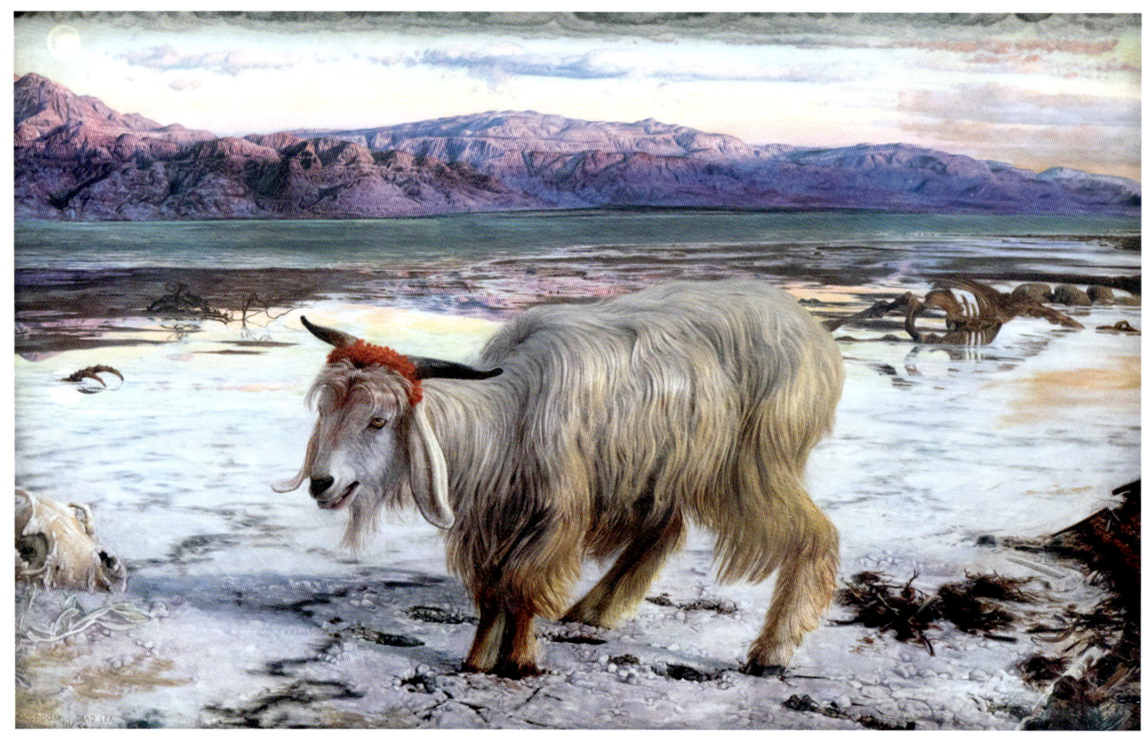

51 William Holman Hunt, *The Scapegoat*, 1854–5, oil on canvas, 87 × 139.8 cm, The Lady Lever Art Gallery, Liverpool, UK.

depicting such a large object on a single sheet of paper. It was necessary 'to take a smaller specimen to paint, in order to get it into my half-sheet of paper life-size'. North writes that the plant was called a 'Brookiana lily' in Borneo but that the Kew 'magnates call it *Crinum augustum*'; boasting that another crinum had been named '*Northiana* [*sic*; *northiana*]'.[35] On another occasion North writes of painting coconuts in Jamaica, stating 'cocoanuts [*sic*] are very difficult to draw, being so exceedingly high that unless one gets too far away to see the detail one cannot get both ends in'.[36] Huxley's claims that North never wrote about painterly technique or problems relating to painting are inaccurate.[37]

A likely influence on North's botanical paintings is the botanist, poet, painter and philosopher Dr Robert Thornton's (1768–1837) *The Temple of Flora* (1812), a book containing numerous illustrations of exotic flowers commissioned from well-known artists;[38] an engraving is also present of the ancient Greco-Roman gods Aesculapius, Ceres and Flora honouring a bust of Linnaeus.[39] Several famous writers of the time provided accompanying prose, including the poet George Dyer (1755–1841) and the natural philosopher Erasmus Darwin (1731–1802). Botanical historian Judith McKay claims that Thornton's book 'inspired traveller-artists like Marianne North who catered for the public curiosity in the plant life of distant lands'.[40] Several of the illustrations in *The Temple of Flora* are by renowned painter Philip Reinagle (1749–1833). Reinagle's illustration *Large Flowering Sensitive Plant* (fig.45) is paired with a poem by Erasmus Darwin. The image depicts mountains and a hummingbird feeding off the flower. North's painting 047, *Flowers of Datura and Humming Birds, Brazil* (fig.46), depicts a hummingbird feeding from the newly opened flower head of a *Datura cornigera* plant upon which a bird's

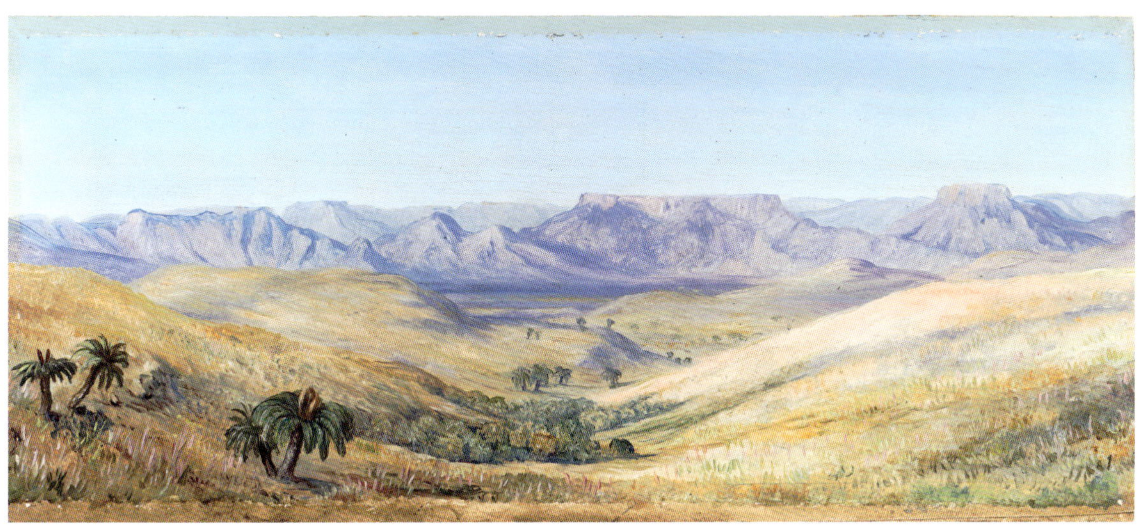

52 Marianne North, 351, *View of the Mountains from the Railway between Durban and Maritzburg, Natal,* oil on board, 15.2 × 35.1 cm, Royal Botanic Gardens, Kew.

nest has been built. Similar compositional tropes can be found in North's paintings 124, *Leonotis nepetaefolia and Doctor Humming Birds, Jamaica* (fig.47), as well as paintings by Martin Johnson Heade of orchids and hummingbirds. North's painting 047 also shows some of the *Datura* plant's structure after the manner of Ehret through the depiction of a flower in addition to a bud, pod and leaves. In Reinagle's illustration a human figure is shown in the distance standing next to a plant, a device later used in colonialist photography as a gauge of measurement. North uses the same device in painting 383, *A Remnant of the Past near Verulam, Natal* (fig.48). The scene depicted by North in painting 047, which shows the *Datura* plant adjacent to a riverbed, is compositionally like Reinagle's illustration *The Night-Blowing Cereus*, also included in *The Temple of Flora*. As directed by Thornton, the settings depicted in illustrations included in *The Temple of Flora* are largely imaginary. North may well have adapted that approach by depicting plants in their actual environments. Other paintings by North that indicate an indebtedness to *The Temple of Flora* include painting 170, *Flowers of Jasmine Mango or Frangipani, Brazil* (fig.49), 301, *Foliage, Flowers, and Fruit of a Tree Sacred to Krishna* (fig.50), and 305, *The Gool-Achin or Caracucha*, all of which include landscape settings with a plant conspicuously placed in the foreground of the painting. Lys de Bray describes how North continued working when it rained in the tropics, and how 'she would arrange her plants as foreground subjects or quite often as flower-pieces, which might have been due to the influence of her early teacher Miss von Fowinkel'.[41]

North was a great admirer of William Holman Hunt's painting *The Scapegoat* (1854–5; fig.51), which depicts the goat described in the Bible's book of Leviticus – used to take on communal sin and then banished into the wilderness – amidst the landscape of the Dead Sea in Palestine. North writes of walking up to the top of a hill in Palestine during a visit there in 1866 and witnessing 'the wonderful red and purple sunset clouds roll over the dead sea, and the deep dark mountains beyond reminding us of Holman Hunt's wonderful picture of the Scapegoat', adding that it was 'perhaps the finest of modern English pictures'.[42] Some of North's landscape paintings are similar in their composition, colouring and detail to *The Scapegoat*. North's painting 351, *View of the Mountains from the Railway between Durban and Maritzburg, Natal* (fig.52), for example, echoes the vastness and vibrant colouring of the landscape depicted by Holman Hunt, who is known to have applied colour on top of a layer of 'wet white paint' creating 'vibrant results'.[43] Other members of the Pre-Raphaelite Brotherhood used a dry white ground underpainting technique upon which to build highly coloured realistic painterly detail, prompting Delacroix to label the Pre-Raphaelites as the 'Dry School', while admiring their 'feeling for truth towards what is real and characteristic in detail'.[44] North may have imitated the Pre-Raphaelites' technique; the botanical expert Wilfrid Blunt (1901–87) criticised the 'curiously dry and unattractive quality' of some of the artist's painting.[45] *The Gardeners' Chronicle* notes how North made use of 'little or no medium', with the colours being applied just as they were 'pressed out of [...] tubes', and that no turpentine was used for cleaning the brushes, they were 'merely wiped clean with a piece of rag'. North's paintings are further described as a 'noble collection of oil-colour sketches' which have been 'dashed off with such bold and truthful drawing and colouring that the fruits themselves seem to be before the visitor in a living state'.[46]

The Scapegoat was not completed by Holman Hunt in situ. It was begun in front of the landscape at the Dead Sea during a visit to Palestine in 1854–5 accompanied by the painter Thomas Seddon (1821–56), but Holman Hunt was forced to complete it from sketches in Jerusalem and London after the goat used as a model died.[47] While in Jerusalem, Holman Hunt met Scottish photographer James Graham (1806–69), who reputedly 'photographed the goat that served as the chief protagonist in Hunt's *The Scapegoat*'.[48] Graham also photographed views for Seddon, and these photographs were used as a point of reference for Seddon's painting *Jerusalem and the Valley of Jehoshaphat from the Hill of Evil Counsel* (1854–5) and towards the completion of Holman Hunt's paintings of Palestine. A watercolour, *Nazareth* (also known as *A Distant View of Nazareth*; completed 1861), was initially worked on by Holman Hunt in situ over three days from 24–27 October 1855. Graham took a photograph of the same scene, *Nazareth from the North* (1855), presumably alongside Holman Hunt on 27 October. Holman Hunt did not complete the watercolour in Palestine and used Graham's photograph as an aide-memoire. Art historian Carol Jacobi concludes that the techniques of 'traditional Picturesque landscape painting were abandoned [by Holman Hunt] for the striking exaggerated perspective and tonal geometries brought out by the camera'.[49] Jacobi cites the critic Philip Hamerton, who 'compared Holman Hunt's seascape effects' to the photographs of the French painter turned photographer Gustave Le Gray.[50] Holman Hunt claimed that photography had been sent by providence to 'show painters their shortcomings'.[51]

Letters from North to Hemsley raise questions regarding North's own possible use of photography as an aid to painting. Referring to paintings of India to be hung at the North Gallery in Kew, North writes, 'I send you the old photograph & two Indian sketches in answer to the last part of your note, thinking it better to give you such scrapes, than the promise of paintings while I may never have time to make'.[52] Although cryptic, North's comments indicate the possession of photographs which may have been used as a visual aide-memoire in support of the completion of paintings. In another letter to Hemsley, North refers to a map that the cartographer Trelawney Saunders (1821–1910) had been asked to paint on the ceiling of the North Gallery. North writes of Saunders, 'I fear he is not business like character & if we do not get his answer in time must do whatever [...] & find my photographs', adding, 'I will do my plants you fix in'.[53] If North did indeed use photographs as an aid to painting, they would have found ready precedent in the working processes of Holman Hunt and other highly regarded Victorian artists. North's sketchbook painting *Palace Yard and Female Elephant and Child, Udaipur, India* (fig.53), held in Kew Archives with several related sketches by North, provides further evidence of North's possible use of photographs. Three elephants are depicted, with one being represented by only its head and forelegs at the edge of the painting. This severe cropping of the subject is indicative of similar effects brought about by the taking of photographs. The use of photography

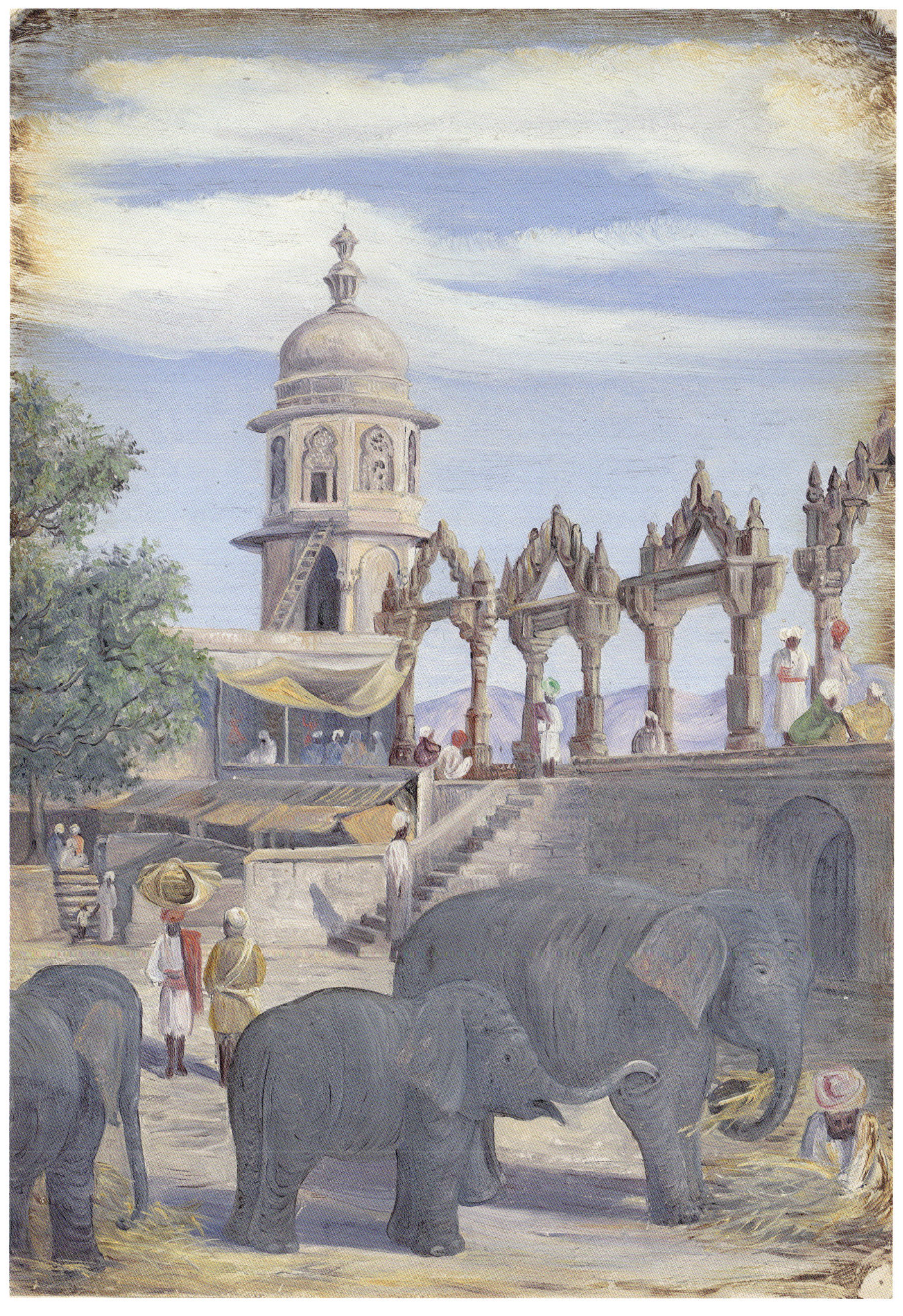

53 Marianne North, *Palace Yard and Female Elephant and Child, Udaipur, India*, oil on paper, 35.5 × 25.2 cm, Royal Botanic Gardens, Kew,

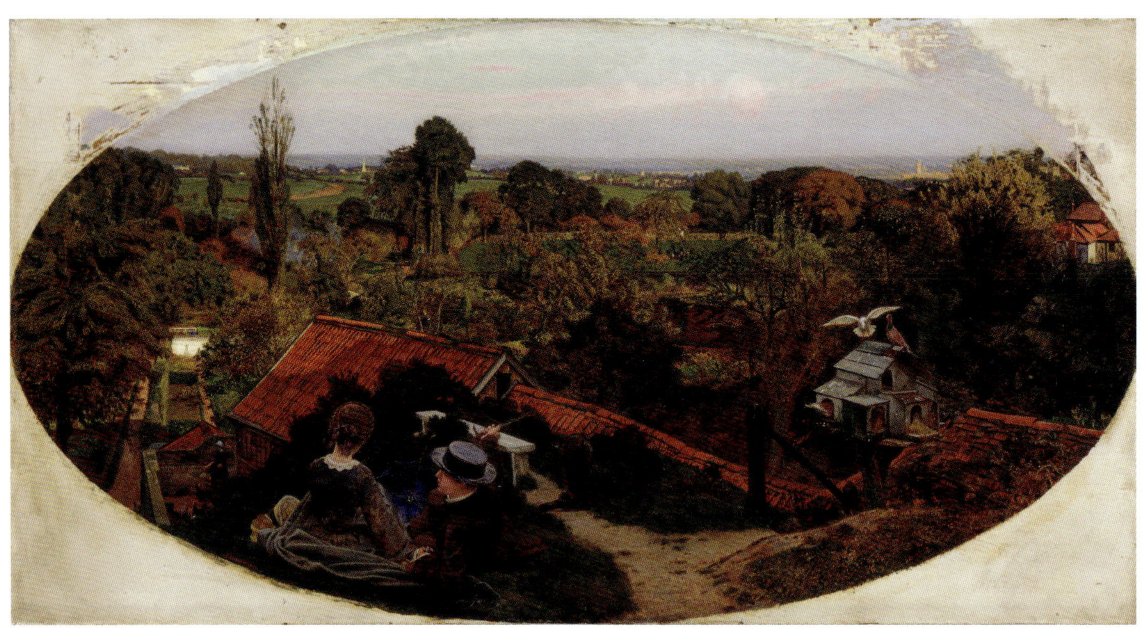

54 Ford Madox Brown, *An English Autumn Afternoon*, 1852–3, oil on canvas, 71.7 × 134.6 cm, Birmingham Museums Trust.

as an aid would explain how North was able to produce paintings in such large numbers over a relatively brief period.

Tensions have persisted regarding the use of photography in relation to botanical illustration. Some regard it as unnecessary. Writing in the 1980s, Sacheverell Sitwell, for example, asserts that there is 'no reason to think that the fine flower book is ended' because the medium of photography 'can never possibly equal the drawn and coloured portrayal by the human hand'.[54] By contrast the botanical illustrator Keith West, writing in the same decade, argues that in some situations where it 'would be criminal to pick' plants to draw, when a 'detailed study is [. . .] impractical' or when 'lack of time' may be of concern, 'a photograph can be taken and a simple line drawing can be carried out in situ'. West stresses, however, that 'photographs should be used only where there is no other sensible means of access to the necessary information' and that painters should not use a photographic image of a plant 'taken by anyone else'.[55] West concludes that photographs are 'poor substitutes for living plants' while accepting that the availability of 'good quality prints backed up by notes, sketches and voucher specimens may be sufficient for many purposes, and as aid towards illustration'.[56] As the artist David Hockney argues, the 'use of outside intervention horrifies the layman', especially via the 'use of optical aids', since it is perceived as 'cheating [and] attacking the very idea of innate artistic genius'. Hockney adds, 'optics do not make marks, only the artist's hand can do that and it requires great skill' – the 'popular conception of an artist is of an heroic individual like [. . .] Van Gogh, struggling alone to represent the world in a new and vivid way'.[57] Given these tensions, it is unsurprising that the possibility of North using photography as a visual aid has not been widely discussed. North firmly refused a gift of photographs in a letter to J.D. Duthie, stating 'photographs, [and] native drawings though most excellent in their way would be little use to me, as I have my own way of doing things & only care to paint from nature', ending 'it was very good to lend them to me'.[58] As Hockney asserts, artists do not like their secrets exposed to the public. North may not have wished 'my own way of doing things' to be exposed to an inner circle of friends, let alone the public. The flat lighting and overall detail of North's paintings has a distinctly photographic quality.

Both artists and scientists in the 19th century questioned formulaic ideas concerning pictorial representation. Madox Brown's painting *An English Autumn Afternoon* (1852–3; fig 54) depicts, in almost photographic detail a vista surrounding a couple depicted on a Hampstead hilltop. Ruskin incorporated photography into art-making and writing in 1840, and Madox Brown in 1847. The art historian Christopher Newell writes that '[f]rom the first, Ruskin used daguerreotypes [an early form of photography] both as aides-memoire and to test his observation of buildings against what was seen in the photographic record'.[59] Jacobi cites a contributor to the *Art Journal*, one of the most important art magazines of the 19th century, who writes that 'the study of photographs was already an established practice among some landscape painters'.[60] Jacobi also writes that 'one of the consequences of the Enlightenment and the Industrial Revolution was the spread of printing and literacy, making a new generation of artists aware of events of science, philosophy and history', and that 'early photographers were frequently artists or closely associated with artistic and literary circles', adding, '[t]he liaison between art and photography was, from the start, transformative to both media'.[61]

The partnership between David Octavius Hill (1802–70), a painter, and Robert Adamson (1821–48), a pioneer in photographic experiments at St Andrews University, Scotland, is indicative of the interaction between art, science and photography in 19th-century Britain. Hill and Adamson's partnership was largely concerned with portraiture, but it also drew on the traditions of genre and landscape painting. Jacobi states that the two were 'inspired by J.M.W. Turner' to produce pioneering 'photographic panorama in two series, one taken from Calton Hill, and the other from Edinburgh Castle'. Jacobi also attests that Hill and Adamson's Rock House studio was on the slopes of Calton Hill, 'which had long served as a panoramic platform'. The site's 'observatory [with] large camera obscura was used by artists'. Jacobi writes that Hill's painting *Edinburgh Old and New* 'updates these precedents with observations from photographic panoramas made with Adamson between 1844 and 1846.'[62] The line between art and photography was further blurred by some early photographers looking towards art as a source of inspiration, and some painters becoming photographers. One such English artist/photographer was Roger Fenton (1819–69), who took photographs of the Crimean War. Photographs by Fenton such as *The Double Bridge of the Machno* (1857) demonstrate a compositional indebtedness to 19th-century British landscape painting.

Photographs were certainly used as aids to the making of paintings by artists within North's immediate social circle. Frederic Church is known to have utilised photographs to help 'hold onto various and direct impressions'.[63] Katherine Manthorne has identified landscape photographs within the Olana collection that were taken in Jamaica, in the 1860s, by an unknown photographer. One of these, titled *Shore with Isthmus, Jamaica* (1860), reveals close similarities to Church's painting, *Palisades near Kingston, Jamaica* (1865; fig.55).[64] Art historians Katherine Bourguignon and Christopher Riopelle argue that Church 'may have purchased [a] photograph of Niagara Falls at the time of his visit' as a 'supplement to the oil sketches and drawings he made there', and that at 'a later date he worked over the photograph *Niagara from the American Side*, 1858 [fig.56], in oil paints, translating its entirely tonal values into the first hints of colour'.[65] Wealthier 19th-century artists commissioned professional photographers to accompany them on their travels – Church is recorded as having enlisted the aid of photographer Peter Bergheim (1813–95) in 1868. Most artists travelling to Egypt and the Middle East without the means to commission an accompanying photographer purchased photographs in local photographic studios, where 'they could stock up on material to help them with their compositions once they had returned home'.[66] In Europe, commercial photographers targeted the artist market by 'producing what were known as *études après nature*, images of a

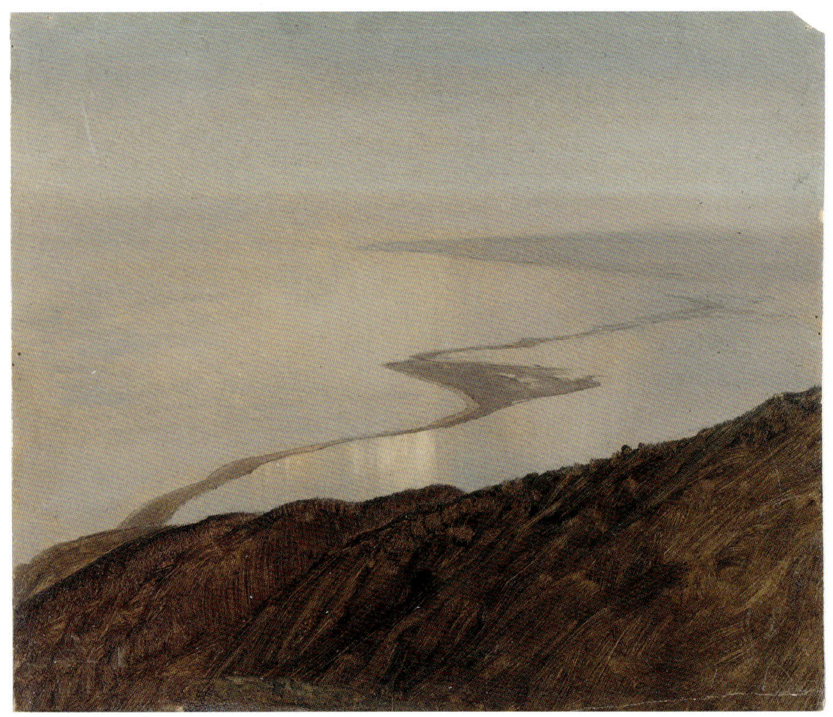

55 Frederic Edwin Church, *Palisades near Kingston, Jamaica*, also known as *Coastline of Jamaica*, 1865, brush and oil paint, graphite on paperboard, 26 × 30.5 cm, Cooper Hewitt, Smithsonian Design Museum.

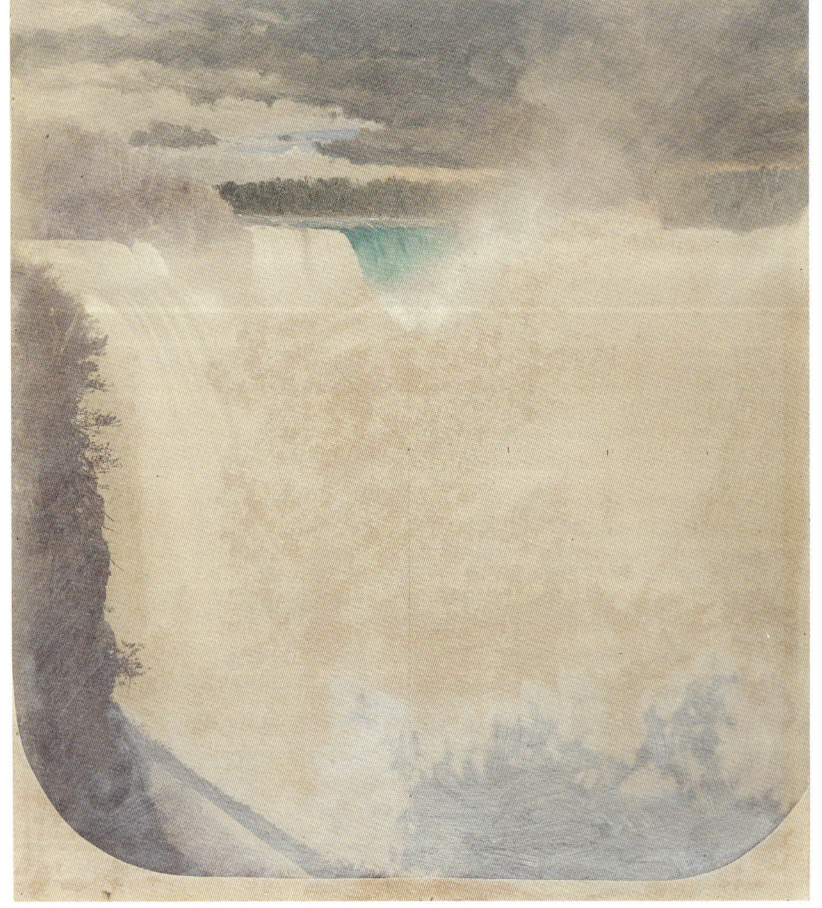

56 Frederic Edwin Church, *Niagara from the American Side*, August 1858, brush and oil paint over albumen silver print, 32.7 × 29.5 cm, Cooper Hewitt, Smithsonian Design Museum.

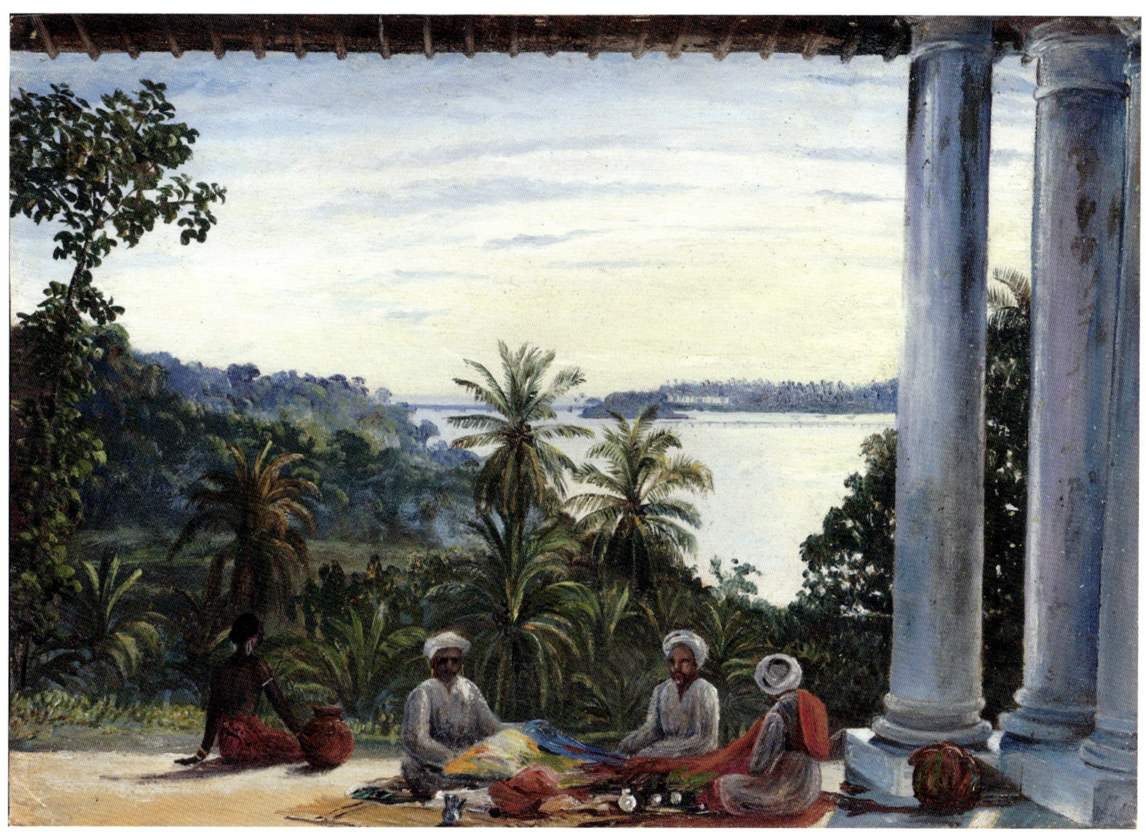

57 Marianne North, 248, *Bombay Pedlars on Mrs Cameron's Verandah, Kalutara, Ceylon*, oil on board, 24.9 × 35 cm, Royal Botanic Gardens, Kew.

variety of objects, scenes, and people that were taken specifically to suit the requirements of artists looking for guidance in detail'.[67]

North was photographed by the pioneering photographer Julia Margaret Cameron during visits to Cameron's home in Ceylon (Sri Lanka) in 1876 and 1877. North describes the walls of one room being covered with 'magnificent photographs', while others were 'tumbling about the tables, chairs, and floors' with 'quantities of damp books, all untidy and picturesque'.[68] North's sister Catherine writes of the artist bringing photographic material back to England after spending time at Cameron's house, alongside sketches and paintings.[69] North made several paintings at Cameron's house while Cameron was taking photographic portraits of Tamil workers, including *A Group of Kalutara Peasants* (1878). Two paintings in the North Gallery were made while North was with Cameron in Ceylon: 240, *Some of Mrs Cameron's Models, with Cocoanut [sic] and Teak Trees, Kalutara, Ceylon* (Sri Lanka) – which depicts a river with tall trees near its banks looking out from the veranda of a house, with a boy holding an urn, and accompanied by animals; and 248, *Bombay Pedlars on Mrs Cameron's Verandah, Kalutara, Ceylon* (Sri Lanka; fig.57) – depicting a group of peddlers sitting on the lawn in front of Cameron's house appearing to sell silk scarves. In painting 240, three trees to the left of the painting frame Cameron's garden. In painting 248 there is a tiled veranda just in view and three Greek classical-style pillars framing the garden, which is set on a hill sloping down to a river. The view of

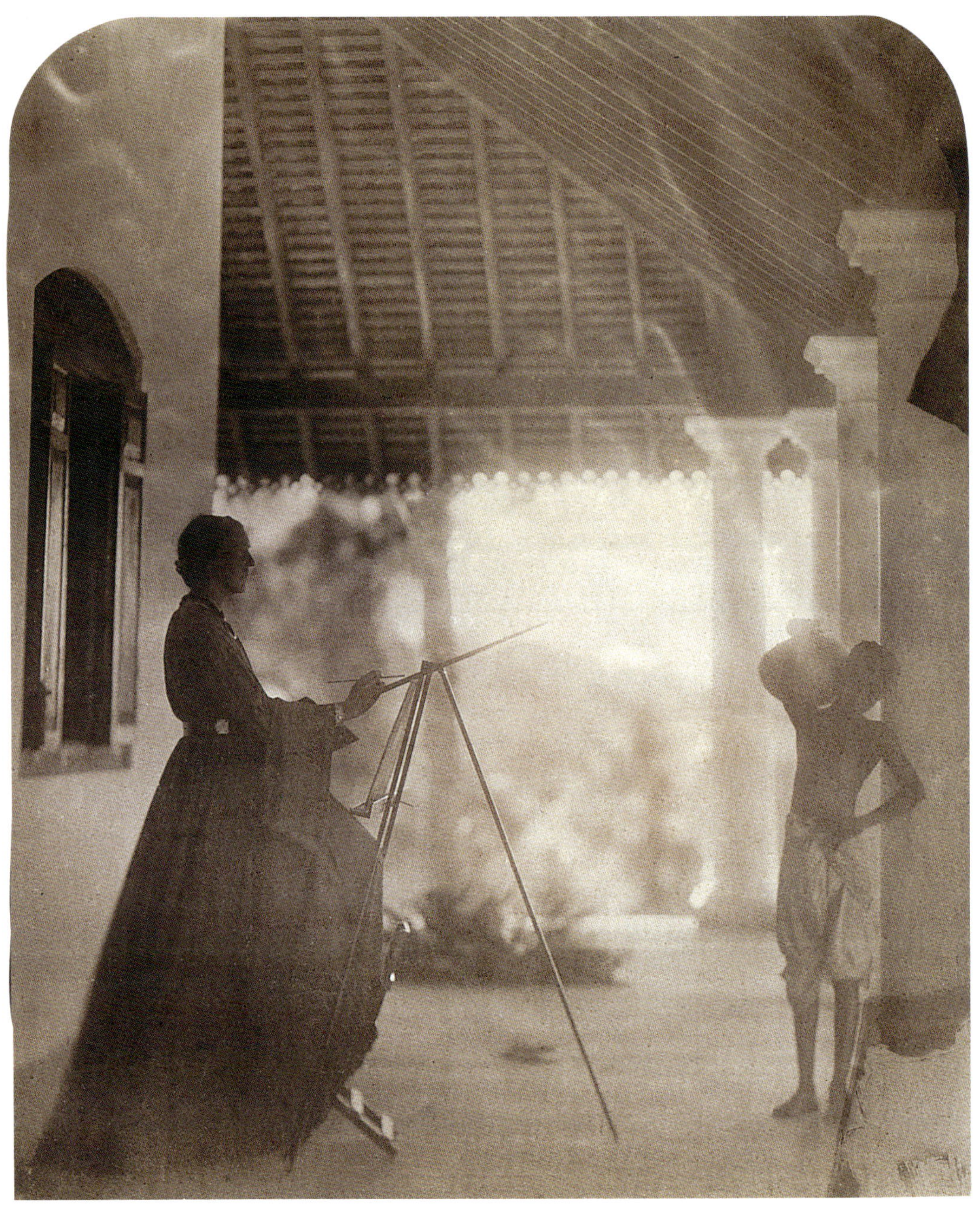

58 Julia Margaret Cameron, Marianne North with a boy holding an urn, 1877, photograph, Tom North for the North family archive, Rougham, Norfolk, UK.

the garden and river is identical in both paintings. The stance of the boy depicted in painting 240 is like that of a boy holding an urn photographed by Cameron (fig.58). The boy appears to be posing for North, who stands at an easel outside one of the buildings set within Cameron's garden. There is a small window with shutters behind North and a tiled roof with Greek pillars to the right of the picture. These are very similar to features depicted in North's painting 248. North may have used Cameron's photograph as a starting point upon which to elaborate imaginatively in paint. Kew photographer Andy McRob, on an assignment to catalogue and confirm some of the sites and vistas in North's paintings, found discrepancies in North's depiction of Cameron's house. McRob could only find pillars fitting a round-square-round format, while all the pillars in North's painting are round. The only three pillars North could have depicted in this way are on the front porch of the house, and these pillars are situated on the left side of the porch. McRob also notes that the only area with a tiled roof was a series of buildings at the back of Cameron's house which appeared to be servants' quarters or utility rooms, and that the pillars there were square. McRob confirmed that, because the house is positioned upon a hill, it did comply with the view in painting 248 and it was also evident that the view from the back of Cameron's house corresponded with the river view directly beyond the garden vegetation in both paintings, 240 and 248.[70] All of this indicates that North produced painting 248 from differing viewpoints. Photographic prints at the Cameron house, and four portraits of North taken by Cameron in January 1877, could have been used to inform North's paintings in a composite way. Historian of photography Colin Ford writes that during North's visit, Cameron was inspired to produce the 'nearest photograph to a landscape' in one taken of a 'group of estate workers (or possibly itinerant peddlers) close to the veranda of her home'.[71]

Even if photography was not used consistently by North as an aid, the paintings are nevertheless undeniable composites, both in terms of compiling differing representations over time – as is also the case with Dutch flower painting of the 17th and 18th centuries – and the use of secondary sources. North's letters unequivocally reveal the use of illustrations by others as reference points alongside studies made in situ. North was extraordinarily prolific in producing paintings of a wide range of botanical and landscape subjects using differing media and techniques, and may well have chosen not to reveal the complexity of those uses to a wider public who expected paintings of scientific authenticity from an intrepidly heroic female traveller. North's evident artistic aspirations may also have influenced that lack of candour. Perhaps the artist felt that there could be greater frankness with close friends and professional associates such as Hemsley, who understood the actual methods used in the production of botanical paintings and illustrations.

Today, the contemporary art world embraces the use of lens-based technologies such as photography and video as well as techniques associated with collage-montage and de-familiarisation. Global travel related to the making of art is commonplace. A pre-modernist blurring of the boundaries between art and science has also become a focus for the work of contemporary artists. North's work as a travelling botanical illustrator at a time during the 19th century of precipitous technological and social change is in many respects a precursor for these developments. Viewed in this light, it becomes necessary to reappraise North's contribution to visual culture. North's paintings sustain established approaches to image-making associated with the European post-Renaissance painterly tradition. They are also part of the initiation of ways of making images beyond those established approaches, since they incorporate new approaches to technologies, as well as technologies that can be used to make not only images, but also art objects and installations.

4

Travels as a Botanical Painter

North's enthusiasm for world travel and travel writing was not entirely unusual for upper-middle-class British women of the mid- to late 19th century. Several of North's female friends were also travellers and travel writers. They include the British novelist Amelia Edwards, with whom North corresponded frequently over several years. Edwards was well known as the author of the book *A Thousand Miles up the Nile* (1877), which gives an account of Edwards's life in Egypt along with accompanying sketches as illustrations. Seeing a growing threat to Egypt's architectural heritage brought about by colonialism, Edwards 'became an avid advocate for the greater protection of Egypt's monuments' and would eventually abandon painting and writing for campaigning and fundraising in support of the cause.[1] Many who travelled from Britain, Europe and America to what was then referred to as the 'Orient' found it to be 'a life-changing experience'. On returning home they often adopted lifestyles that reflected their travels abroad and continued, as art historian James Parry indicates, to have a deep 'affection for a part of the world that had played such a defining role in their careers and lives'.[2]

From 1871, North travelled extensively in search of botanical subjects to paint. Between 1871 and 1872 the artist journeyed to the United States, Canada and Jamaica, and then spent eight months in Brazil producing over 100 paintings. In 1875 North travelled to Tenerife and the Canary Islands before beginning a two-year journey around the world between 1875 and 1877, which included visits to California, Japan, Borneo, Java and Ceylon (Sri Lanka). North visited India in 1878 and 1879, producing 200 paintings there. In 1880 the artist returned to Borneo, also visiting New Zealand and Australia, where 300 paintings were produced, before returning to the United States in 1881. Between 1882 and 1883 North visited South Africa, in 1884 the Seychelle Islands, and between 1884 and 1885 Chile. North's diaries were published posthumously, and contain recollections of these travels as a botanical painter; travels that were at times conducted under gruelling conditions, with an indifference on North's part to conventional dress codes. North's adventures abroad include sitting unromantically all day painting in a 'mangrove swamp' without catching a fever. Catherine Addington Symonds states that North 'could live without food, without sleep, and still come home, after a year or two, a little thinner, with a more careworn look in the tired eyes, but ready to enjoy to the full the flattering reception which London is always ready to give to any one who has earned its respect by being interesting in any way'.[3] Despite its privations, North remained an indomitable traveller, writing in a letter to Arthur Burnell about the time 'when summer comes and the country house dressed up for parties [. . .] put as counter temptations to wandering away quietly with my easel and old portmanteau to unseen wonders the other side of the world, I think both you and I can guess which will carry the day'.[4] North also writes that 'Mrs. Agassiz and I agreed that the greatest pleasure we knew was to see new and wonderful countries' and 'the only rival to that pleasure was the one of staying at home', adding, 'only ignorant fools think because one likes sugar one cannot like salt; those people are only capable of one idea, and never try experiments'.[5] North's travels were of continuing interest to the British public. *The Times* newspaper of London reported regularly on where North would travel next.[6]

Among North's more adventurous travels as a botanical artist was an expedition to Borneo and Java (the present-day north-west of Borneo island and part of Malaysia; Java is now part of Indonesia) in 1876. As part of this expedition North visited Sarawak, arriving with letters of introduction (a then customary means of connecting with strangers within upper-middle-class and high Victorian society) to Charles and Margaret Brooke, the then Rajah and Rani of Sarawak, provided by Sir William Hooker.[7] Margaret, formerly de Windt (1849–1936), had married Charles Brooke (1829–1917), the nephew of the first colonial European Rajah of Sarawak. Charles was apparently 'dedicated [. . .] to his adopted country and believed his mission was to preserve Sarawak from the exploitation and influence of the Europeans'.[8] Sarawak was ruled by the Brooke family, who installed their own 'curious version' of the Indian British Raj, for over a century from 1841.[9] Margaret Brooke's book, *Good Morning and Good Night* (1934), gives an account of the Brookes' time as the rulers of Sarawak. Margaret, who was generally indifferent to visiting Europeans, writes of North's visit, 'Miss North's arrival in Sarawak is a great and happy landmark in my life [. . .] Many of my English friends were devoted to her.' Margaret goes on to describe North as a 'hurtling energetic'.[10] Throughout North's visit to Sarawak, Charles Brooke had a band play every night. Other entertainments included the playing of croquet and lawn tennis, as well as 'constitutional walks and occasional dinner parties'.[11] It seems that Margaret gave North 'entire liberty, upon her visit to their home'. The artist was not made to accompany Margaret upon the 'somewhat monotonous' constitutional walks the Brookes took every afternoon, although North did occasionally go with Margaret on evening boating trips 'before the splendid sunsets were over' (fig.59).[12] Margaret writes, 'the first evening of her [North's] stay in Kuching we went for a row on the river, and the sunset behind Matang was, as she said, a revelation'.[13] North was placed in 'a most luxurious room' at the Brookes' palace from where it was possible to 'escape by a back staircase into the lovely garden'.[14]

North's ragged travelling attire on arriving in Sarawak was subject to Margaret's critical attentions; especially the 'undraped knees' which were thought to be 'risqué'.[15] North sent for 'a bit of undyed China silk and a tailor' so that a new garment could be made.[16] North recalled a conversation held with a local chief of police during a painting trip to Brazil in 1872–3, in which the policeman 'was extremely curious to know why I was travelling alone, and painting. Did the government pay my expenses? I certainly could not pay them myself, as I was too shabbily dressed for that!' North informed the policeman that, upon returning to Britain, the artist hoped to 'paint the Organ Mountains and to sell it for so much money that it would pay for all my expenses', concluding ironically, 'then at last he understood what I travelled for, for is not money the end of all things?'[17]

Margaret Brookes was somewhat irritated by North's extensive knowledge of plants, including pitcher-plants

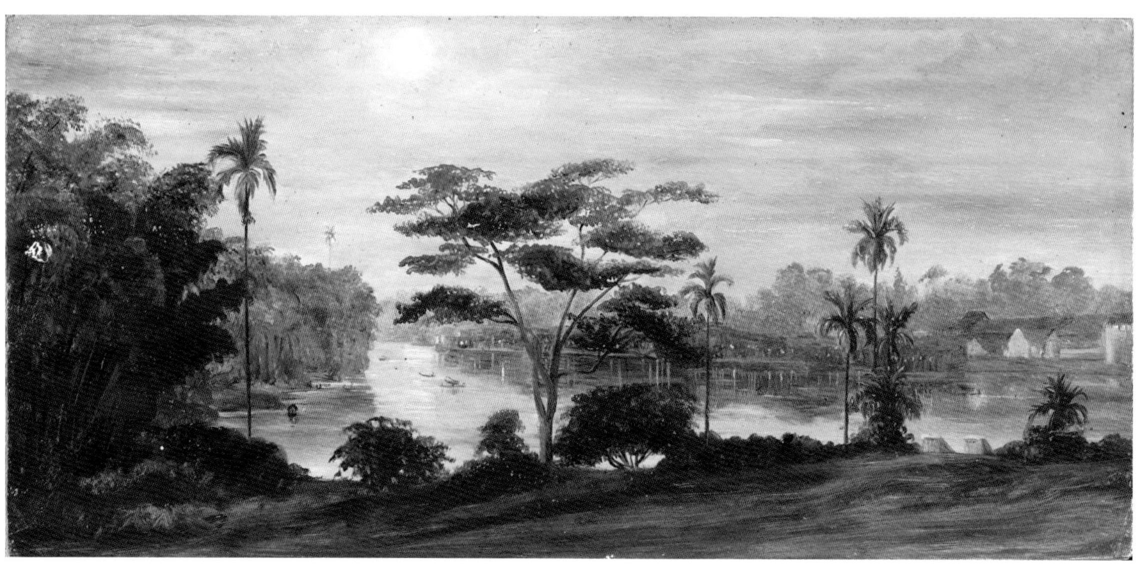

59 Marianne North, 540, *Moonlight View from the Istana, Sarawak, Borneo*, oil on board, 24 × 50.8 cm, Royal Botanic Gardens, Kew.

that Margaret had never heard of. In trying to impress North, Margaret made up bogus Latin names for plants, but North gave Margaret a 'kindly scolding' and observed that the names were 'nonsense'.[18] This friction extended to Charles, who had some knowledge of horticulture. Open disputes arose between Charles and North 'over identifications and methods of cultivation' with, according to Margaret, arguments erupting especially on nights when curry was on the menu.[19] North stayed with the Brookes for around six weeks, during which time the artist apparently painted all day. Margaret thought 'this must be bad for [North]' and 'sometimes tried to get her away early in the afternoon for excursions'.[20] To avoid an official visit to Charles and Margaret by the new consul of Labuan, North retreated via canoe to the Brookes' mountain-farm at Mattange to be comfortably alone, with 'a cook, a soldier, and a boy' and a 'coopful [*sic*] of chickens'. North writes, 'Life was very delicious up there. I stayed till I had eaten all the chickens, and the last remains of my bread had turned blue [with mould].'[21] Despite their disputes, Margaret recalls accompanying North 'very sorrowfully' to a departing steam ship but feeling 'something new and delightful had come into my life, for she had not only introduced me to pitcher-plants, but to orchids, palms, ferns, and many other things of whose existence I had never dreamed'. Margaret adds, 'Miss North was the one person who had made me realize the beauties of the world'.[22]

During the visit to Sarawak, plants were collected for North to paint. They included orchids and pitcher-plants which, North writes, were 'pulled for me most ruthlessly, the latter being of several varieties'.[23] The variety of pitcher-plant named after North, *Nepenthes northiana*, was brought to the artist by a 'Mr. E.', the cousin of the British painter John Everett Millais, who accompanied North 'into the great forest' while visiting Tegoro in Sarawak. North writes that Mr E. travelled up a mountain and brought down 'some grand trailing specimens of the largest of all pitcher plants'. North 'painted a portrait of the largest', remarking that 'my picture afterwards induced Mr. Veitch to send a traveller to seek the seeds [...] from which he raised plants and Sir Joseph Hooker named the species'.[24] On their travels Mr E. made illustrations in pen and ink which North tried 'hard to make him publish'.[25]

As mentioned in the previous chapter, North visited photographer Julia Margaret Cameron in Ceylon (Sri Lanka) between 1876 and 1877. North writes that Cameron had 'made up her mind at once [she] would photograph me' and 'for three days she kept herself in a fever of excitement about it'.[26] Cameron effectively invented the close-up photograph through 'taking a series of soft focused portraits',[27] and was famous for adopting an 'intentional blurring of her images'.[28] That practice was coincidental with John Ruskin's aestheticising conception of the ideal photograph. As photography historian Carol Jacobi indicates, Ruskin 'praised photography that did not seek sharpness at all costs', believing painters and photographers should both explore 'the implications of focus and indistinctness'.[29] Cameron dressed North 'in flowing draperies of cashmere wool', with loose hair and standing in front of 'spiky cocoa-nut [*sic*] branches' with the rays of the noonday sun projecting between the leaves as a slight breeze moved them. North was then placed against 'a background of breadfruit leaves and fruit, nailed against a window shutter'. Cameron told North 'to look perfectly natural' with the thermometer standing at 96° Fahrenheit. The injunction failed, 'and though she [Cameron] wasted twelve plates, and enormous amount of trouble, it was all in vain she could only get a perfectly uninteresting and commonplace person on her glasses, which refused to flatter' (fig.60).[30] Cameron's photographic portrait of North depicts its subject in Middle Eastern style dress and holding a pose akin to that conventionally used by European painters to represent the Virgin Mary. Similar stylings were used in orientalist paintings by 19th-century Western artists. The genre of orientalist painting 'developed and diversified during the eighteenth and nineteenth centuries in Britain' with individuals projecting 'different identities, whether delusory, transitory or contradictory'.[31] Such portraits 'were conceived specifically for public display' or for 'wider distribution' through Victorian 'print media culture'.[32] Prominent examples include Thomas Phillips's (1770–1845) portrait of Lord Byron, *Nobleman Dressed as an Albanian*, also known as *Lord Byron in Albanian Dress* (1813). Cameron's portrait of North could be described as a reprising of these existing painterly formats.

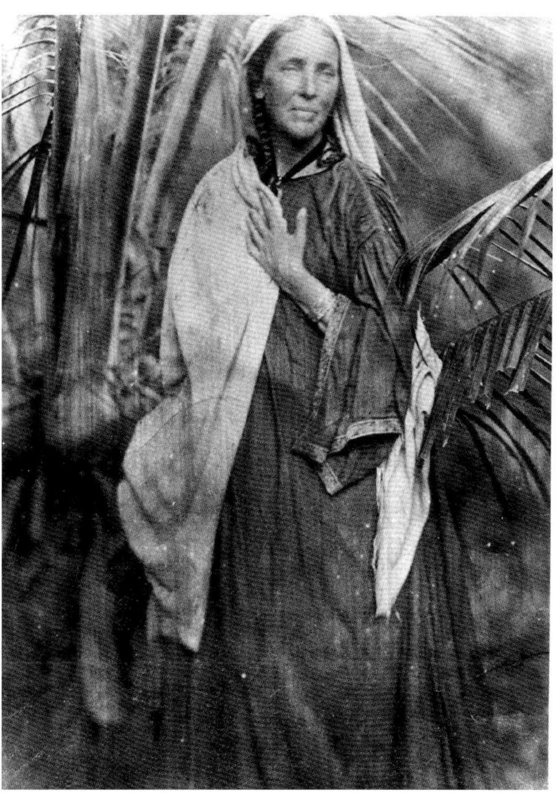

60 Julia Margaret Cameron, Portrait of Marianne North, 1876–7, photograph taken at Cameron's home in Ceylon (Sri Lanka), Royal Botanic Gardens, Kew.

The pose adopted by North is 'consistent with the romantic adoption of Oriental dress by other 19th-century Western travellers'.[33] The *Portrait of George Cummings in Turkish Dress* (1817) by Andrew Geddes (1783–1844), for example, depicts the sitter wearing

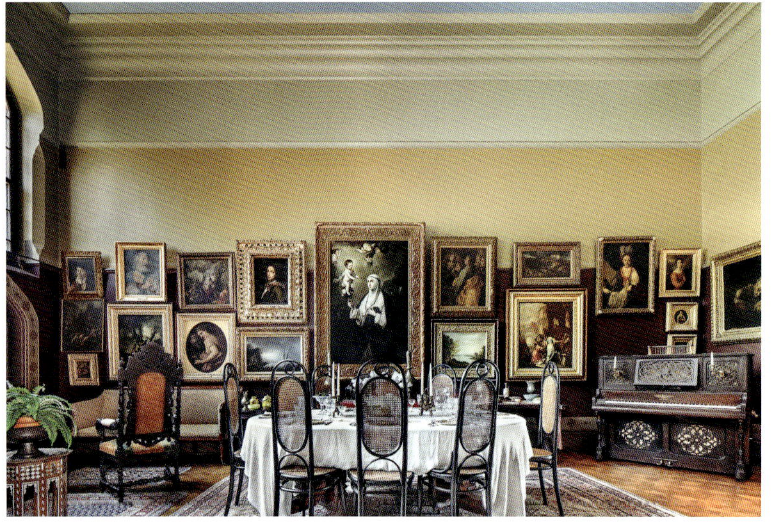

61 Peter Aaron, The dining room inside Olana's main house, looking east, photograph, The Olana Partnership.

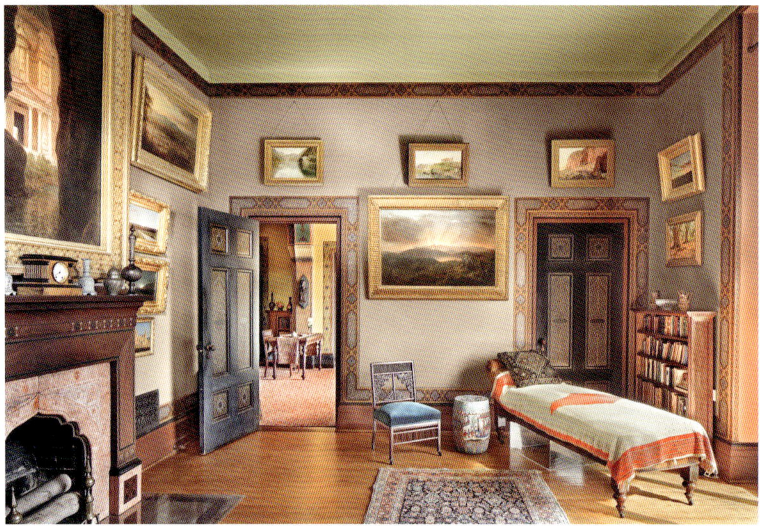

62 Peter Aaron, The sitting room inside Olana's main house, looking east, photograph, The Olana Partnership.

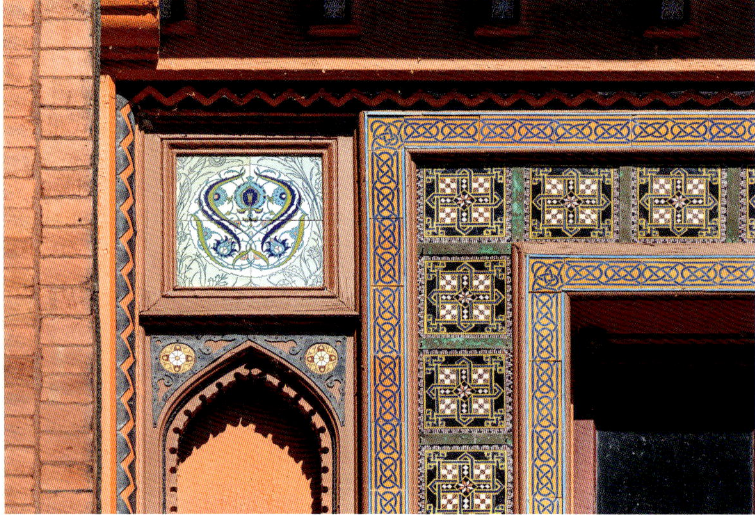

63 Peter Aaron, Detail of the second storey of the east facade of the main house at Olana, photograph, The Olana Partnership.

Palestinian clothes. William Holman Hunt did not dress up in this way while travelling in the Middle East, however, and ridiculed Thomas Seddon for doing so.[34] Holman Hunt was 'unconvinced by what they considered an unnecessary "adaptation of the costume" and initially refused to wear any local apparel',[35] but was photographed 'in similar guise by Cameron in 1864 and was depicted the following year by John Ballantyne [one of North's painting tutors] as a figure dressed in Biblical attire in the painting *The Finding of The Saviour* (1865)'.[36] North's discomfort while being photographed by Cameron may have echoed Holman Hunt's concerns with dressing up.

While travelling to the US for the second time in 1881, North visited New York, where a party was given in conjunction with the showing of a series of paintings that the artist had produced in Australia. North writes of being 'interviewed in turn by everybody, till I got tired of perpetual roaring'.[37] The show was well received, with the *New York Times* reporting on North's 'tour around the world to paint the distinctive wild flowers of each country'.[38] North also writes that 'Mr. Church heard one evening in an omnibus of my being in New York, and came off at once to see me about nine o'clock, making me promise to go home with him the next day to see his new house, and Mrs. Church up the Hudson', adding that 'He [Church] looked through all my paintings with real interest; which pleased me, for I still think him the greatest of living landscape-painters'.[39] While visiting Church's home, Olana, North witnessed the American artist's growing collection of oriental *objets d'art* and cheek-by-jowl hanging of paintings in the dining room, in addition to painted architraves and doors throughout the house (fig.61). According to Katherine Manthorne, Olana 'integrated the memorabilia of travel, from decorative arts to tourist souvenirs, into the fabric of their [the Churches'] home'.[40] On this second visit to Olana, North was able to see the finished results of what had been in the initial stages of planning in 1871. North describes a walk with Church in the hills above Olana:

> We mounted 700 feet above it [Olana] by a new zigzag road through the forest, and came to the clearing on the top, in which was the picturesque Eastern-looking house with its Moorish arches and windows and coloured tiles, having a grand view of the winding Hudson beneath, and distant Catskill Mountains. Mrs. Church [. . .] made a perfect centre to the curious Damascus hall with its high pointed arches, oriental divans, and central fountain. She [Church] had contrived to make the whole collection of curiosities look like the natural parts of a comfortable living-house: exquisite Persian rugs, bronzes, carvings, porcelain, etc.[41] (figs 62–3)

North also writes of sleeping in 'a Chinese bed which was a marvel of wood, horn, ivory, and even jade carvings, and its coverlet and pillows (by day) were made of the richest Japanese embroidery'. Church advised North to visit 'New Granada, where he said the spurs of the Andes were so high that each of the valleys between them had a different flora, that the people were kind and hospitable, and travelling not difficult'.[42] Frederic Church's travel letters include references to flora and fauna, local people, and exotic foods similar to those found in North's diaries.[43]

Throughout the 19th century the British surveyed lands across the globe for military, scientific and economic purposes. Those involved include cartographers, geologists and geographers, archaeologists, ethnographers, food producers and plant hunters. Painters and cartographers were employed to make topographical representations of land based on empirical data as part of this process. Such representations, which included maps, sketches and watercolour paintings, were used to illustrate travel literature. Some of the images produced were panoramas.[44] As historian Richard Neville indicates, panoramas 'emerged in the early nineteenth century as a form of popular entertainment, at a time when the reach of the British Empire was expanding' and paintings of locations across the world were being

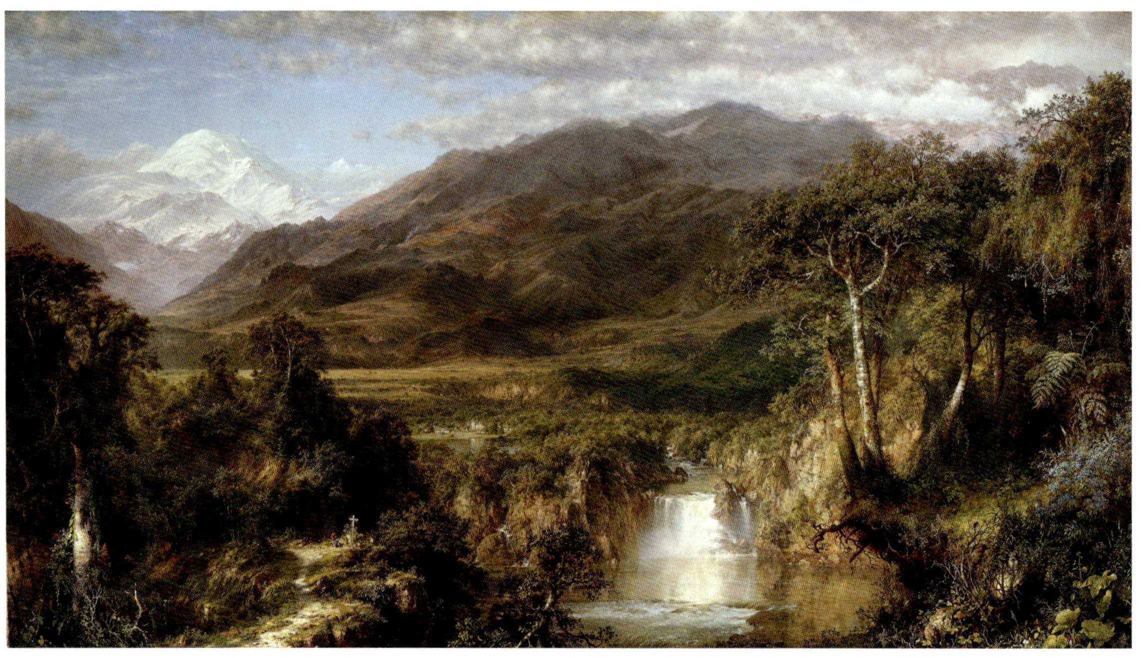

64 Frederic Edwin Church, *Heart of the Andes*, 1859, oil on canvas, 168 × 302.9 cm, The Metropolitan Museum of Art, New York.

'exhibited throughout England in purpose-built structures'.[45] The fashion for painted panoramas was introduced by the Englishman Robert Barker (1736–1806) and marketed with varying degrees of success by entrepreneurs, including several artists who 'enjoyed a brief but splendid popularity in Europe, England, and to a lesser degree America'.[46] Painted panoramas were 'usually large in scale and either stationary or moving on rollers', and 'surrounded the viewer with a remarkably realistic image of a chosen scene'.[47] As Neville also indicates, panoramas in 'their wide-angled [. . .] breadth of view and emphasis on both scale and detail' reflected the 'confidence of Empire' and, for 'many people, panoramas were their first introduction to worlds beyond their own'. Panoramas 'were presented as educational' and 'often supported by printed texts' that explained 'the detail of painting which focused on a dramatic mix of the exotic and the curious'.[48] Neville also states that typically 'panoramas were drawn on many sheets of paper, with the sheets joined after execution of the artwork' and 'were often rolled for storage'[49] in a similar manner to that of a Chinese scroll. Panoramas were also sometimes made, part-by-part, using lensed technologies. The Australian colonial topographical and panorama painter John Rae (1813–1900) writes in a letter to the British artist John Skinner Prout (1805–76) on 21 January 1848 that the

> camera has been finished for some time now and consequently I have got tired of it. You must know however that I made a very good job of it. I call it a camera but it answers also as a small panorama – I made it all with my own hands and tools and it has given much amusement to many spectators at different times.[50]

Many 19th-century artists travelled abroad to produce more conventional landscapes. Among the most prominent are Edward Lear, William Holman Hunt and Frederic Church. Some artists, such as Frederic Leighton,

David Wilkie (1785–1841) and John Frederick Lewis (1805–76) became topographical painters. There were also photographers, such as James Graham, whose 'heavy photographic equipment was an impediment to progress when travelling' according to Holman Hunt.[51]

North's output as a botanical painter while travelling was prodigious, amounting to many hundreds of paintings and sketches of botanical subjects and landscapes over 14 years. While each of these works can be appreciated separately, they are also parts of a vast more-or-less systematic record of botanical subjects across the world given concrete expression by the North Gallery at Kew, in which many of the paintings are brought together according to region for public viewing. Could North – an amateur artist in many ways – have completed that record simply by painting subjects at first hand in situ? Or was its production a technically more complex and drawn-out process? North's approach is certainly akin in some ways to that of panorama painters in its stitching together of individual images to make a representative whole. The North Gallery, as a purpose-built site for presenting a visually expansive topographical representation of the world, is very much in keeping with the displaying of panoramas more generally in the 19th century; albeit one that gives viewers a sweeping global representation of nature through bringing together detailed topographical fragments, rather than a single composite or moving image. North's use of manufactured canvases of standard sizes – a by no means uncommon practice for painters of the outdoors during the 19th century – made the orderly arrangement of paintings in standard black japanned frames at the North Gallery possible. Did North also employ photography and/or lensed technologies as an aid to the making of individual paintings? Other travelling painters of the 19th century, such as Holman Hunt and John Rae, would appear to have done just that. As suggested in the previous chapter, the use of photography as an aid to painting would go some way to explaining North's ostensibly superhuman productivity. Today, such uses would not be seen as unusual but as part-and-parcel of modern visual productivity. North's paintings were not produced in splendid isolation but, as the diaries and other accounts attest, with the support of others as part of an informal worldwide network. Movement across continents combined with colonially supported connectivity and the possibilities provided by 19th-century technology are the crucial prevailing context of North's achievements as a travelling botanical painter.

Quasi-panoramic approaches to the representation of nature were taken up by other travelling 19th-century artists, among them North's friend Church, whose vast and expansive painting of the South American landscape, *Heart of the Andes* (fig.64), was exhibited at the German Gallery on Bond Street in London in 1859. A critic writing in the *Art Journal* commented that the 'picture combines more than any other we know, the minute and literal truth at which the Pre-Raphaelites aim imperfectly, with Turner's greatness and grace of conception'. Other critics were not so impressed by Church's combination of observed detail and sublime excess.[52] A perceived boundary between high art and the topographical detail provided by panoramas and their display for public entertainment may well have lain at the heart of those less-than-positive responses. Enduring distinctions of this sort between high artistic expression, descriptive detail and public entertainment may also account, in part at least, for the critical discrediting of North's paintings and the North Gallery (fig.67). A more fulsome appreciation of North's work as a travelling botanical painter requires a nuanced understanding of the prevailing discursive and practical contexts of the mid- to late 19th century, in addition to information found in the artist's diaries (figs 65–6).

North's lifelong friend Edward Lear produced numerous paintings and topographical illustrations as well as diaries while travelling. As a child, North had watched Lear complete several paintings based on travel sketches, among them *The City of Syracuse from the Ancient Quarries where the Athenians were Imprisoned BC 413* (1853). Lear added a rendering of a

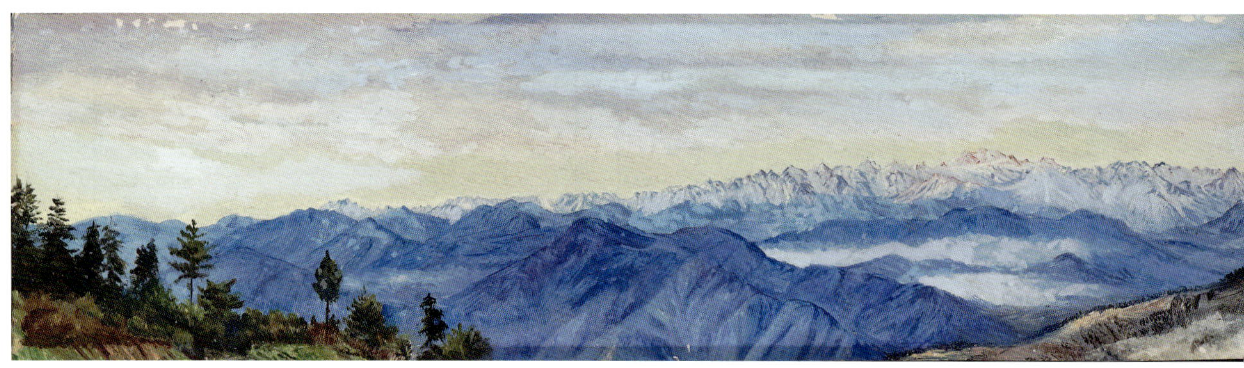

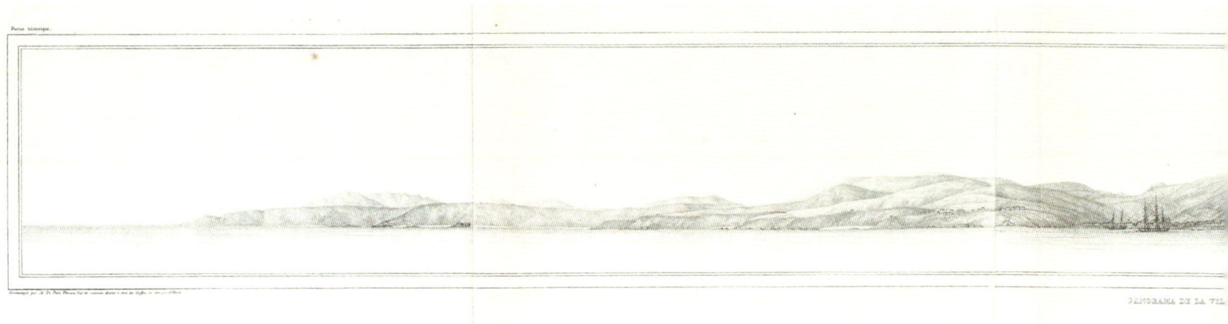
Partie historique.
PANORAMA DE LA VIL

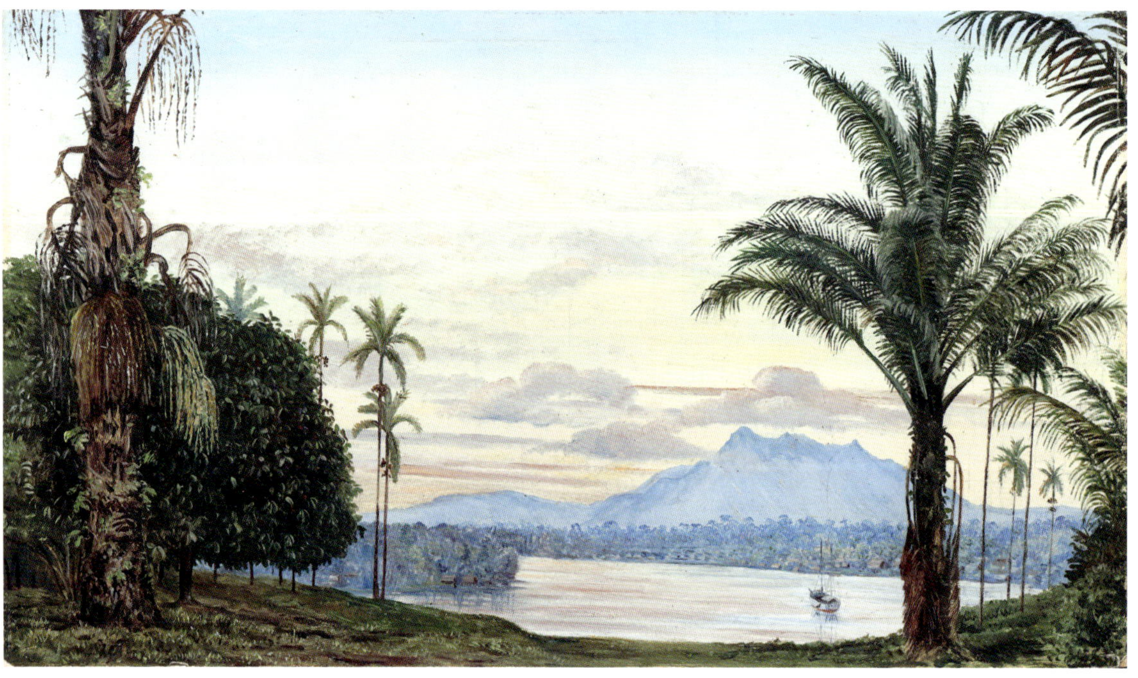

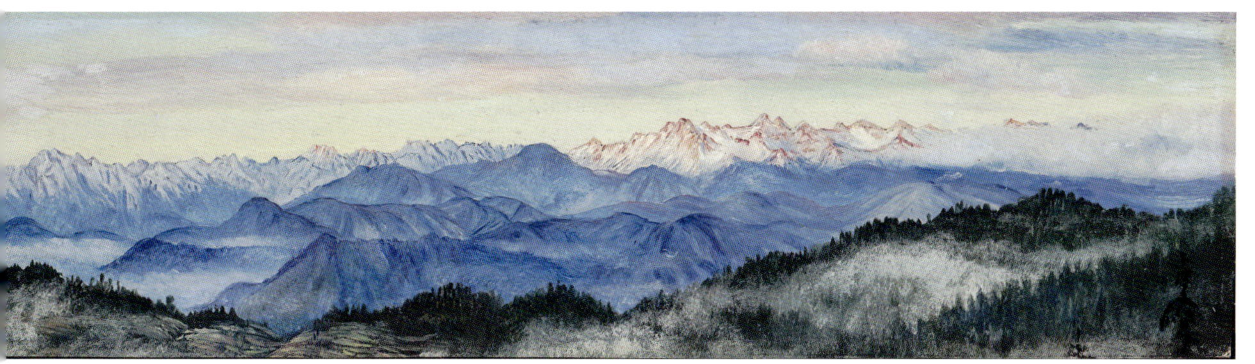

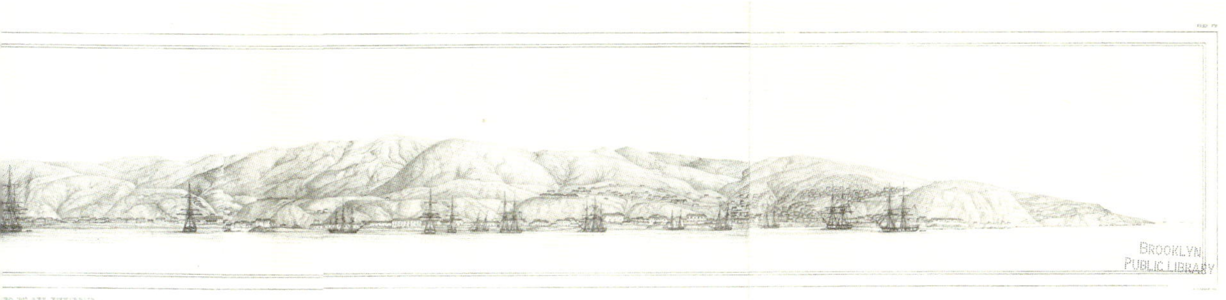

65 (top) Marianne North, 290, *Pine-clad Slopes of Nagkunda, North India, and View of the Distant Mountains*, oil on board, 12.8 × 35.2 cm, Royal Botanic Gardens, Kew.

66 (middle) Philipp Von Martius, *Panorama. Executed during the Years 1826–1833*, in Alcide Dessalines d'Orbigny, Jean François Camille Montagne and Karl Friedrich Philipp von Martius, *Atlas*, 1846–7, 147.4 × 19.5 cm.

67 (left) Marianne North, 557, *View of Matang and River, Sarawak, Borneo*, oil on board, 28.6 × 50.2 cm, Royal Botanic Gardens, Kew.

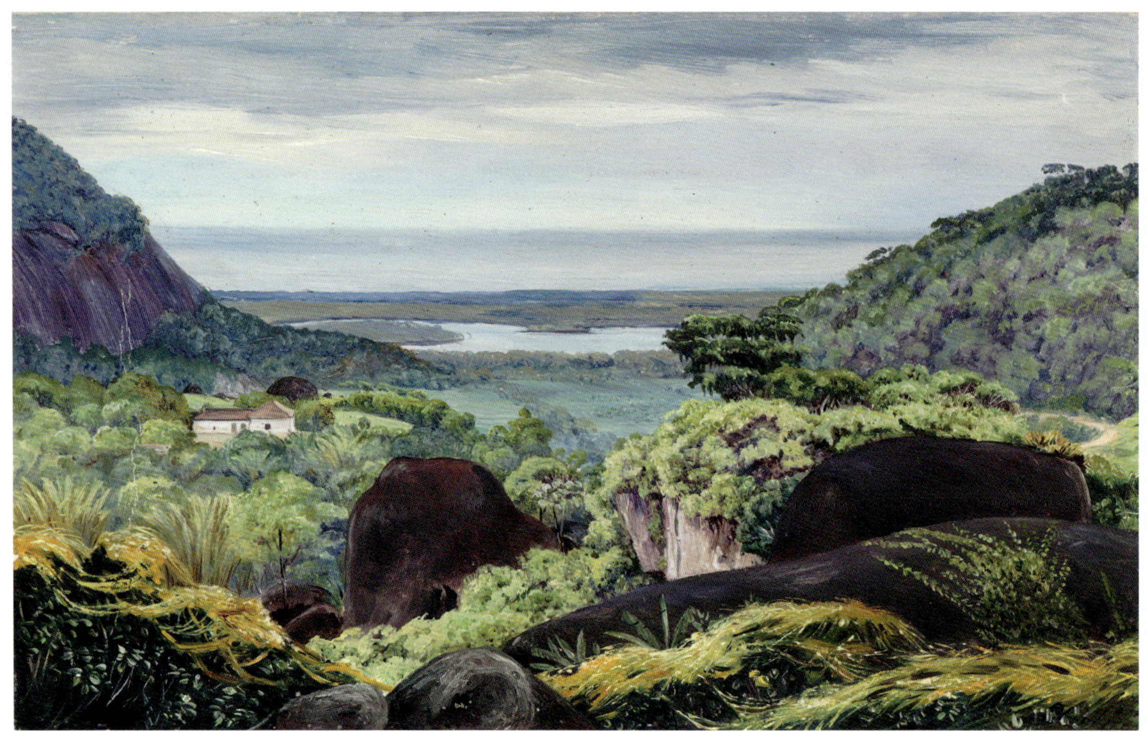

68 Marianne North, 821, *View near Tijuca, Brazil, Granite Boulders in the Foreground*, oil on board, 25.2 × 35.6 cm, Royal Botanic Gardens, Kew.

69 (opposite top) Marianne North, 787, *A Bush Fire at Sunset, Queensland*, oil on board, 25.5 × 35.5 cm, Royal Botanic Gardens, Kew.

70 (opposite below) Marianne North, 035, *View of the Jesuit College of Caracas, Minas Geraes, Brazil*, oil on board, 25 × 35 cm, Royal Botanic Gardens, Kew.

fig tree found in North's garden in Hastings as part of the foreground of the painting, and a group of ravens to another painting, all of which were drawn from 'one old specimen with a broken leg, which was fastened to an apple tree' outside the windows of North's home.[53] This composite approach by Lear is described in North's diaries prior to May 1854, placing it within the same time frame as Lear's completion of another travel painting, *The Temple of Apollo at Bassae* (1854–5). Lear had returned to England armed with preparatory watercolour sketches for the painting, and added an oak tree and rocks to the foreground of the canvas while in Leicestershire.[54] This composite approach would seem almost certainly to have influenced North.

North may also have been influenced by Lear's travels. As well as travelling in the Middle East, Lear visited India in 1872. After visiting India personally in 1878 and 1879, North began to take the possibilities of travel painting seriously. Both artists painted the Himalayas. Many of North's paintings of the region are in a topographical style that incorporates Lear's characteristic compositional use of a birds-eye view leading down towards an expansive landscape across water, for example 821, *View near Tijuca, Brazil* (fig.68), as demonstrated in Lear's

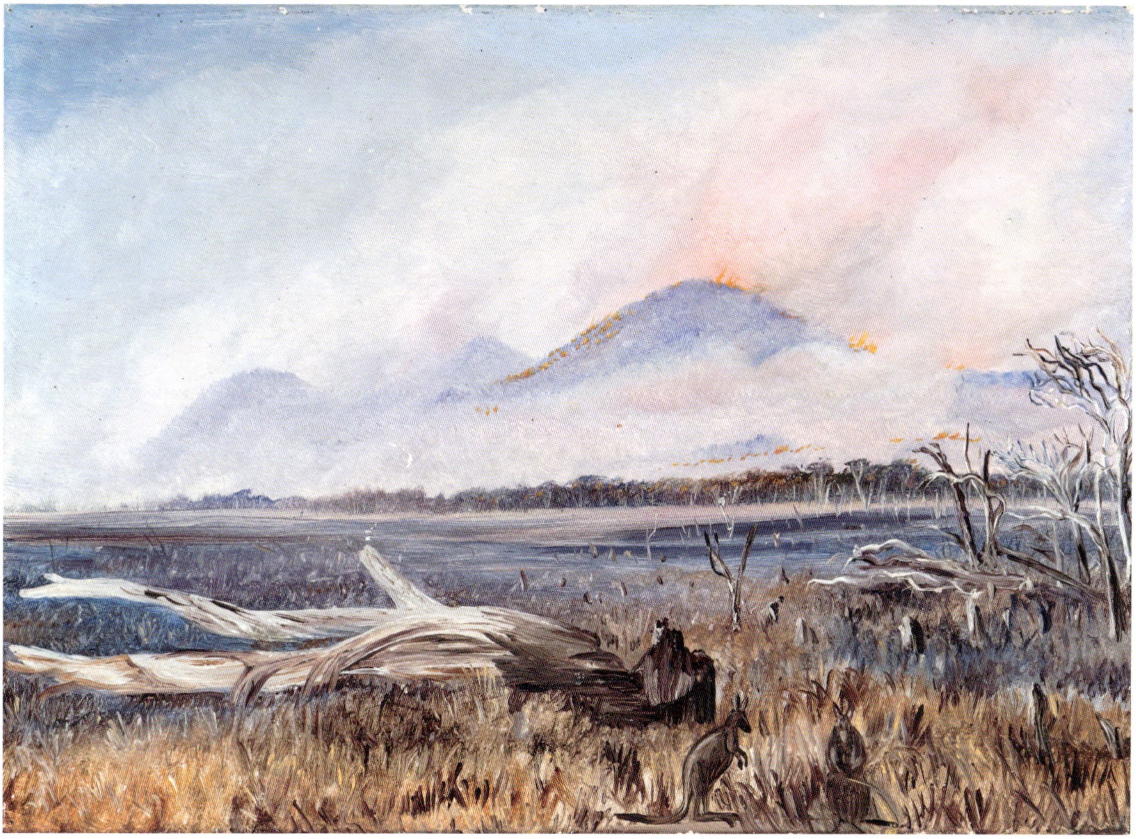

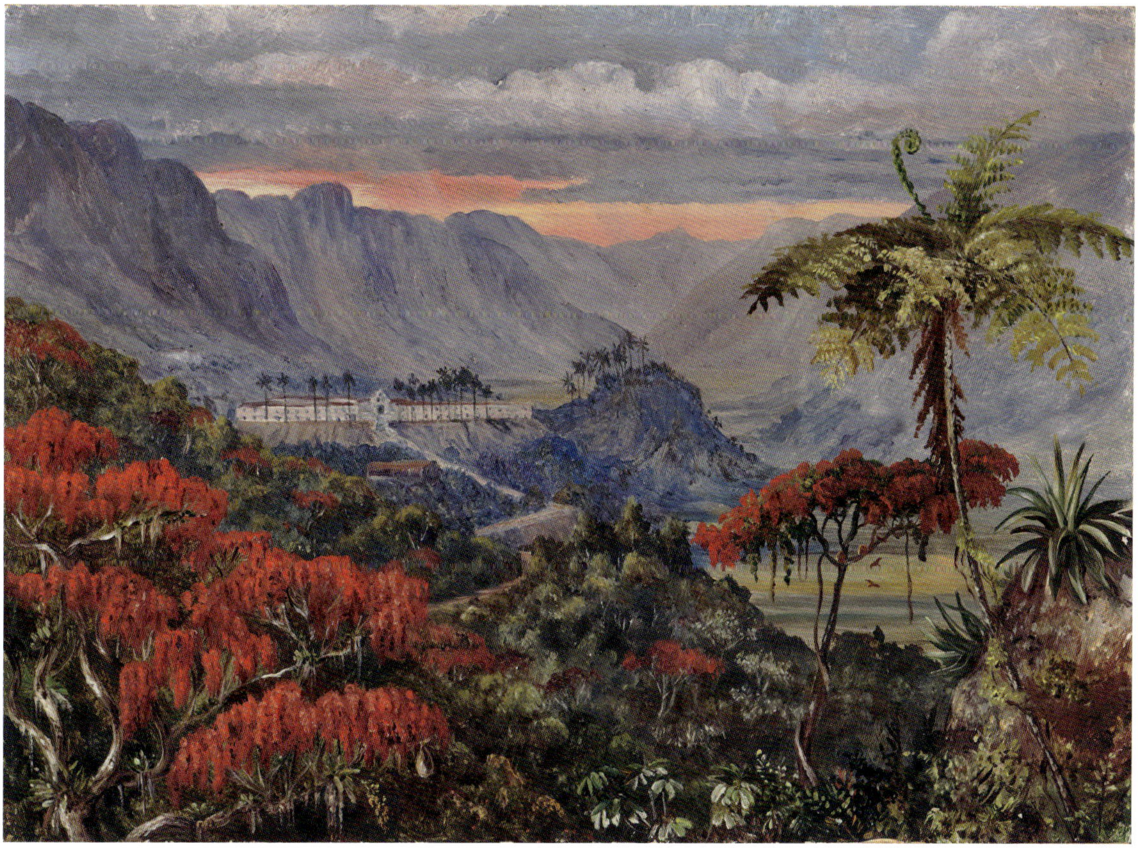

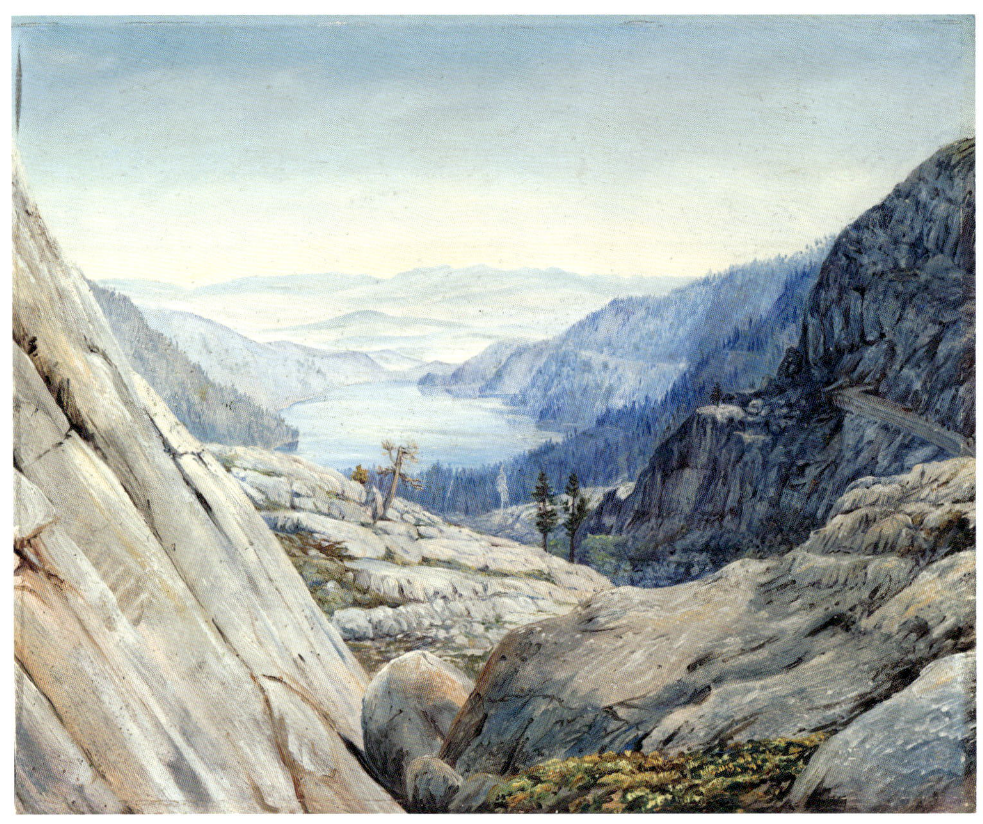

71 Marianne North, 201, *View of Lake Donner, Sierra Nevada,* oil on board, 35 × 44 cm, Royal Botanic Gardens, Kew.

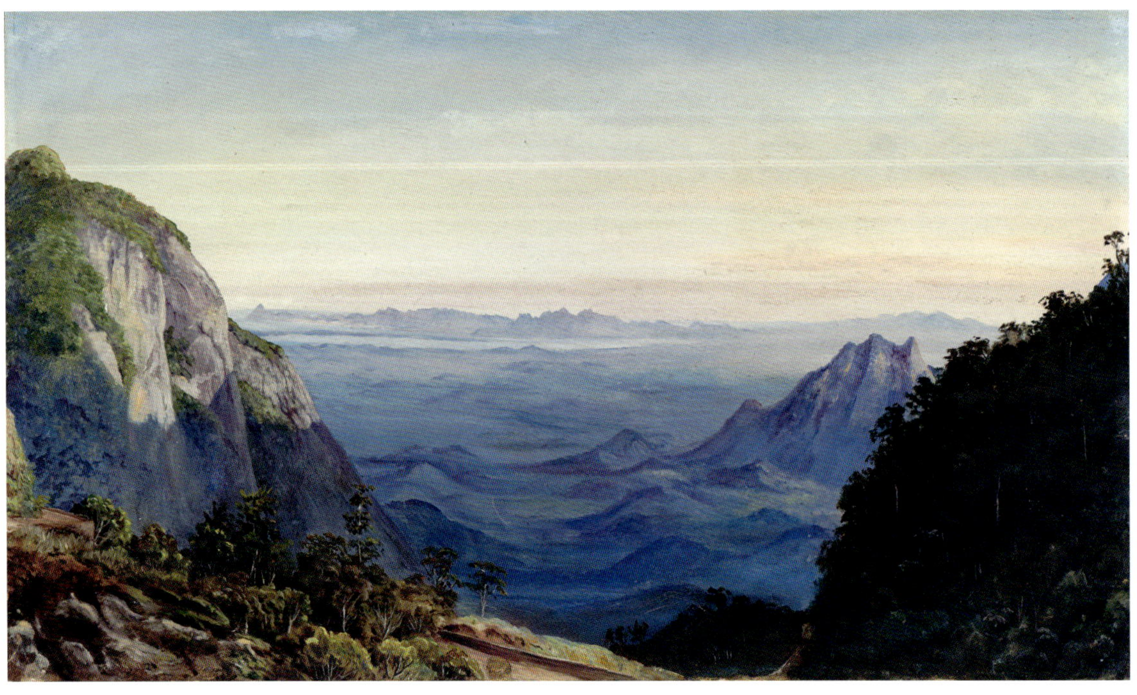

72 Marianne North, 075, *View from the Sierra of Petropolis, Brazil,* oil on board, 19 × 50 cm, Royal Botanic Gardens, Kew.

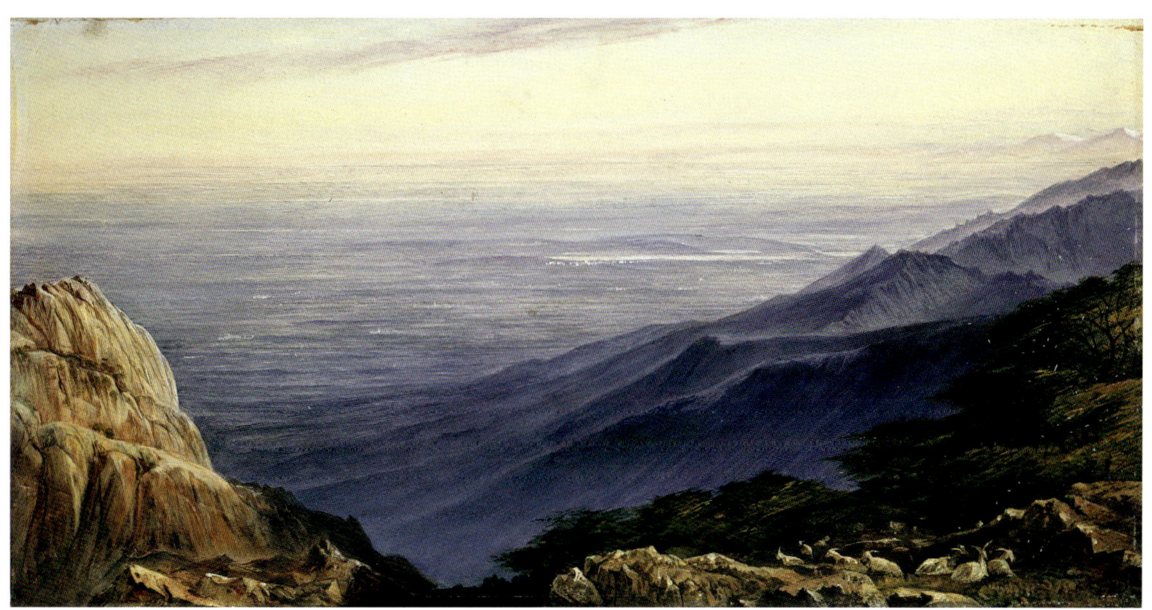

73 Edward Lear, *The Plains of Lombardy from Monte Generoso*, 1880, oil on canvas, 24 × 47 cm, The Ashmolean Museum.

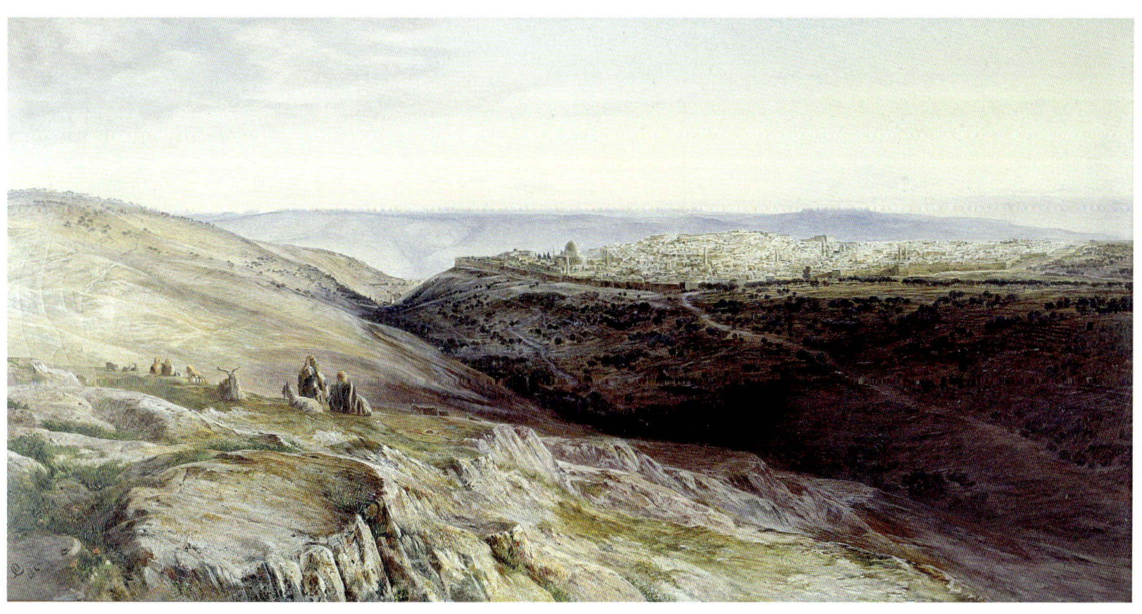

74 Edward Lear, *Jerusalem*, 1865, oil on canvas, 121 × 199.5 cm (framed), The Ashmolean Museum.

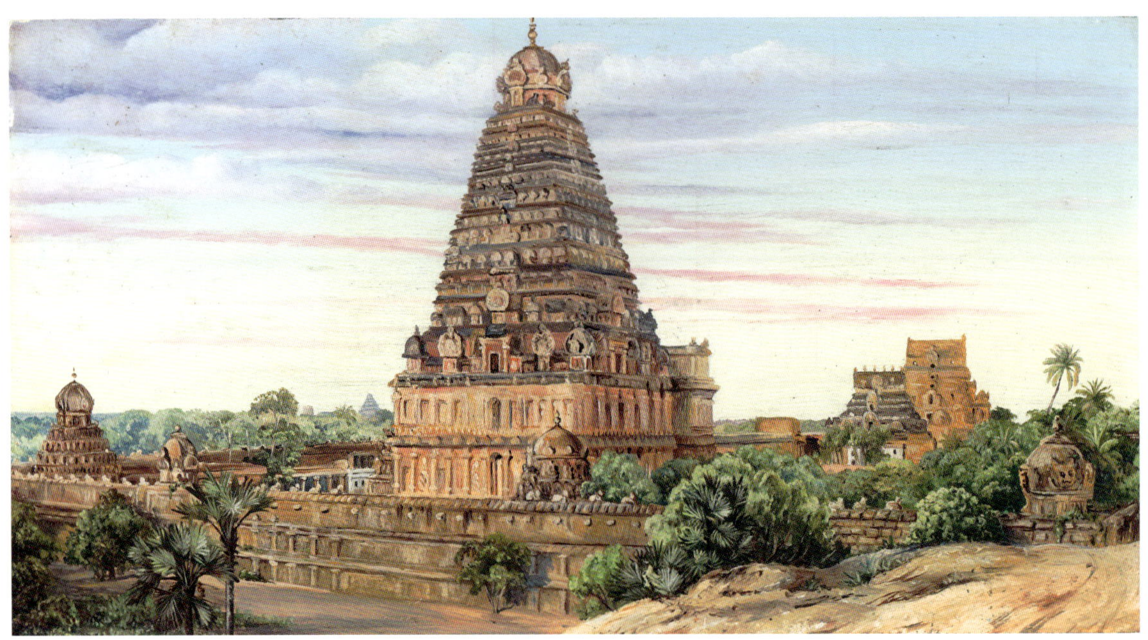

75 Marianne North, 331, *Temple of Tanjore, Southern India*, oil on board, 26.7 × 50.2 cm, Royal Botanic Gardens, Kew.

painting, *Petra* (1859). Lear's topographical paintings have aesthetic qualities but also reveal geological structures present in the landscape, matching the depiction of fine naturalistic detail by Holman Hunt. In the view of the art historian Nicholas Tromans, Lear's 'views of Beirut and Damascus' and '1865 painting of Jerusalem [. . .] all seem to carry echoes of Hunt's influence'.[55] The two were friends, with Lear referring to Holman Hunt as 'PRB [Pre-Raphaelite Brotherhood] Daddy',[56] and briefly taking 'Pre-Raphaelite instruction' from the younger artist in 1852. The quasi-panoramic expansiveness of Lear's landscape paintings is at the same time reminiscent of paintings by the Hudson River School. Landscapes by Lear and Church are most definitely similar in this respect. It is consequently possible to perceive a nexus of landscape styles related to travel among artists – Lear, Holman Hunt and Church – that North knew and/or admired. Lear's paintings of Beirut, Damascus and Petra also echo the sublimity of landscapes by Caspar David Friedrich which North may have been exposed to while travelling in Europe in the 1840s.

Traces of the styles, techniques and compositional tropes used by Lear, Holman Hunt and Church are discernible in numerous landscape paintings produced by North while travelling, for example: 390, *Vegetation on the St John's River, Kaffraria*; 787, *A Bush Fire at Sunset, Queensland* (fig.69); and 035, *View of the Jesuit College of Caracas, Minas Geraes, Brazil* (fig.70). North's paintings 201, *View of Lake Donner, Sierra, Nevada* (fig.71), and 075, *View from the Sierra of Petropolis, Brazil* (fig.72), are notably close in their execution, composition colouring and choice of subject matter to Lear's paintings *The Plains of Lombardy from Monte Generoso* (1880; fig.73) and *Jerusalem* (1865; fig.74); both paintings depict a cutting running centrally through a rugged mountainous landscape. In Lear's painting there is a bright blue sea in the far distance, while in North's there is a clear blue lake. Although similar in many respects, there are also significant differences between North's paintings and those of Holman Hunt, which North admired. Holman Hunt's paintings are usually symbolic and the landscapes they depict provide

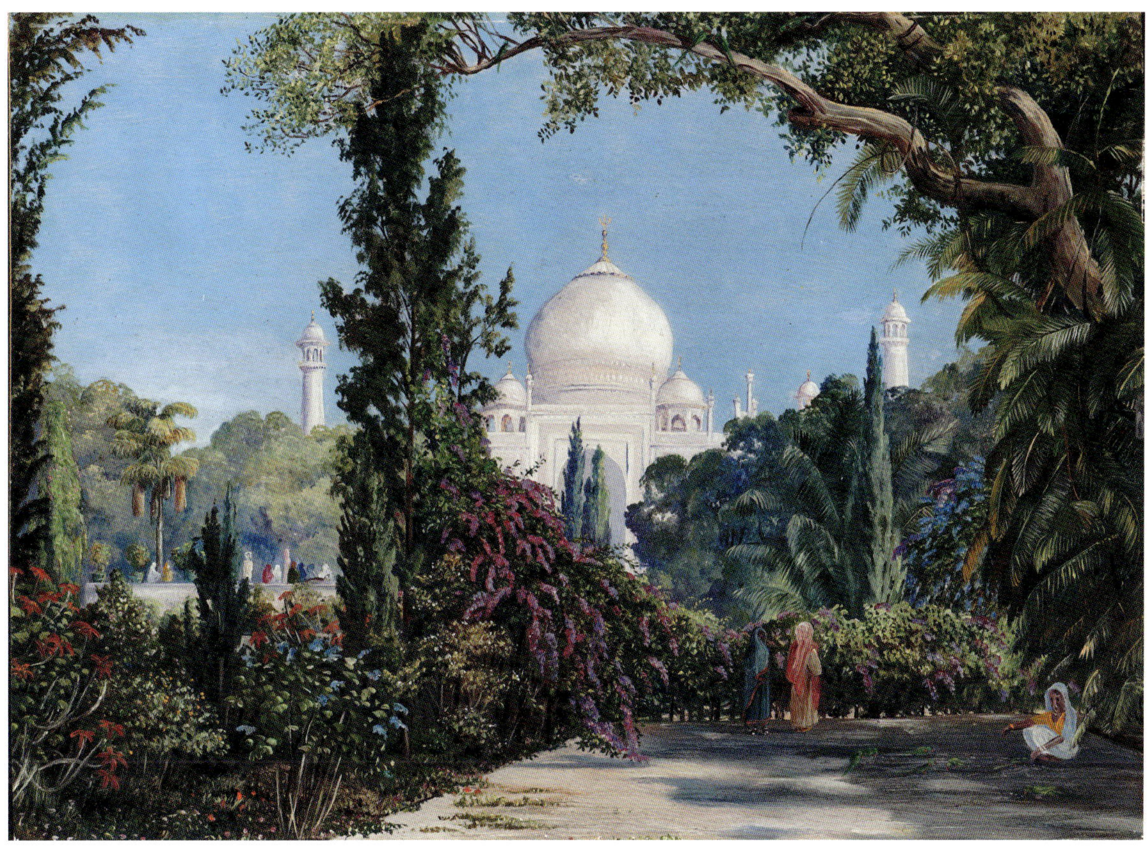

76 Marianne North, 228, *The Taj Mahal at Agra, North-West India*, oil on board, 34 × 47.2 cm, Royal Botanic Gardens, Kew.

the setting for a particular narrative, with the stylistic tropes and techniques turned towards scientific rather than purely artistic purposes. North's paintings, by contrast, concentrate simply on nature and are primarily attempts to capture a visual record without narrative or symbolism. The colour palette of North's paintings of the Middle East, however, depicting the rich oranges and yellows of the local architecture, is similar in intensity to Holman Hunt's.

North's travel paintings not only combine possible influences from topographical landscape painting but also from photography. Paintings 321, *Mosque of Delhi from the Lahore Gate of the Citadel*, and 323, *Mosque of Lahore from the Palace*, are both recognisably topographical representations of urban space, with the addition in both cases of musicians playing on the roof of a nearby building and women conversing in a courtyard. In the North painting 331, *Temple of Tanjore, Southern India* (fig.75), there is a visual similarity with the composition and painterly texture of Holman Hunt's painting *The Sphinx at Gizeh* (Giza, Egypt) (1854). Both paintings present a monumental structure that could have been painted entirely in situ. However, since it has been alleged that Holman Hunt and Seddon used photography as a visual aid in the making of some of their artworks, North too could easily have completed painting 331 from a tourist photograph or postcard used as an aide-memoire. In North's painting 228, *The Taj Mahal at Agra, North-West India* (fig.76), foliage abruptly cuts off the view of the monument, leaving only the dome and larger

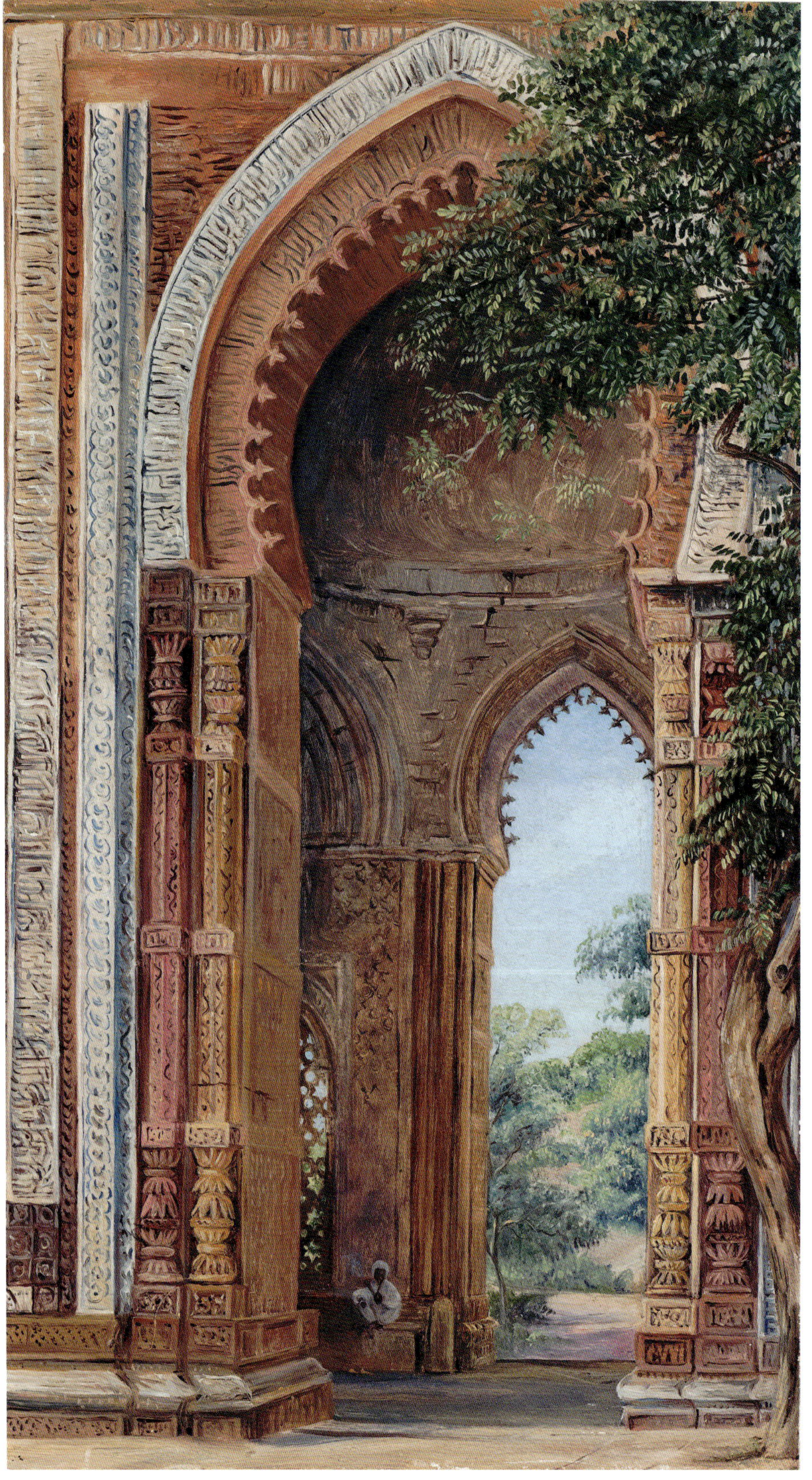

77 Marianne North, 241, *Tomb of Ali ud Deen and Neem Tree, Delhi*, oil on board, 50.7 × 28.5 cm, Royal Botanic Gardens, Kew.

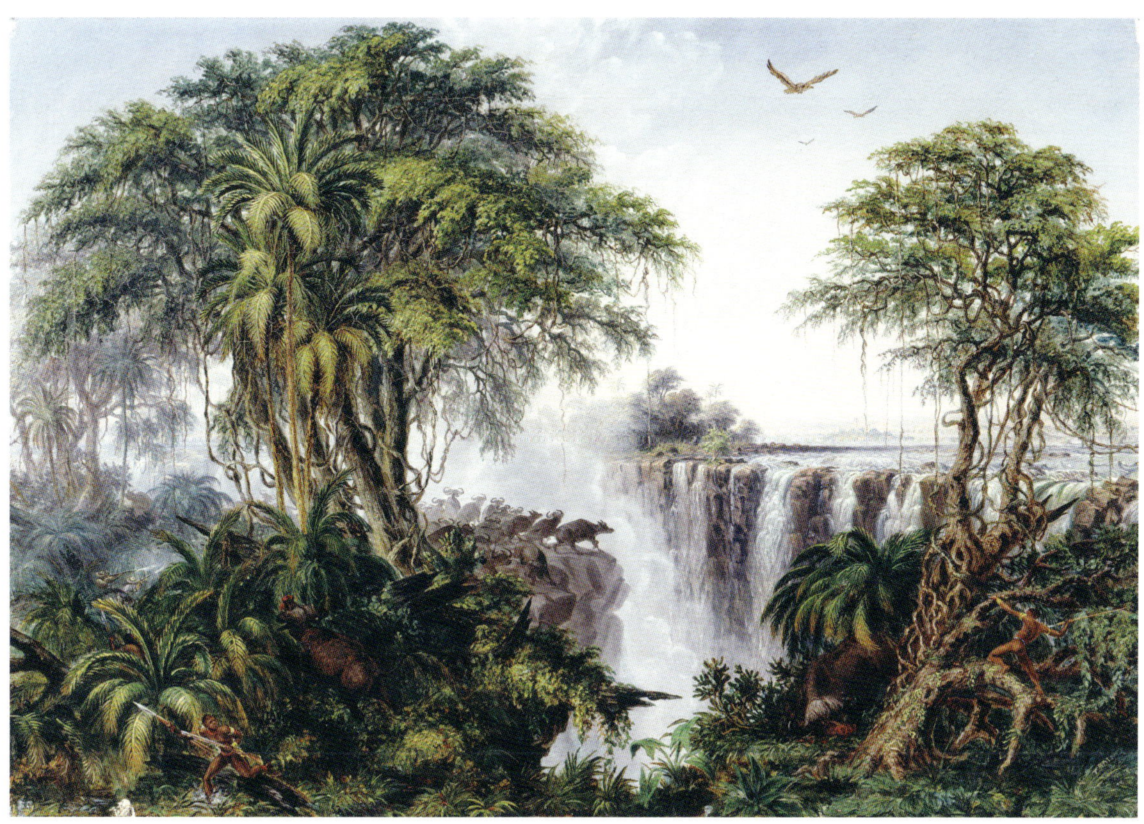

78 Thomas Baines, *Herd of Buffalo, opposite Garden Island, Victoria Falls*, 1862, oil painting, 74.5 × 54 cm (framed), Royal Geographical Society.

minarets visible. North includes local women walking upon the path and another working some palm leaves on the floor. The painting involves strong white and blue tonal/colour contrasts between the foreground and background. Its composition suggests that it may have been based on a locally acquired tourist photograph. As with North's paintings of Cameron's home and garden in Sri Lanka, the composition is redolent of the accidental perspectives and compositional incidents of photography.

The North Gallery at Kew houses numerous architectural paintings alongside the botanical paintings and landscapes. Among the former are depictions of monuments and buildings in Japan and South-East Asia which North visited while travelling. North's architectural renderings are similar in style to those produced by the British travelling painter John Frederick Lewis, who was reportedly a self-fashioned 'oriental gentleman, in life and in art'.[57] North's painting 241, *Tomb of Ali ud Deen and Neem Tree, Delhi* (fig.77), is similar in composition and style to works by Lewis such as *Courtyard of the Painter's House, Cairo* (1850–51) and *Interior of the Hagia Sophia* (1840–41). North and Lewis both depict recessed spaces in urban settings, often with a lone figure, near to monumental buildings. Other significant paintings by Lewis include *In the Bezestein, El Khan Khalil*, also known as *The Carpet Seller* (1860). Lewis's paintings, while to some extent romanticised and orientalising, are nevertheless testimonies to lost urban environments. From the 1880s, North African and Middle Eastern cities such as Cairo

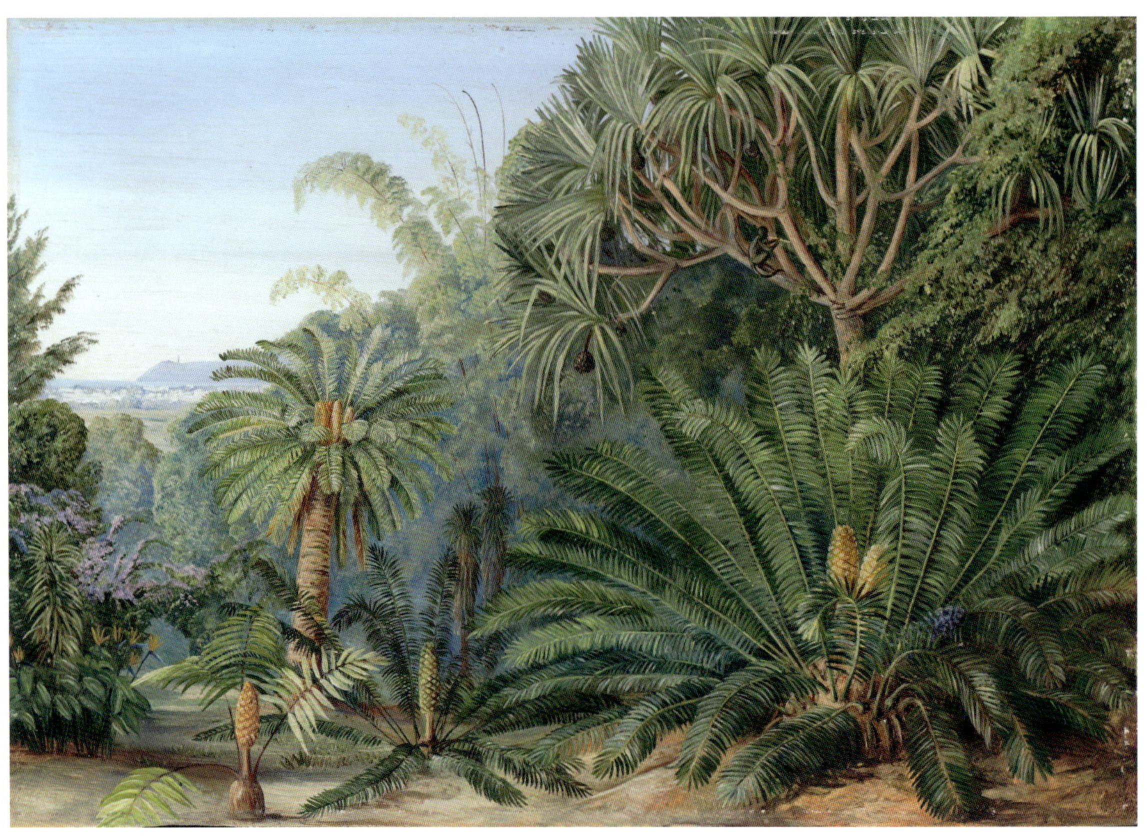

79 Marianne North, 389, *Cycads, Screw-pines and Bamboos, with Durban in the Distance*, oil on board, 35.4 × 50.8 cm, Royal Botanic Gardens, Kew.

and Alexandria would be radically transformed by the impact of European colonialism.[58] North's architectural renderings may well have been made to preserve a record of buildings and urban landscapes in places that might also be similarly transformed. On a visit to Baalbek, in present-day Lebanon, North writes of how 'the barbarians were still doing their best to spoil the place by taking away loads of stone for house-building in the town, and excavating the pillars to get at their iron clamps', and that they 'had lately discovered a fine headless statue, and I have little doubt more might be found by judicious digging'.[59]

Another 19th-century British painter of note who set a precedent for North's work as a travelling botanical painter was fellow of the Royal Geographical Society, Thomas Baines (1820–75). Baines accompanied the Scottish anti-slaver, evangelist and naturalist, David Livingstone (1813–73) on expeditions along the Zambezi in search of the origin of the River Nile. Baines recorded landscapes as well as animals, birds and plants seen during the expedition, working primarily in watercolours and pencil on paper. Sketches produced in the field were used to produce detailed topographical paintings in the studio. In addition to topographical paintings, Baines also produced a lavish folio edition of lithographs, *The Victoria Falls and Zambezi River* (1865), completed after Baines's dismissal from Livingstone's expeditionary party.[60] Marion Arnold writes that Baines was not only 'stirred by the spectacle of space and the natural elements' but also had 'a well-developed interest

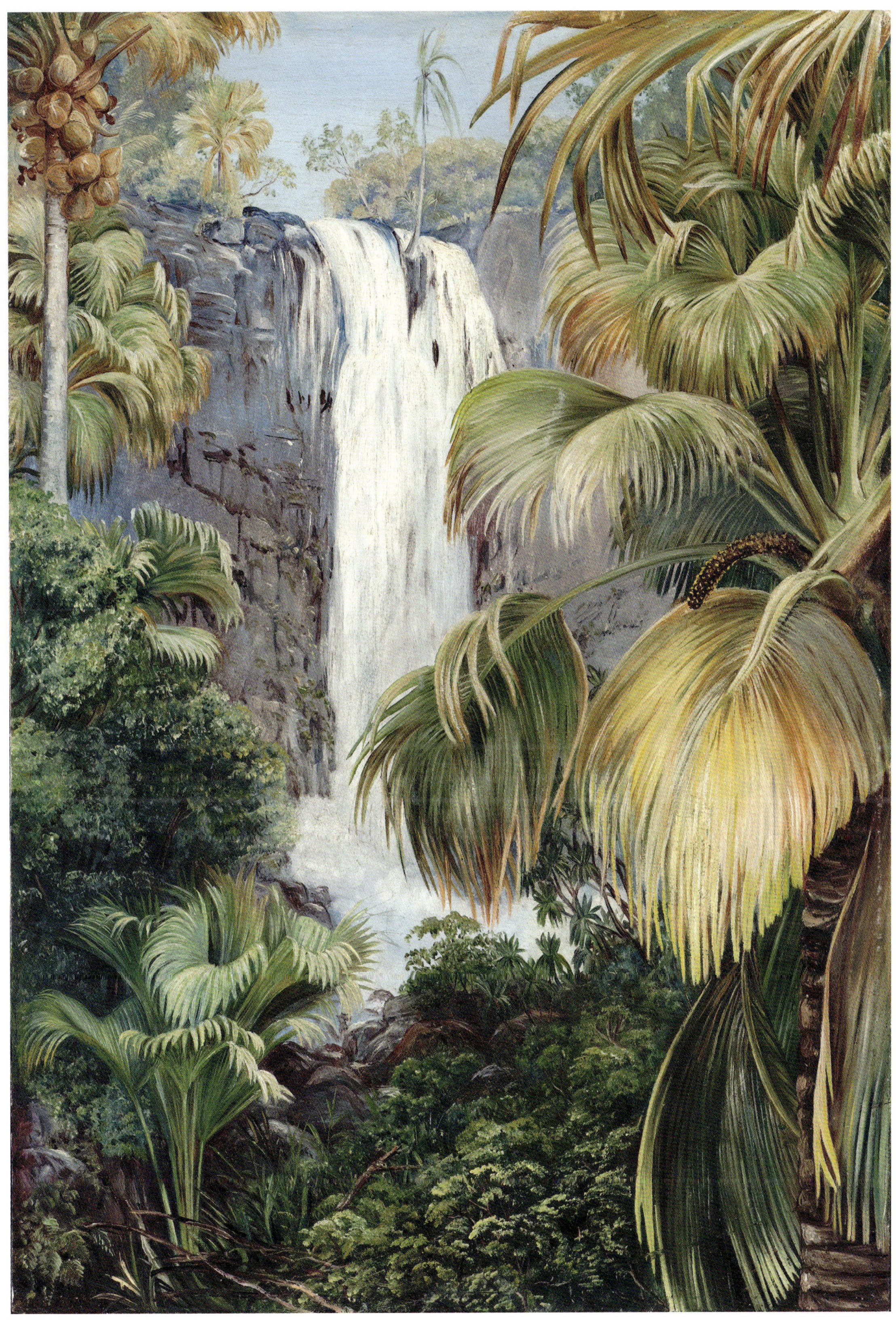

80 Marianne North, 479, *Waterfall in the Gorge of the Coco de Mer, Praslin*, oil on board, 50.5 × 35.3 cm, Royal Botanic Gardens, Kew.

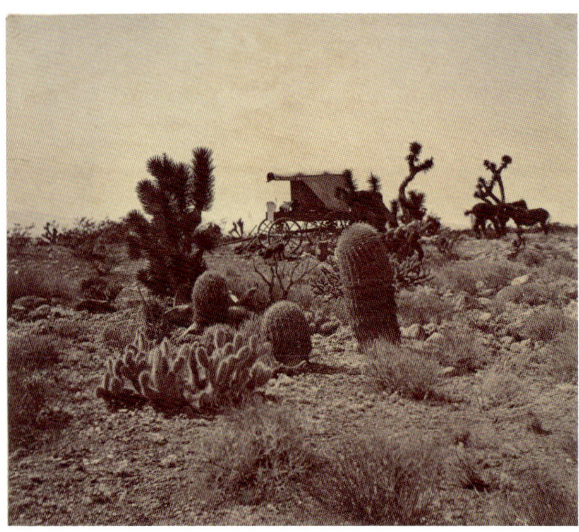

81 Barrel cactus, *ferocactus cylindraceus asp leocontei*, photograph taken during Joseph Hooker's trip to Utah, US, 1861, Royal Botanic Gardens, Kew.

in natural history' and that 'he collected plants'. Some of these plants were sent to Kew Gardens for classification, and Baines corresponded with William and then Joseph Hooker as its successive directors.[61]

Though not a trained botanical illustrator, Baines's working methods as a travelling topographical painter, including sketches of plants that are accurate and meticulous enough to have been useful to science, are nevertheless close to those adopted later by North.[62] Topographical landscape paintings by Baines often include depictions of animals in their natural habitats; for example, the painting *Herd of Buffalo, opposite Garden Island, Victoria Falls* (1862; fig.78), which shows the herd coming to the edge of a cliff in a dramatic state of agitation, while other buffalo are being hunted down by a local tribe. North's method of working in oils directly from the motif, often without the assistance of preliminary sketches, echoes Baines's initial use of watercolour and pencil, and both artists share a very similar attention to detail when painting plants and trees in the landscape. In North's paintings 389, *Cycads, Screw-pines and Bamboos, with Durban in the Distance* (fig.79), and 479, *Waterfall in the Gorge of the Coco de Mer, Praslin* (fig.80), foliage is depicted in a manner very close to that of Baines's paintings *Victoria Falls, Zambezi River from the West End of the Chasm (with Rainbow)* (1862) and *Herd of Buffalo, opposite Garden Island*. Both painters shared a similar topographical approach to landscape painting required by scientists and colonial developers alike. North does not simply replicate Baines's painterly approach, however. North's painting 374, *Looking up Stream from the Mouth of the St John's River, Kaffraria*, for example, which depicts a river, a ravine and a mountainous background in a manner akin to Baines, does so without any accompanying narrative or dramatic incident. North's landscape paintings, while aestheticised and using similar compositional tropes, maintain a certain detachment distinct from Baines's residual Romanticism.

As discussed in the previous chapter, letters to William Hemsley indicate North's possible use of photography and published reproductions as aids to the painting of individual plants. This usage could easily have extended to North's painting of topographical landscapes. The use of photography in scientific fieldwork, by the likes of Baines, was prevalent well before North's travels abroad. The still relatively new medium had become increasingly practical and affordable with the development of new portable photographic technologies which extended the use of photography from studio-based professionals to a growing middle class with disposable income. By the time of North's travels, photographic images were ubiquitous in Victorian society. Moreover, '[f]aster reproduction techniques and intense competition between studios saw a growth in nakedly commercial photographic work' that could be easily accessed.[63] The British artist and photographer Roger Fenton made reportage photographs of scenes during the Crimean War (1853–6), using a wagon to transport the necessary photographic equipment. As photography historian Quentin Bajac explains, by the mid-19th century photography was endowed 'with a

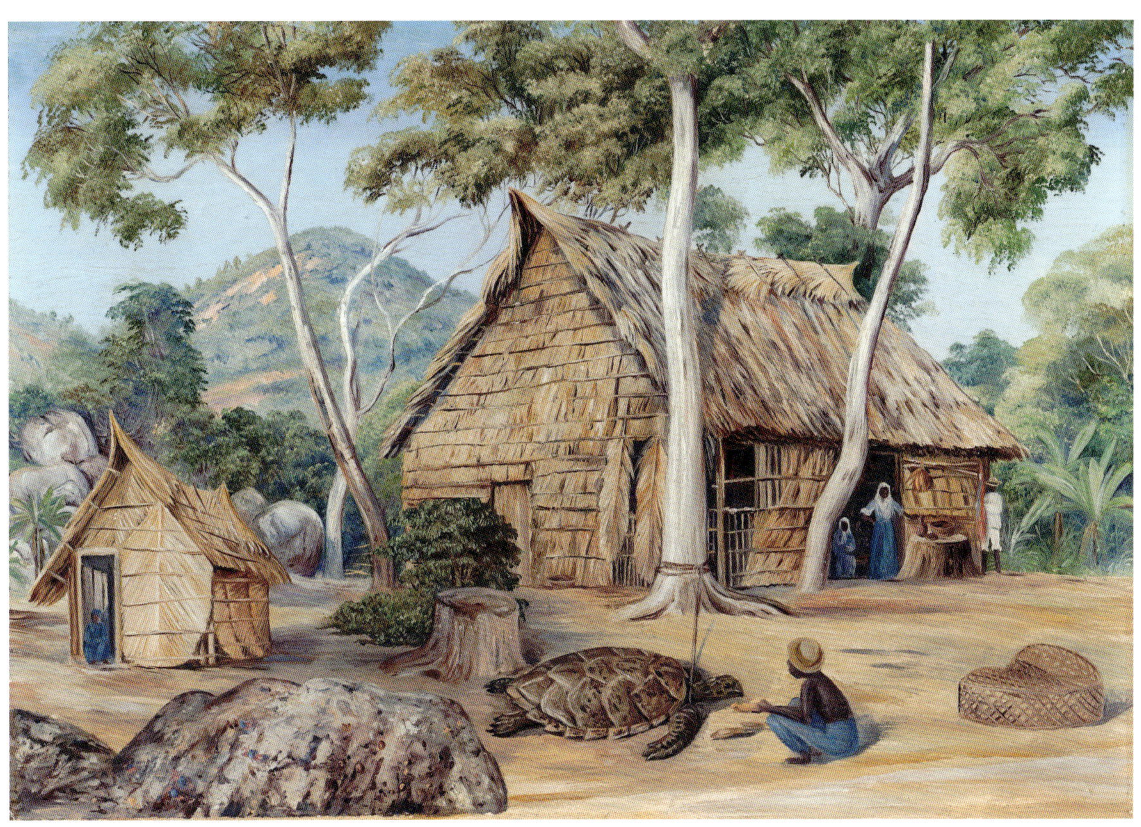

82 Marianne North, 483, *Emile's Palm House, Praslin, Seychelles*, oil on board, 35.2 × 50.6 cm, Royal Botanic Gardens, Kew.

certain technical maturity' that 'gradually supplanted all other techniques used to reproduce images', which had up until then been limited to drawing, printing or casting. The relative 'speed of execution' as well as the 'accuracy of the resulting image [. . .] in the eyes of the public' made photography a valuable 'aid-document'.[64] North's exposure to photography in the context of science is likely to have come about in different ways. Kew Gardens possessed an extensive collection of botanical and landscape photographs dating back to the 1830s. The collection was housed for many years in Kew's Museum of Economic Botany, which North had been introduced to as a young woman by the museum's founder William Hooker. North's botanical and topographical landscape paintings were produced in the context of an accepted use of photography by artists and scientific illustrators. The scientifically led 19th-century fashion for panoramas saw the combining of photography and painterly image-making. North's role models Lear, Holman Hunt and Church were users of photography as an aid to painting.

Among the thousands of photographic images contained in the collection of the Museum of Economic Botany at Kew are government commissions and postcards published across the British Empire. They include photographs of tea plantations, botanical gardens and expeditions.[65] Many of these photographs are in very high definition; in them, plant life can be read visually in sharp detail. Other images related specifically to the specialist, horticulturalist and gardener were commissioned at Kew by both William and Joseph Hooker. An albumen photographic print related to Joseph Hooker's visit to south Utah, in

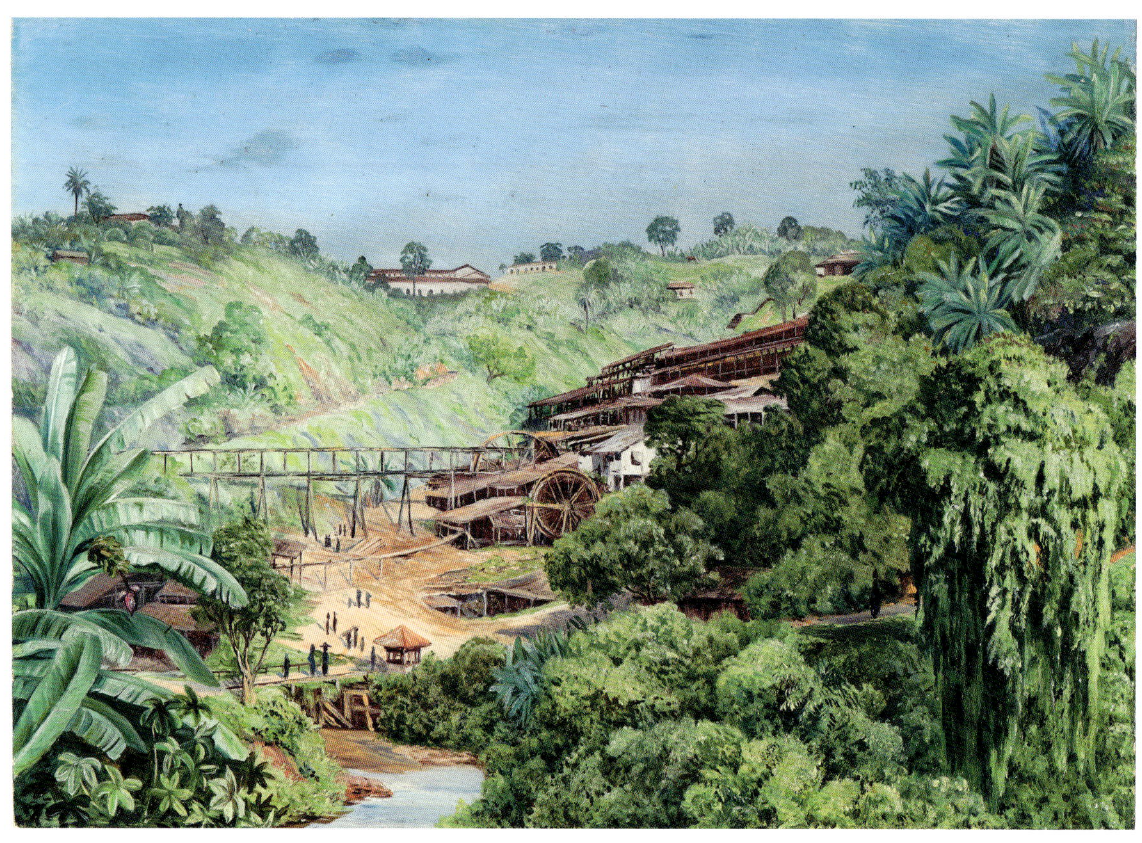

83 Marianne North, 079, *View of the Old Gold Works at Morro Velho, Brazil*, oil on board, 25 × 35 cm, Royal Botanic Gardens, Kew.

the US in 1861 has recently been rediscovered. The photograph depicts in sharp detail a desert landscape containing a barrel cactus, *ferocactus cylindraceus asp lecontei* (fig.81), with two horses, two men and a carriage/wagon that was probably used to carry the camera equipment as well as Hooker's field tools, present in the background.[66] Another photograph found in the Economic Botany collection, known to have been taken by the photographer James Chapman (1831–72), has an almost identical composition to Hooker's described above. It strongly resembles a watercolour field sketch in Kew's collection painted on 29 December 1861 by Thomas Baines.[67] Chapman and Baines would work together on expeditions in West Africa with Livingstone in 1864.

North's experiences while travelling were not confined solely to interactions with European colonialists, but included active attempts to engage with indigenous societies and their cultures. While travelling in Canada, North writes of visiting some of the 'less civilised' and 'more interesting' inhabitants of the village of Loretta, befriending a young Canadian man described as having 'long lank hair and high cheek-bones'. On insisting upon being taken by the man to a local school, North found the children to be 'a sight worth seeing' as there were 'plenty of genuine Indian faces among them, mixed up with French'. The children sang 'several wild Indian hymns with soft-sounding words', which impressed North as the songs 'had never been written down'. The nomadic lifestyle of indigenous Canadians struck North as similar to the way of 'our [own] gypsies . . . at home'.[68] North writes of visiting Japan in 1876, 'I much preferred my quiet life in Kioto [Kyoto] among the purely Japanese people and picturesque buildings, to that in the European settlements',[69] going on to comment that the Japanese are 'like little children, so merry and full of pretty ways, and very quick at taking in fresh ideas'. North then adds, 'they don't think or reason much [. . .] have scarcely any natural affection towards one another' and '[e]verybody who has lived long among them seems to get disgusted with their falseness and superficiality'.[70] North's interest in non-European cultures and disdain for European colonialist society is mixed with what we now regard as distinctly orientalising attitudes towards non-Western otherness. Yet again, North is revealed as a contradictory figure whose indeterminate crossing of boundaries between science and art, disregard for the limits imposed by Victorian patriarchy, and desire to go beyond the limits of European social and cultural experience, is mixed with an ingrained sense of colonialist-imperialist superiority.

Some of North's paintings include depictions of local people. In painting 483, *Emile's Palm House, Praslin, Seychelles* (fig.82), for example, a woman is shown cooking in a hut and a boy toying with a turtle on a beach. The depiction of these figures, using only a few daubs of paint, is merely cursory, little more than a decorative accent to the overall composition. North's attention is focused more on the form of a palm tree central to the painting. The image includes enough information to comply with the requirements of topographical representation but tells us nothing in detail about the material facts of the everyday lives of the people represented or their individual identities and subjectivities. As Suzanne Le-May Sheffield points out, 'human beings do not often appear in North's paintings' and, when they do, they are locals within their 'natural settings'. Colonialist buildings are occasionally depicted, for example in North's paintings of Cameron's house in Sri Lanka, but no Europeans are ever included. Sheffield describes North's depictions of local people as a 'positive rather than negative gesture towards them'.[71] The placing of figures within their natural settings is, however, also in keeping with North's contextualising approach to botanical painting. Human beings are rendered as objects. Copying from available photographic materials and printed illustrations would have added further distance. Other paintings by North include depictions of colonial industrialisation. In painting 079, *View of the Old Gold Works at Morro Velho, Brazil* (fig.83), a mill is shown with local workers in attendance, and in painting, 609, *Tea Gathering in Mr Hölle's Plantation at Garoet, Java*, a tea plantation is set high into a hilltop with a view of mountains in the background. These paintings are similar in format to colonialist photographs and topographical illustrations. Such images helped to inform European audiences about how colonial industry and agriculture operated and how it looked. They do not usually present the brutal working conditions of the people represented or the wider impact of industrialisation on the environment. North's topographical paintings of colonial industry are similarly lacking in detailed information. Given North's sensitivity towards environmental issues and alignment with the Emersonian outlook of the Hudson River School, they may nevertheless have been intended as testaments to the destruction of a pristine nature.

North's global travels came to an end after a visit to the Seychelles and Jamaica in 1885. While in quarantine during a smallpox outbreak, North developed delusions that the other inmates were plotting and might even turn to robbery and murder. North writes of hearing imaginary voices and observes that 'my nerves broke down from insufficient food and overwork in such a climate'.[72] On returning to Britain, North nevertheless found the strength to complete necessary changes to the North Gallery after its extension, writing that in addition to rehanging, 'Every painting had to be re-numbered so as to keep the countries as much together as possible'.[73]

5

The Marianne North Gallery

A major part of Marianne North's contribution to botanical painting is the gallery purpose built to permanently house a large representative body of the painter's work at the Royal Botanic Gardens, Kew (fig.84). The gallery, designed by the architectural historian and amateur architect James Fergusson (1808–86) in collaboration with North, was opened on 7 June 1882 and has remained open to the public, with occasional periods of closure for extension and renovation, ever since. The gallery currently houses 832 of North's botanical and topographical paintings, 16 large decorative panels, several decorative door panels and surrounds and a dado (the lower part of a wall inside a room of about waist height whose decoration and/or facing contrasts with the upper part) running throughout its main exhibition spaces composed of 246 abutting strips of wood from around the world. Following an extension to the gallery in the mid-1880s, its display of North's botanical and topographical paintings has remained largely unaltered. Today the North Gallery stands adjacent to the Shirley Sherwood Gallery of Botanical Art which was opened in 2008. The Sherwood Gallery is a world-recognised centre for displays of modern and historical botanical painting as well as exhibitions of contemporary art related to the natural world.

The North Gallery is, from the outside, an unremarkable, largely brick-built, structure – similar in its general appearance to a Victorian domestic villa – situated in an unassuming position at the east-facing boundary of Kew Gardens. To enter the gallery visitors first ascend a flight of stone steps to a veranda supported by decorated cast-iron columns before passing through double front doors leading to a vestibule containing a bust, supposedly of Marianne North but more likely of North's niece, Katharine Furse, placed there sometime after the artist's death. The gallery's main exhibition space, comprising two large, connected rooms and a first-floor balcony with Roman classical-style iron balustrades, lies beyond a further set of double doors (fig.85).

The extraordinary spectacle confronting visitors on entering the main exhibition space contrasts powerfully with the North gallery's rather plain exterior. The rooms contain an overwhelming array of paintings in black japanned frames depicting flora and fauna, as well

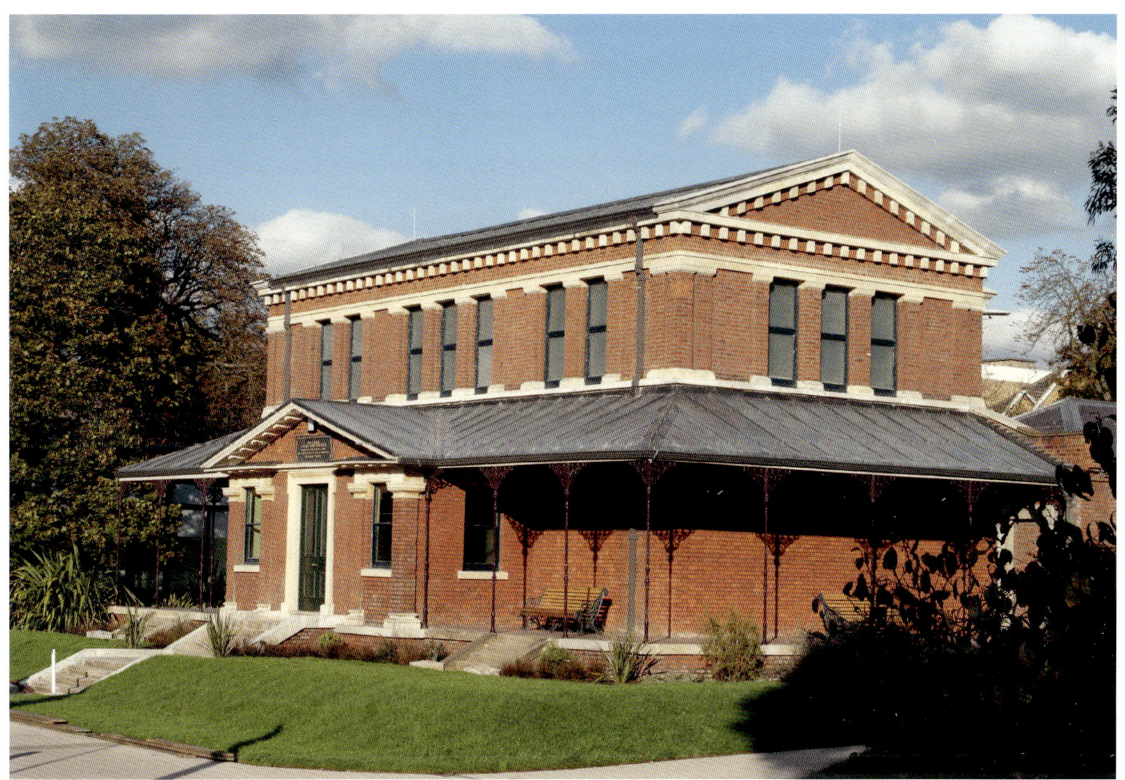

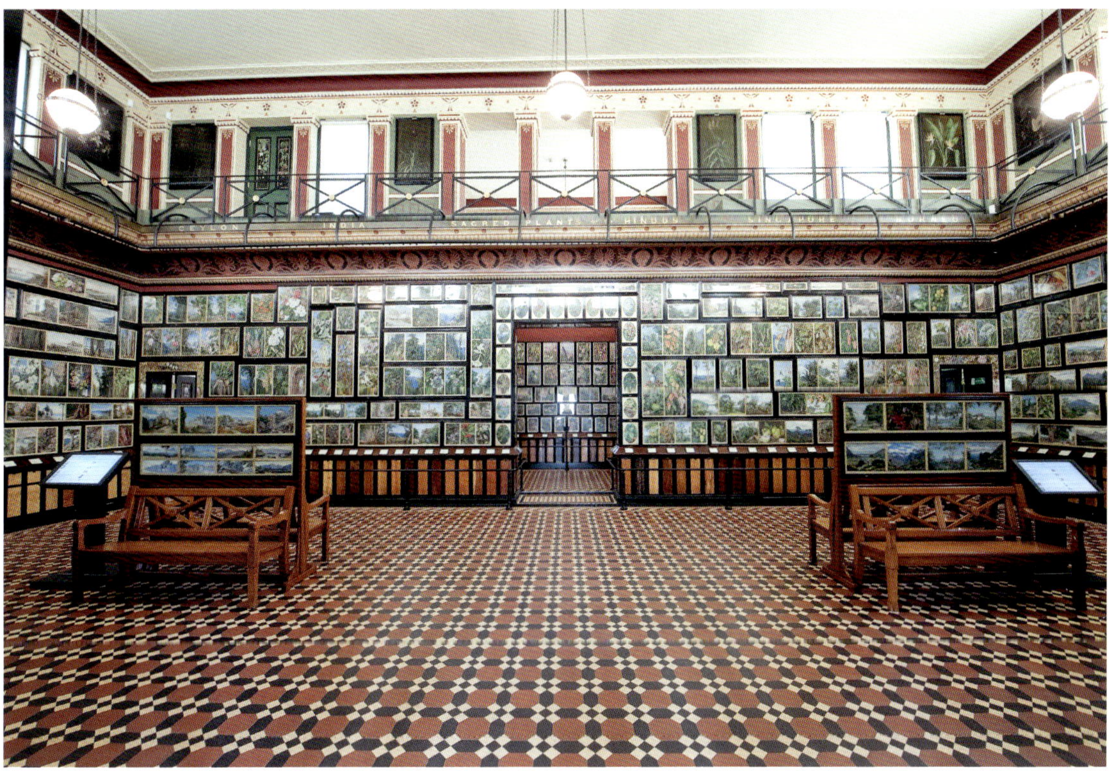

84 The exterior of the Marianne North Gallery, *c.*2007, photograph, Royal Botanic Gardens, Kew.

85 Restored interior of the Marianne North Gallery, photograph, Royal Botanic Gardens, Kew.

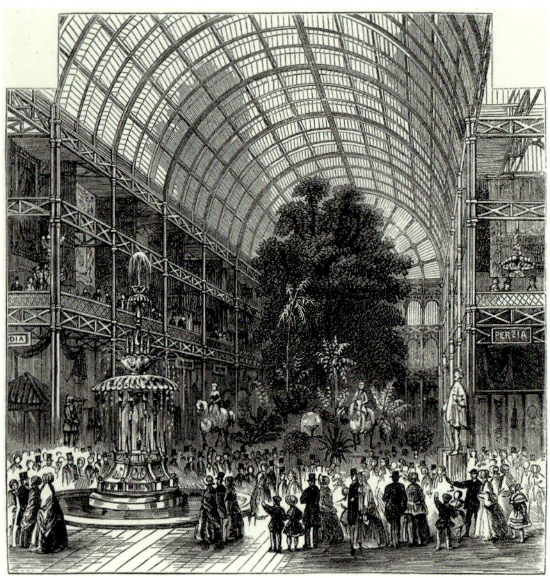

86 Nave of the Great Exhibition of 1851, in Edward Walford Cassell, *Old and New London*, c.1880.

as landscapes from across the globe hung from the top of the dado to the ceiling without intervening gaps. In front of the dado are protective railings that survived proposals to remove them as part of a renovation in 1937. There are also paintings incorporated into supporting wooden screens above the benches situated in the middle of the gallery, that replaced originals as part of the 1930s renovation, in addition to decorative panels painted with floral motifs on and around the doors and on the walls of the ground and upper floor. The framed paintings of flora, fauna and landscapes are arranged systematically in groupings under the titles Tenerife, Brazil, Jamaica, the United States, California, Ceylon, India (with a series of sacred plants of the Hindus), Singapore, Borneo, Java, Japan, New Zealand and Australia, representative of North's global travels as a botanical artist. Unlike modern white cube gallery spaces – where the setting is intentionally made subordinate to the objects on display – viewers are compelled to move continually between an appreciation of individual paintings and a sense of immersion in the entirety of the gallery's interior. In recent years, newly built vitrines have been included in the main gallery with the intention of presenting rotating displays of objects belonging to the artist – one such object was a taxidermy platypus given to North as a gift.

A further room off the main exhibition space, originally intended as a studio for North, is situated towards the rear of the gallery. Following a major restoration in 2010, the room now contains digital and other displays providing information about North's life and work. The gallery building also incorporates spaces intended as accommodation for a resident caretaker that are currently used as offices by Kew's administration. The original siting of benches on the veranda and in the gallery's main exhibition space invited visitors to sit in leisured contemplation of nature outside the gallery and its multifaceted global representation inside.[1]

North first proposed the gallery in a letter to Arthur Burnell dated 9 August 1879, writing,

> I should like to build a gallery close to the pleasure grounds (or in them) at Kew, hanging my pictures and have coffee and tea for all the poor tired visitors – with a cottage attached to boil the kettle in a spare room for myself to go and sulk and paint in when I want rest [...] If Sir Joseph [Hooker] could find me a bit of ground I would build this – and leave it to him and future directors of the gardens, pictures, cups and saucers and all.[2]

The idea of the gallery appears to have been prompted by favourable reviews of an exhibition of North's paintings at the Conduit Street Gallery, London in 1879, published by *The Spectator*, *The Times* and *The Pall Mall Newspaper*.[3] North responds to those reviews in a letter to Burnell by stating, 'they all [...] give me credit for truth which is the one thing I am at'.[4] On 11 August 1879, North writes to Joseph Hooker, director and chair of the Board of Governors at Kew, enquiring

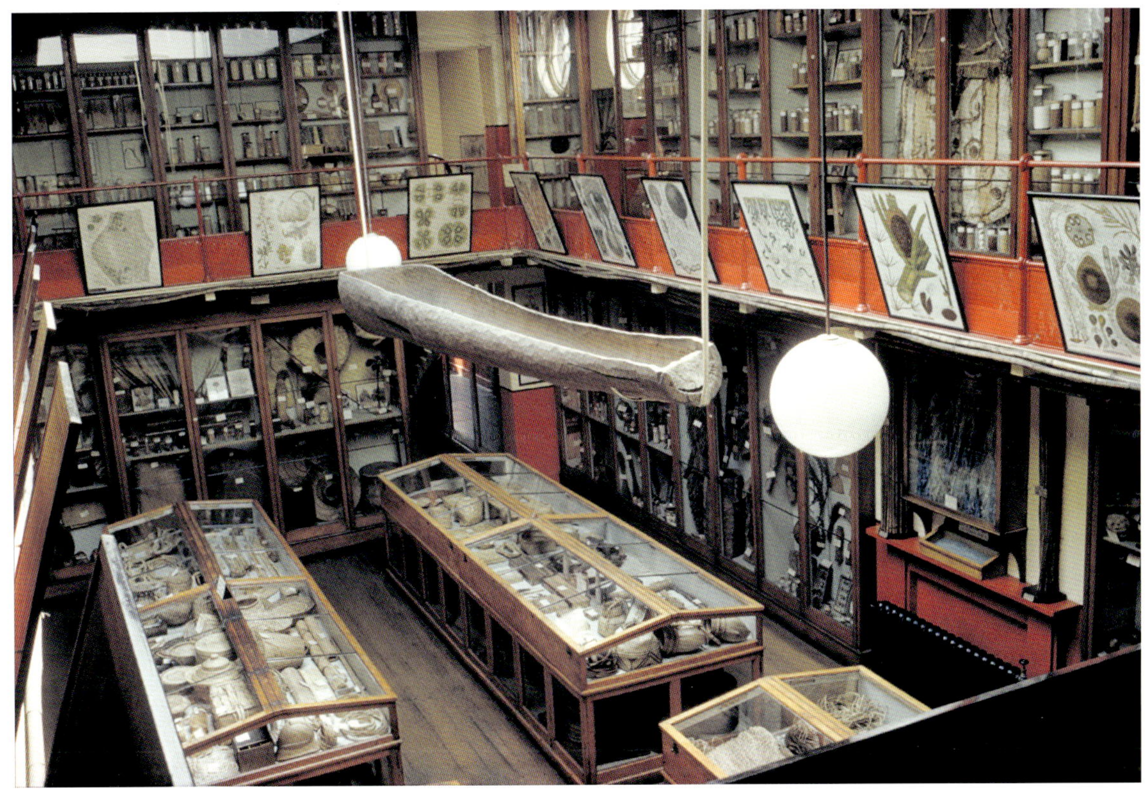

87 The interior of Sir William Hooker's Museum of Economic Botany, 1960s, photograph, Royal Botanic Gardens, Kew.

about the possibility of building the gallery, indicating a willingness to provide 'a thousand or even two thousand pounds on the building' and that the whole sum be made available 'even at my death'.[5] Hooker replied quickly, agreeing to North's request.[6] Letters from North to Hooker on 23 August indicate Fergusson's willingness to join the project.[7]

James Fergusson was born in Scotland and, after leaving school, worked for ten years as an employee of the family trading company at Calcutta (Kolkata) in India. While there, Fergusson made a fortune from managing an indigo factory, enabling him to retire from business to pursue a second career in architecture and as an architectural historian. Fergusson published several books on architecture and architectural aesthetics, including the *History of Indian and Eastern Architecture* (1876), a richly illustrated survey of buildings throughout India and other parts of Asia which remains a key reference work today. Fergusson was not only a leading figure in the 19th-century European study of Indian and Asian architecture but is also credited as 'the first historian to make extensive use of photography in recording and comparing buildings'.[8] Fergusson was an advisor to numerous public works, including the design and construction of the Royal Albert Hall and the display of Indian art at the Great Exhibition of 1851 in London (fig.86).[9] Fergusson was elected a member of the Royal Asiatic Society in 1840 and awarded a gold medal by the Royal Institute of British Architects in 1871, despite receiving little or no formal training as an architect and designing only a very small number of buildings. Buildings by Fergusson still standing today include the Jamaican Parliament and the North Gallery at Kew. North's extensive network of connections with expatriate British society, which enabled the artist's global travel, along with Fergusson's lucrative time as a trader in India, make the North Gallery a direct beneficiary of colonial surplus value.

North's idea for a gallery at Kew may have been prompted by visits there as a younger woman with Frederick North, who was a friend of the garden's then director, William Hooker, father of Joseph.[10] William Hooker oversaw the construction of the Museum of Economic Botany at Kew visited by North and Frederick. The museum – which was converted from a fruit store and foreman's residence on the former site of Kew's Royal Kitchen Garden by the architect of the Temperate House and Palm House at Kew, Decimus Burton (1800–81) – opened in 1848 and was eventually extended to four buildings before being closed in the 1960s (fig.87). It accommodated a large collection of textiles, drugs, gums, dyes, timbers and associated manufactured objects accumulated by William Hooker over more than a quarter of a century. The museum was not only intended as a site of scientific record and pedagogy but also one where professionals of all kinds outside the scientific community – such as merchants, manufacturers, physicians and artisans – could expand their knowledge of available botanical materials and their potential uses.[11] Photographs of the museum, taken not long before its closure, record a space very close in its design to that of the North Gallery, with a ground-floor exhibition area and first-floor gallery. The photographs also show pictures of botanical subjects in black japanned frames like those in the North Gallery. A possible source of inspiration for the North Gallery's dado may have come from the artist's travels to the United States. North writes of having seen 'different sorts of wood', including 'black walnut, butternut, hickory, ash, and pine', used for 'floors, staircases, and chimney-pieces', inside Mr and Mrs Adams's house at Quincy in 1871 – the Mr Adams in question was the grandson and son of former US Presidents, John Adams (1735–1826) and John Quincy Adams (1767–1848). North describes the various woods as being 'beautifully put together, with very little ornament, sometimes a line or simple geometrical pattern cut and filled with blue or red, and the rich natural colour of the wood kept as a ground-work'.[12]

Correspondence related to the planning of the North Gallery indicates partly contrasting views regarding its intended function. North and Joseph Hooker both envisioned the gallery as a site of scientifically led enlightenment corresponding to the pedagogical and utilitarian imperatives that underpinned other public museum and industrial displays in mid- and later 19th-century Victorian Britain – as exemplified by the Great Exhibition and the subsequent establishment of the Victoria and Albert Museum at South Kensington in London. However, despite agreeing to North's request to build the gallery, Hooker and Kew administrators strongly resisted the suggestion that it should provide visitors ready access to refreshments.[13] As a government-funded institution Kew was required to make its gardens accessible to the public.[14] Hooker was nevertheless continually vexed at the damage caused to Kew by visiting members of the public and remained adamant that the gardens should be first and foremost a site of scientific enquiry. A resistant Hooker was criticised for 'planting trees everywhere, sacrificing spacious lawn' as part of a series of changes made after being appointed director at Kew.[15]

Hooker's views ran contrary to those of successive Commissioners of Works in London, who ruled that the gardens had to cater for 'pleasure seekers'.[16] During the 1860s, the British parliament sought to promote science and art education in conjunction with what was described as healthful recreation and improvement of the people. In part, this entailed making museums and other publicly owned institutions accessible to all, along with, in some cases, on-site sale of food and alcohol.[17] Henry Cole (1808–82) – who had, along with Prince Albert, spearheaded the staging of the Great Exhibition – gave substance to Parliament's wishes by designing decorative architectural elements for the Royal Horticultural Society's exhibition of 1862 as a way of making the gardens 'attractive in winter as well as summer'.[18] Cole supported the opening of public museums during the evening so that working people could visit more easily and advocated the clear labelling of exhibits as a way of making the purchase of expensive catalogues unnecessary.[19] The London Commissioners' rulings were underscored by obligations placed on Kew from 1886 to supply bedding plants for London parks and the city's poor.[20]

North reluctantly gave up plans for the provision of refreshments in the face of Hooker's recalcitrance, as confirmed in a letter from Hooker to the secretary of Kew Gardens.[21] An attempt was made by Hooker's wife to reconcile their differing positions. In a letter to William Hemsley, North writes, 'after all Lady Hooker has persuaded me to give up refreshments & is going to put up a card inviting my friends to come to her for them'.[22] This attempted reconciliation, while no doubt intended kindly, betrays the ingrained elitism of bourgeois Victorian society in its limitation of hospitality to a limited circle of the same class.

A site for the North Gallery was eventually found next to an unused railway lodge designed by W. Eden Nesfield (1835–88), at the edge of Kew. North had previously rejected a prominent site behind the Temperate House (first opened in 1863) because it would have involved the felling of 'some noble trees'.[23] In a letter to Burnell dated 17 January 1880, North writes, 'have you heard my Kew scheme, I am going to build a gallery for all my botanical and plant subjects [. . .] with a house attached [. . .] and a studio for myself or other artist who wishes to paint specimens there'.[24] With plans secured, North embarked on a visit to the US, leaving funds for Fergusson to build the gallery and employing a friend, Miss Ewart, as a proxy supervisor.

Before leaving for the US, North had suggested to Fergusson that the gallery be 'Indian in its outline', with 'faint echoes of the bungalow-type dwellings that Europeans built in India'.[25] Fergusson – who like other European architects of the time privileged the architecture of classical Graeco-Roman antiquity above all others – did not adhere strictly to that vision, however.[26] As Professor J.P.M. Brenan (1917–85), a former director of Kew, indicates, the facade of the North Gallery resembles that of 'a Greek temple with oriental verandas'.[27] Fergusson was distinctly Ruskinite on architectural styling and did not share in the popular mid-Victorian taste for ornament.[28] In *The Stones of Venice* (1851–3), John Ruskin declares that one should never 'demand an exact finish for its own sake, but only for some practical or noble end'.[29] In letters to Hooker, North writes of Fergusson's plans being far simpler than first hoped. However, being nevertheless pragmatic towards Fergusson's stewardship of the gallery's design and construction, instead of requesting wholesale changes North thought of adding creepers to cover the gallery's plain, almost suburban, exterior brickwork.[30] The unadorned exterior of the North Gallery also appears to have troubled Fergusson, who wrote to Hooker on the subject, referring to the building as a 'single ugly shed'[31] after previously declaring, perhaps despairingly, 'I am not a practicing architect & have no staff'.[32]

The £1000–£2000 budget provided for the building of the North Gallery (approximately equivalent to £300,000 today) was modest for such an ambitious project. Fergusson responded by making use of inexpensive, readily available materials, such as brick, ceramic tile and cast iron, mass-produced in industrial Victorian Britain and circulated at home and throughout the British Empire. The gallery is to some extent a kit building whose appearance and construction corresponds to semi-prefabricated British colonialist architecture still in evidence today in places such as India, southern Africa, South America and Australia. The heyday for semi-prefabricated structures of this sort in Australia was between 1840 and 1880,[33] with portable iron-frame structures being widely used there after the discovery of gold in 1851 – the demand for decorative ironwork, especially in the construction of terraced houses in Australia, increased significantly after that date.[34] It is a style often referred to as 'Federation' by Australians.

Another Antipodean building style – the 'Queenslander', named after the Australian state from which it was derived – deliberately incorporated features similar to Asian architecture, as well as some design aspects found within the Federation builds, such as decorated iron railings and columns. Further to this, while in Australia, North would have witnessed the colour palette and formulation of how Australians decorated wall surfaces that deliberately divided the wall into zones, which were then treated in different ways. Colonial Australian homes included a chair rail that divided the wall into two, beneath which the decoration included either a papered or decorated surface that was often divided by colourways. Later, as in the design of the North Gallery, 'this area might be panelled with timber to form wainscotting'. The dado was 'an area at the base of a wall which was roughly equivalent to about a third of its height' and 'came into widespread use in Australia during the 1870s and 1880s'. Above the dado, again, like in the North Gallery, '[t]he colour and design of the filling was often slightly muted so that it did not overpower or compete with pictures or the wealth of decorative ephemera which was commonly found in rooms at the time'.[35] In Australia, the 'frieze was placed beneath the cornice' that provided a 'transition from the wall to the ceiling', moreover, decorative borders consisted of a 'stylised floral motif'. The size and status of these frieze designs became 'a major feature of Australian interior decoration'.[36] The Graeco stencilling designs that North produced in the gallery were also similar in design to those found in Australian colonialist houses that 'reached its peak [. . .] during the late nineteenth century'.[37]

Reproducible brick structures, based on model houses designed by Henry Roberts (1803–76) for the Great Exhibition, became available in Britain and across its empire from the late 1850s.[38] The use of cheap, easily sourced, mass-produced materials enabled Fergusson, who was familiar with colonialist architecture in India, to build at speed and within budget – the period from initial proposal to the opening of the North Gallery was just under three years. The North Gallery's construction, although almost certainly antiquated to modern eyes, is thoroughly contemporary in the context of late 19th-century Britain.

North went to the see the nearly completed gallery building in June 1881, almost immediately on returning to London from a trip to the US, finding 'the building finished (as far as bare walls went) most satisfactorily, its lighting perfect'. North also writes that 'Mr. Fergusson kindly arranged about the decorating and painting of the walls'. The next year was spent hanging paintings in the gallery, with North subsequently commenting 'I had much trouble but also much pleasure in the work'.[39] Fergusson had complained to Hooker during North's absence about the difficulty of framing, glazing and hanging the pictures, concluding 'all this must be left to Miss North [. . .] when she returns'.[40]

North received assistance in hanging the gallery's paintings and the designing of its accompanying catalogue from Hemsley. Almost all the paintings housed by the gallery are individually framed and set behind leaded glass. The frames were manufactured from off-cuts and mostly to standard sizes using paper templates made by North in keeping with Fergusson's use of prefabricated materials.[41] As correspondence with Hemsley shows, North did not complete all the paintings planned for the gallery in situ while travelling; some were produced in London from sketches and other visual sources during the gallery's fitting out.[42] The hanging of the paintings was constantly revised by North and Hemsley to fit in with Fergusson's designing and prior decoration of the interior.[43] Clear labelling of the paintings as well as the abutting strips of wood on display in the gallery's dado echoes Cole's democratising ideas regarding public display.

A review was published in *The Gardeners' Chronicle* at the time of the North Gallery's opening, stating that 'there are in this unique collection no less than 627 oil paintings of plants, and landscapes in which plants form a prominent part'. The article goes on to advise visitors to the gallery that they will be able to acquire from the paintings on display 'a good idea of the natural vegetation of the greater part of the world'. North's importance as a botanist is acknowledged, with the range of flora personally discovered by the artist being listed alongside a statement that 'there are several handsome and remarkable plants here represented that are at present unknown both in gardens and herbaria'. North's paintings are described as 'an adjunct to a botanical garden' and compared favourably to the work of other botanical painters which, it is argued, 'seldom or never give life-like representations of plant life, habit, and natural surroundings'. The author of the article praises the verisimilitude of North's paintings, suggesting that nearly all the plants represented could be readily named by botanists and the numerous birds, animals and insects featured alongside them by zoologists and entomologists.[44]

As the article also indicates, within the gallery 'a great number of timber trees are portrayed, and the whole dado of the room is made up of polished specimens of the woods derived from the trees sketched above', with each example named. Also mentioned is the gallery's catalogue and a handbook that sold for sixpence containing 'all that Miss North knows about the subjects and places painted'. Joseph Hooker is credited as writing a preface to the catalogue. North arranged for the catalogue to be 'cut up, framed and glazed in pages, and hung under the pictures, so that every person who desires to see and learn may do so [. . .] without expenditure of a penny' – another echo of Cole. The article also ventures that '[e]very person interested in horticulture, botany, and art will join with Sir Joseph Hooker in feeling "grateful" to Miss North for her fortitude as a traveller, her talent and industry as an artist, and her liberality and public spirit'.[45] In an interview for *The Daily News*, North describes the paintings on display at the North Gallery as 'an instructive collection' and its catalogue 'finished for the use of students who may wish to paint pictures of specimens in the grounds outside'.[46]

Despite its praise for North's paintings and work as a botanist, *The Gardeners' Chronicle* review criticises the North Gallery as being 'really much too small for the pictures to be properly seen' and that 'a room two or three times the size of the present one is required'. The review is equally critical of the North Gallery's interior decoration, stating, '[w]e were not quite pleased with the big and heavy classical ornament under the cornice, and we think the shiny black frames are too strong in colour'.[47] The main exhibition space at the time of the North Gallery's opening consisted only of one large room, but North may have already been contemplating an extension. In a letter to Hemsley dated 27 June 1882, North proposes an extension, suggesting that it be built in the court at the back of the gallery, where paintings of 'the sacred plants are'.[48] The North Gallery was extended between 1884 and 1885 to include a second connected exhibition space, at which time a further 221 paintings were added to the initial 627. The gallery reopened to the public in 1886.[49]

In 1937, the gallery's original ceramic-tile floor was covered over with brown ruboleum (a material similar in appearance to linoleum),[50] the arrangement of paintings straightened out and unsympathetic electric lighting installed.[51] Correspondence from the time indicates that advice concerning 'subsequent varnishing and glazing' had been given by the painter Frederic Leighton some time during the 19th century.[52] There was a further renovation during the 1980s which kept the ruboleum floor in place and imposed a non-period colour scheme. The major restoration in 2010 – involving, among other things, the reinstallation of period-appropriate flooring in addition to the replication of original decorative colour schemes and stencils – returned the interior to a condition close to that at the time of the gallery's opening. At some point, 16 large unglazed decorative panels on the balcony had been removed from the gallery, and these were returned as part of the 2010 restoration.

The design of the North Gallery brings together diverse stylistic elements reflecting the continuing

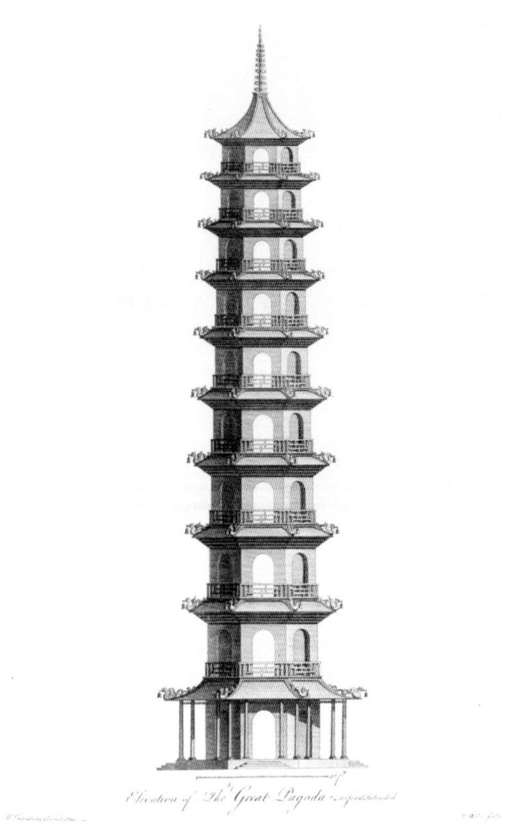

88 Illustration of Sir William Chambers's Pagoda, n.d., engraving on paper, 76.5 × 50 cm, Royal Botanic Gardens, Kew.

eclecticism of Victorian visual culture during the 1870s and 1880s. In addition to British colonial architecture and classical Graeco-Roman architecture, the exterior of the gallery is redolent of ancient buildings in Asia. There are, for example, structural similarities between the North Gallery and traditional Chinese temples. The North Gallery's front elevation – with its entrance steps leading up to a raised veranda and double front doors – is much the same as that of the Hall of Abstinence (1420) built in brick, with a 'hip top' Chinese roof structure, as part of the Temple of Heaven complex in Beijing.[53]

The stylistic eclecticism of the North Gallery's exterior visually counterpoints Sir William Chambers's redesigning of Kew Gardens over a century earlier. At the end of the 1750s and the beginning of the 1760s Chambers constructed and repositioned numerous architectural follies at Kew, including buildings in the Graeco-Roman classical style, such as the Theatre of Augusta (1763), and the now-iconic Chinese Pagoda (1761), situated towards the furthest southern extent of the gardens (fig.88). Like Fergusson, Chambers had travelled to Asia and seen local architecture first-hand. Chambers's design for the Pagoda at Kew, while fanciful in its decoration, includes projected eaves on each floor characteristic of towers constructed traditionally in south-west China and like those covering the North Gallery's veranda. Chambers was largely responsible for the popularisation of Chinese-style gardens in England and across Europe during the late 18th and early 19th centuries.[54] An understanding of the historical setting into which the North Gallery was to be placed is indicated in a letter from Fergusson to Sir Joseph Hooker.[55] North had mentioned to Hooker Fergussson's agreement to build a 'folly' within the gardens at Kew.[56]

The interior of the North Gallery is also stylistically eclectic. The floral frieze on the upper floor of the gallery is antique Greek in influence and the architrave and lintel surrounding the doors to the main exhibition space are replicas of those found at the entrance to the ancient temple of Thebes in Egypt.[57] The top-down natural lighting of the gallery through clerestory windows on the upper floor applies classical architectural principles set out in Fergusson's treatise, *An Historical Inquiry into the True Principles of Beauty in Art* (1849), which includes an account of the interior lighting of ancient classical temples such as the Parthenon.[58] Fergusson included an underfloor heating system beneath the ground floor of the North Gallery, modelled after the use of hypocausts during Roman antiquity.[59]

Further connections between the North Gallery and the architecture of classical antiquity can be made in

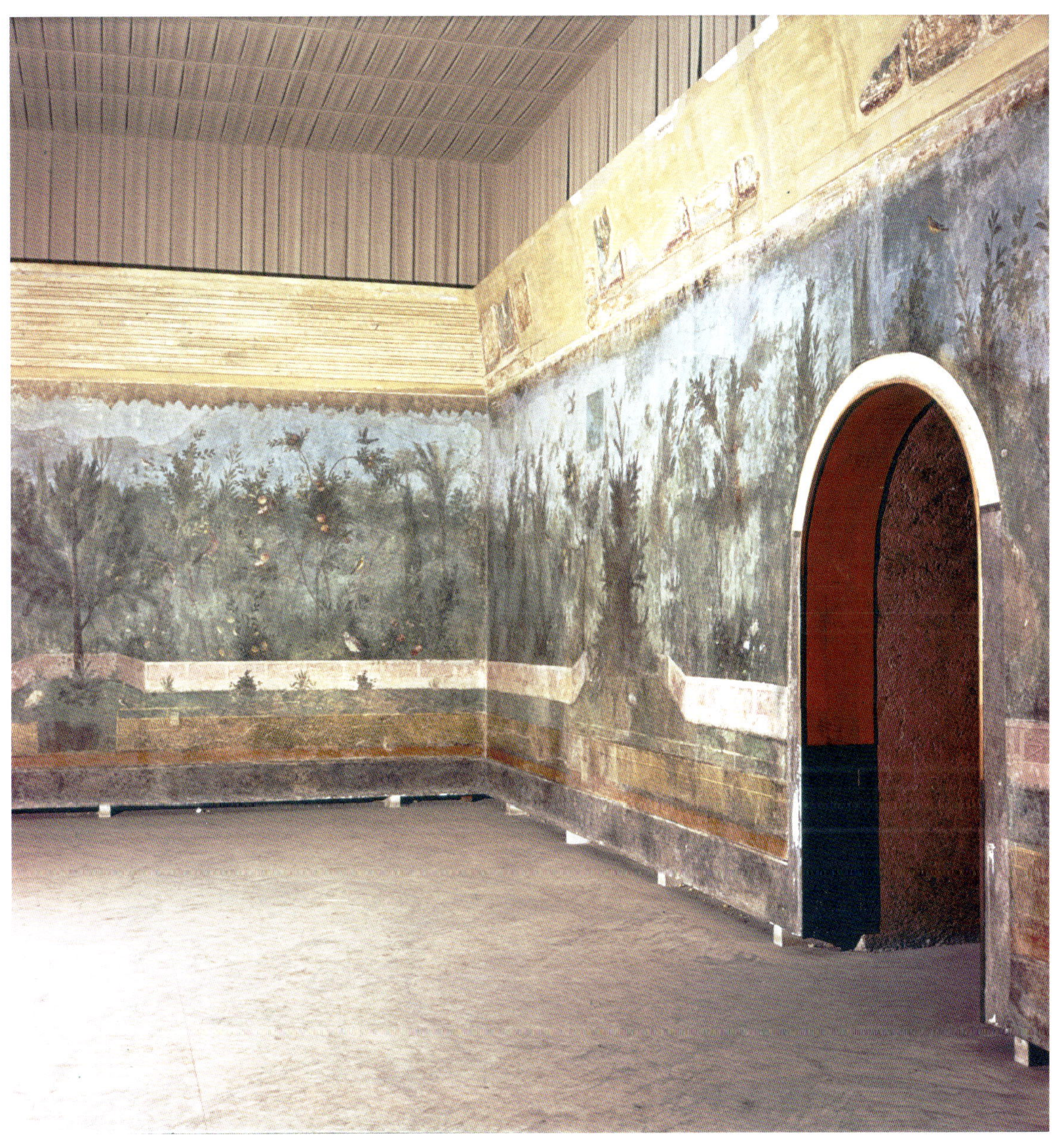

89 Villa of Livia Drusilla, who was married to Octavian, Emperor Augustus, triclinium paintings (dining rooms), Prima Porta, 38–30 BCE, fresco, mural, Museo Nazionale Romano, Palazzo Massimo alle Terme.

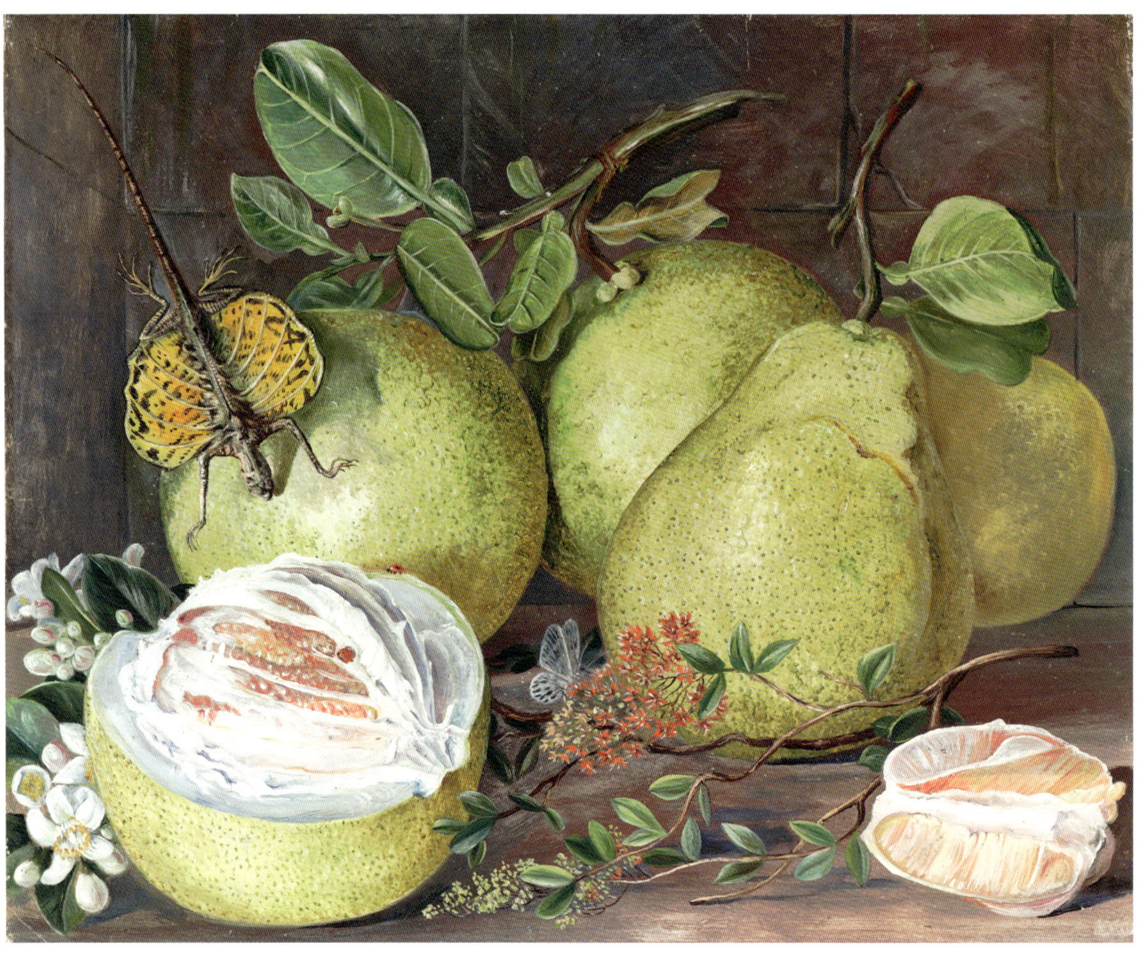

90 Marianne North, 552, *Flowers and Fruit of the Pomelo, a Branch of Hennah, and Flying Lizard, Sarawak*, oil on board, 36.4 × 45.1 cm, Royal Botanic Gardens, Kew.

relation to decorative murals representing flora and fauna found in ancient Roman buildings. Surviving examples include those adorning the garden room of Livia's Villa (38–30 BCE), excavated at Prima Porta during the 1860s, depicting complex arrangements of 'rosettes, bracts, spiral tendrils, and palmettos' alongside 'swans sacred to Apollo and [. . .] a world of tiny beasts, birds, lizards, serpents' (fig.89).[60] The Prima Porta murals decorate a space used for formal dining without intervening architectural structures and mouldings, indicative of a desire to bring nature seamlessly indoors though pictorial illusion.[61] Other similar murals have been discovered at Pompeii, for example in the House of the Golden Bracelet, where a surviving set of murals is 'divided into three horizontal sections' with 'upper and lower zones serving as a theatrical frame for the central scene' which 'completely immerses the viewer in the greenery of a garden'.[62] The panoramic arrangement of paintings within the North Gallery fulfils a comparable function. In some of North's still lifes, small animals and insects are also depicted, as in painting 552, *Flowers and Fruit of the Pomelo, a Branch of Hennah, and Flying Lizard* (fig.90).

The North's Gallery's transhistorical and cultural eclecticism combined decoration that was also

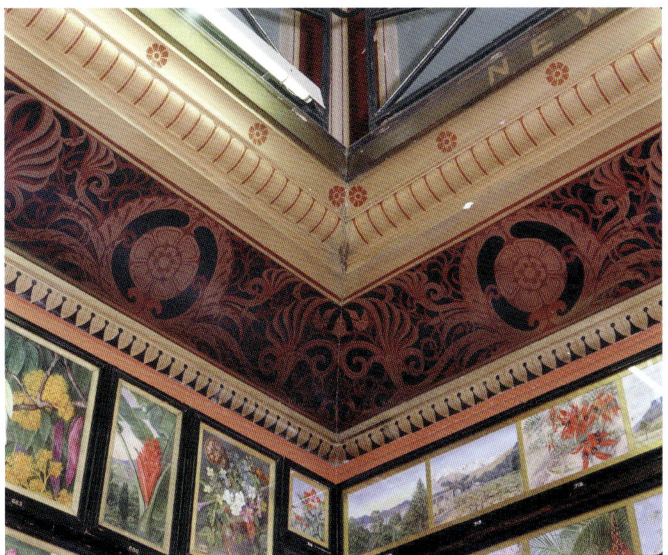

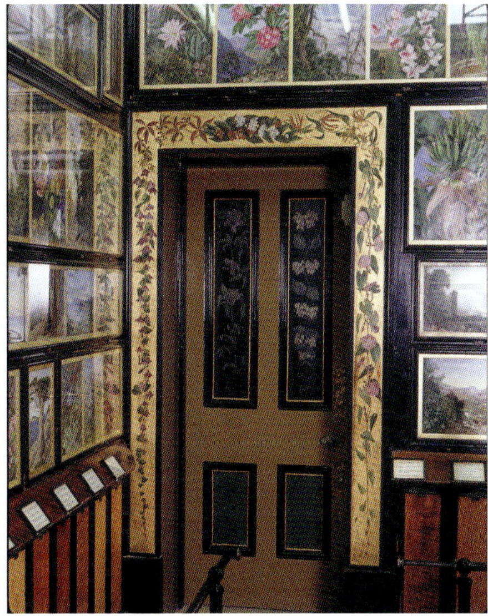

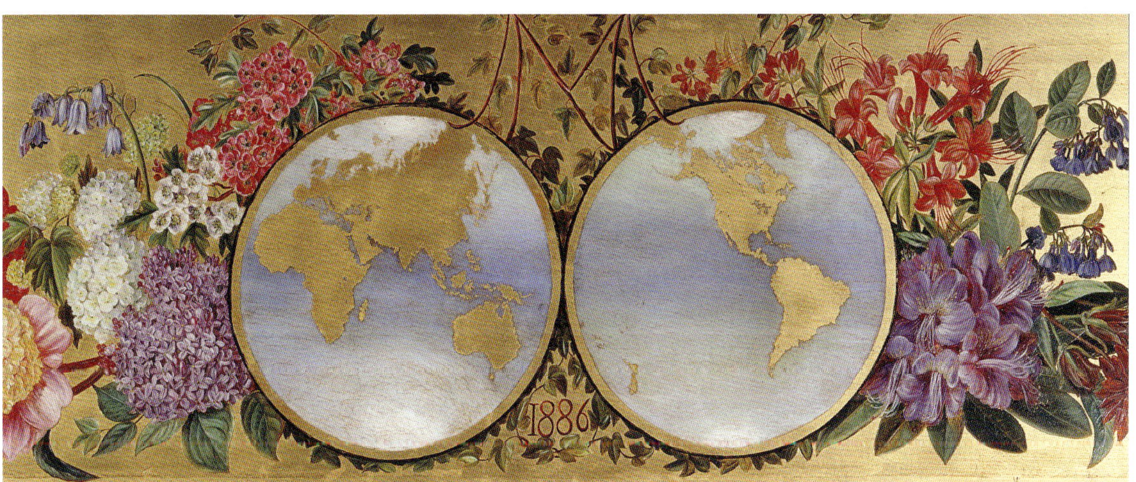

91 (above left) Detail of the cornice within the North Gallery, photograph, Royal Botanic Gardens, Kew.

92 (above right) Detail of the painted door within the North Gallery, photograph, Royal Botanic Gardens, Kew.

93 (below) Detail of gold leaf work, and globes, within the North Gallery, photograph, Royal Botanic Gardens, Kew.

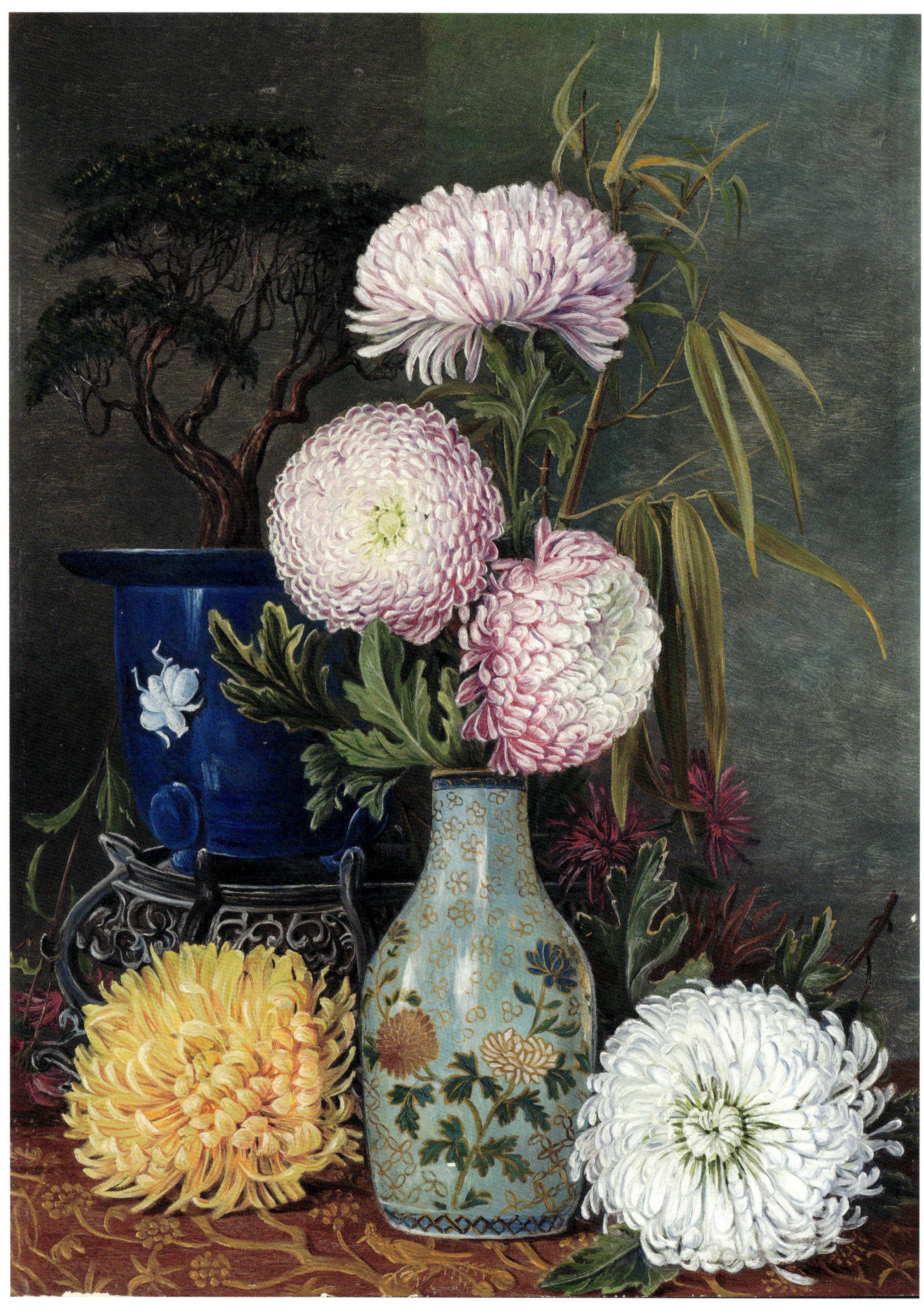

94 Marianne North, 661, *Study of Japanese Chrysanthemums and Dwarfed Pine*, oil on board, 47.2 × 34.5 cm, Royal Botanic Gardens, Kew.

commonly used in British domestic interiors of the late 19th-century . The colours originally adorning the interior of the gallery were muted, including a light dusty pink revealed by the 2010 restoration. This muted colour scheme corresponds to prevailing fashions in Britain during the last quarter of the 19th century, as the development of gas and electric lighting illuminated rooms far more brightly than under candlelight and oil lamps, making the use of intense colour schemes visually jarring.[63] The inclusion of a dado within the gallery also corresponds to then-current approaches to interior decoration. Because of a lack of adequate damp-proofing, the lower interior walls of Victorian houses were often lined with wood panelling.[64]

In addition to its botanical paintings, the North Gallery includes several decorative panels depicting flowers; some attached to the walls and others on the interior doors (figs 91–2). The door panels were most likely painted onto canvas and then marouflaged – that is to say, fixed with adhesive – with the aid of beading. The door panels make use of gilding which, as well as being decorative, gives the appearance of their having been painted directly.[65] North writes to Hemsley about decorating the North Gallery with depictions of 'flowers of the old & new worlds' (fig.93),[66] commenting that the flower hibbertia 'is very lovely but will not show well on the gold – I have half a mind to paint'.[67] The North Gallery's interior was admired by Charles Algernon Swinburne, a prominent member of the Aesthetic movement.[68]

The gilded decorative panels inside the North Gallery are redolent of Japanese-style interiors in Britain during the 1870s and 1880s produced as part of the Aesthetic movement. Such interiors are exemplified by James McNeill Whistler (1834–1903) and Thomas Jeckyll's (1827–81) Peacock Room (1876–7), designed to display a collection of Chinese porcelain owned by the shipping magnate and art collector, Frederick Leyland (1831–92). The Peacock Room incorporates fine gold lacquered murals by Whistler[69] in addition to a dado of semi-gilded panels of Spanish leather. The use of similar stylings inside the North Gallery may have been prompted not just by the Aesthetic movement but also by North's travels in Japan between 1875 and 1877, including a visit to the 'Kyrinitza [*sic*]' temple, the interior of which is described in North's diaries as being 'gilt, full of rich things and colour, with quite a Byzantine look'.[70] The diaries also describe another interior 'richly gilded and painted, with pine trees, storks, flowers, and people, on a gold ground',[71] and an 'especially beautiful' screen that 'had a gold ground with red and white pinks, and pink and white Acacia painted in the most lovely curves on it, as well as two kingfishers and a stork'.[72] Among the botanical paintings on display at the North Gallery are 661, *Study of Japanese Chrysanthemums and Dwarfed Pine* (fig.94), and 641, *Japanese Chrysanthemums, Cultivated in this Country*. Japanese flora was a novel introduction to Britain in the late 19th century.

There are no windows in the North Gallery close to where the decorative gilded panels are situated. In traditional Japanese culture, gold leaf on the surface of decorative screens was used as a way of multiplying the power of artificial and/or indirect light and creating contemplative atmospheres.[73] Such uses of gilding are also resonant with the style of decoration popularised by A.W. Pugin (1812–52) in the first half of the 19th century before the widespread use of gas and electric lighting. The transition between the exterior and interior of the North Gallery, originally signalled using benches on the North Gallery's veranda and in the main exhibition space, resonates with the openness of traditional Japanese buildings to nature – something undoubtedly witnessed by North while in Japan (figs 95–6).

A growing European and American fascination with all things Japanese, after Japan's forced opening to the outside world at the hands of the US Navy in 1853, superseded an earlier European preoccupation with China and the development from the 17th century onwards of the style known as chinoiserie. As Aldous Bertram indicates, '[t]wo of the most celebrated

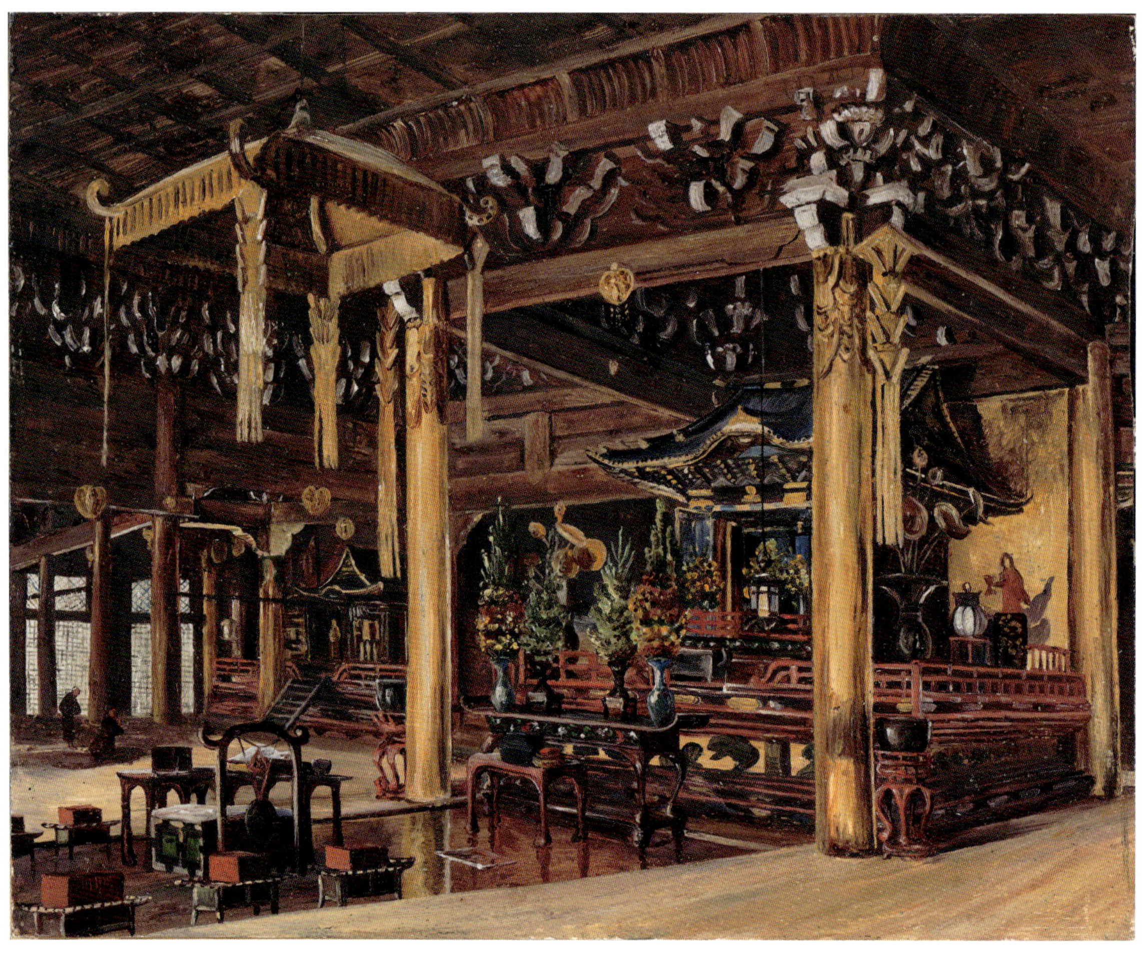

95 Marianne North, 655, *Interior of Chion-in Temple, Kioto, Japan*, oil on board, 35.4 × 44.6 cm, Royal Botanic Gardens, Kew.

attributes of chinoiserie are vibrant colors [*sic*] and intricate patterns. Many of those were first inspired by imported Asian objects such as [...] [gilded] lacquer furniture.'[74] Bertram also states that '[a]t the very heart of chinoiserie is the idea of China [...] as a verdant landscape with exotic plants [...] fruits and flowers [...] All the most influential chinoiserie designers of the eighteenth century made flowers a very prominent aspect of their work.'[75] The incorporation of floral decoration alongside botanical painting within the North Gallery is thus situated as part of an extended and complex relay of East–West cultural exchanges with which North's choice of Fergusson, who had extensive knowledge of Indian and other Asian architecture, as an architect is entirely fitting.

North's decoration of the North Gallery's interior may have been influenced additionally by visits to Frederick Edwin Church's home, Olana, during travels to the US in 1871 and 1881.[76] North describes Olana's interior as being 'after the pattern of a Damascus house'[77] – like the interior of Frederic Leighton's studio-house in London. Conversations between North

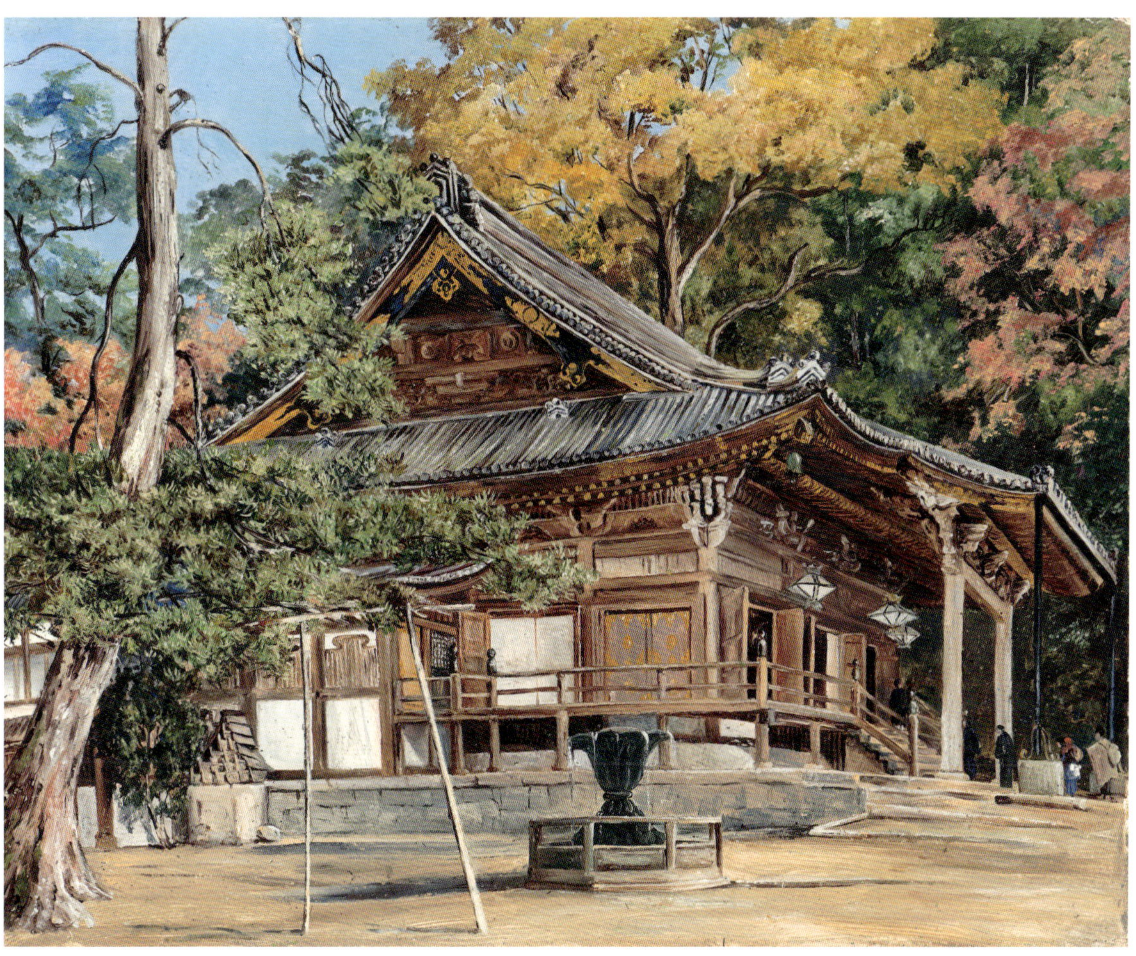

96 Marianne North, 653, *The Hottomi Temple at Kioto, Japan*, oil on board, 36.4 × 45 cm, Royal Botanic Gardens, Kew.

and Church during the visits included discussion of Church's plans for Olana. North writes, 'Mr. Church was going to paint some of his passages in arabesques of luminous paint. The passages had windows to light them by day, but no lamps; and he thought the phosphorous lines would be enough to show the way at night, and that the day-light admitted by the windows would prevent it from fading away.'[78] As noted in North's diaries, Olana was decorated with 'Japanese metal work [. . .] Chinese Fáience and Persian carpets [. . .] Italian pictures, Mexican pottery, and Shaker chairs.'[79] The house was also a setting for the showing of paintings by Church and other notable landscape painters including Claude Lorrain. Church's stylising of Olana's interior draws directly from William Chamber's *A Treatise on the Decorative Part of Civil Architecture* (1759), James Stuart and Nicolas Revett's *The Antiquities of Athens* (1762) and the Society of Dilettanti's *The Unedited Antiquities of Attica* (1817).[80]

The structuring of the North Gallery's display of botanical and landscape paintings relates closely to the German scientist, Alexander von Humboldt's conception of the panorama. Humboldt suggested that, besides museums, 'panoramic buildings, containing alternating

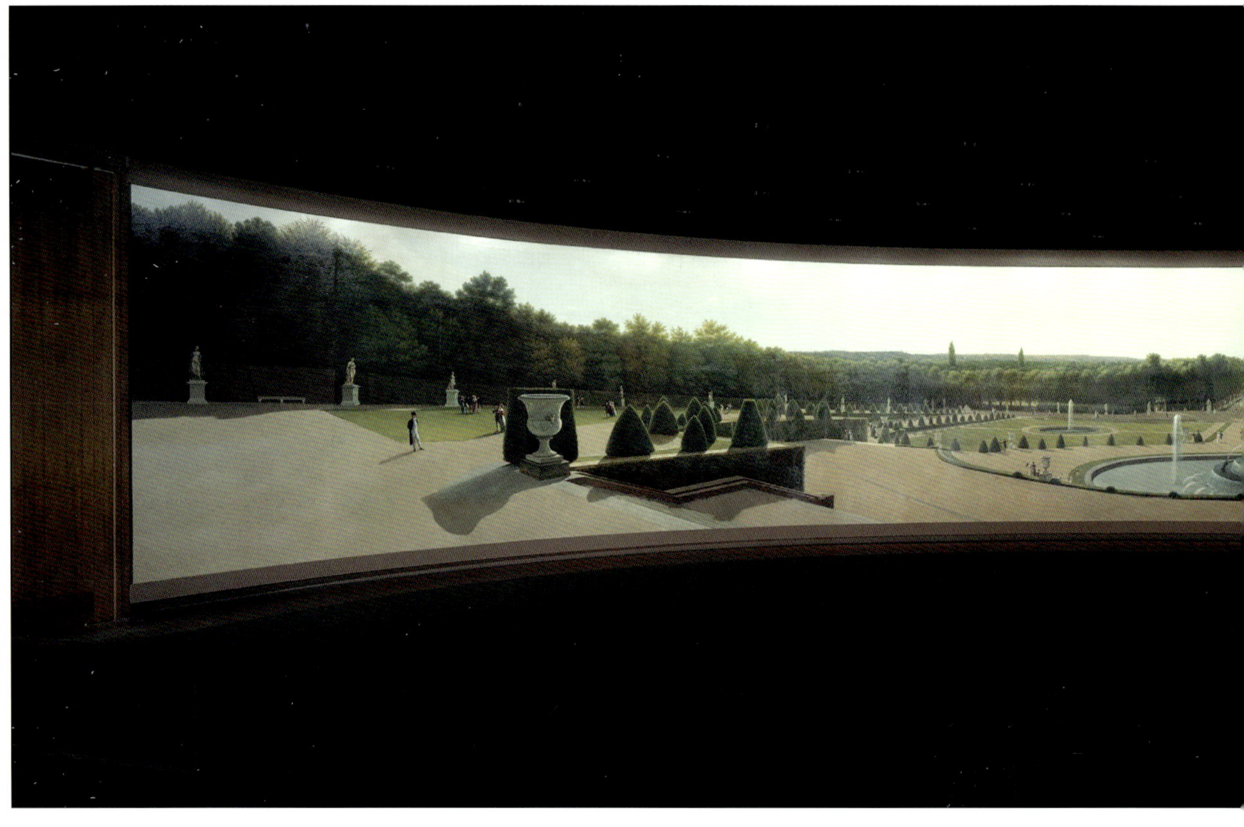

97 John Vanderlyn, *Panoramic View of the Palace and Gardens of Versailles*, 1818–19, oil on canvas, 360 × 4950 cm, The Metropolitan Museum of Art, New York.

pictures of landscapes of different geographical latitudes and from different zones of elevation, should be erected in our large cities [to] raise the feeling of admiration for nature' and 'increase the knowledge of the works of creation.'[81] The word 'panorama' – which derives from the ancient Greek pan (all) and ὅρᾱμᾰ (view) to signify an all-encompassing depiction – was initially coined to describe paintings with a 360° field of representation, but was swiftly applied to 'virtually any painting displaying a broad scene' (fig.97).[82] In the monumental five-volume treatise, *Cosmos: A Sketch of a Physical Description of the Universe* (1845–62), Humboldt looks beyond narrow issues of artistic style to the experimental utility of art, stating that:

> Landscape painting, and fresh and vivid descriptions of nature, alike conduce to heighten the charm emanating from a study of the external world, which is shown us in all its diversity of form by both, while both are alike capable, in a greater or lesser degree, according to the success of the attempt, to combine the visible and invisible in our contemplation of nature.[83]

Humboldt asserts that '[t]he effort to connect these several elements forms the last and noblest aim of delineative art' and that landscape painting 'increases the desire for the prosecution of distant travels, and thus incites men in an equally instructive and charming

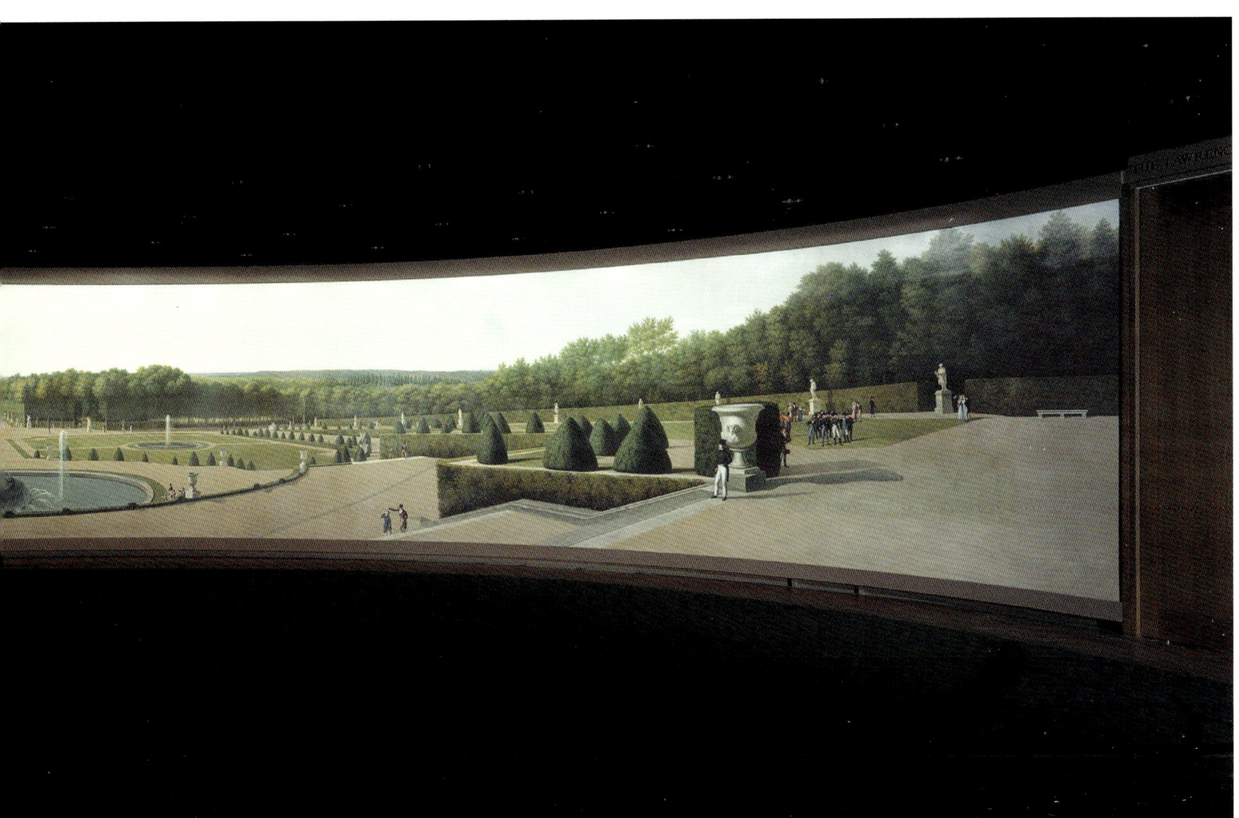

manner to a free communion with nature.'[84] In this, Humboldt can be understood to bring together scientific utility with Romantic ideas of sublimity felt in response to the overwhelming vastness and power of nature.

Humboldt's conception of the panorama impacted significantly on Victorian visual cultural sensibilities.[85] There was a worldwide craze for panoramas during the 19th century, with many artists of the day, including Thomas Girtin (1775–1802) and Philip Reinagle (who had provided paintings for Thornton's *The Temple of Flora*), producing panoramic views.[86] The panoramic manner was formative on the development of the Hudson River School's depiction of nature on a grand scale.[87] North's friend Church was an admirer of panoramas – as were other members of the School, including the group's founders Thomas Cole and Albert Bierstadt (1830–1902) – as exemplified by Church's monumental painting *Heart of the Andes* (fig.64 above). Edward Lear owned a copy of the painting, stating that 'it hangs always before me' and declaring Church to be 'the greatest landscape artist after Turner.'[88] William Holman Hunt reportedly saw panoramas as having a 'global destiny' in which 'painters committed to telling the whole truth about nature' would go into the world 'two by two as Christ had sent out his disciples to preach.'[89] The North Gallery effectively extends Humboldt's idea of the panorama and Holman Hunt's evangelical vision by containing a view of nature with truly global, rather than simply all-round, immersive reach. Horizontally elongated panoramic and dioramic drawings and paintings had become commonplace globally as part of a colonialist pictorial representational surveying of land.[90] Several of North's topographical paintings strongly allude to such formats, including 801, *Another View at Pushkar* (fig.98), and 001, *Victoria regia* (fig.99) –

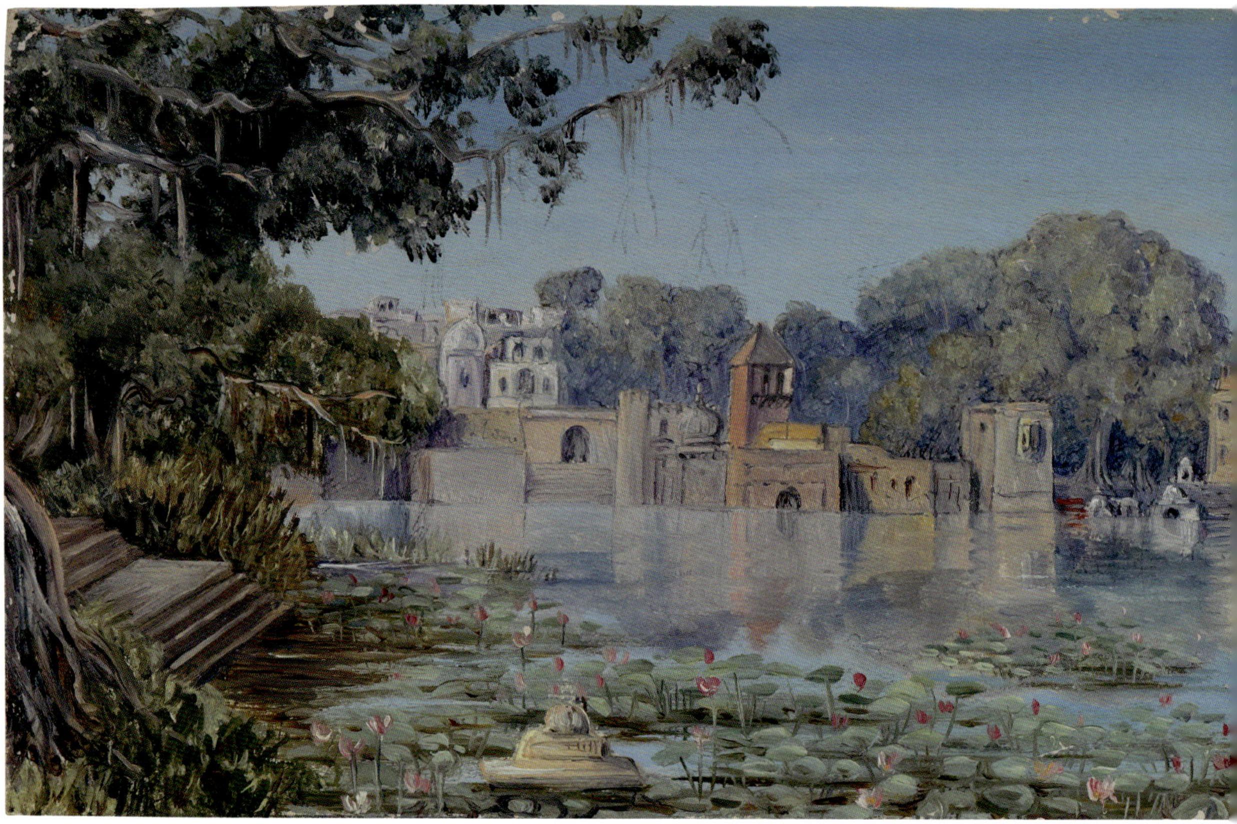

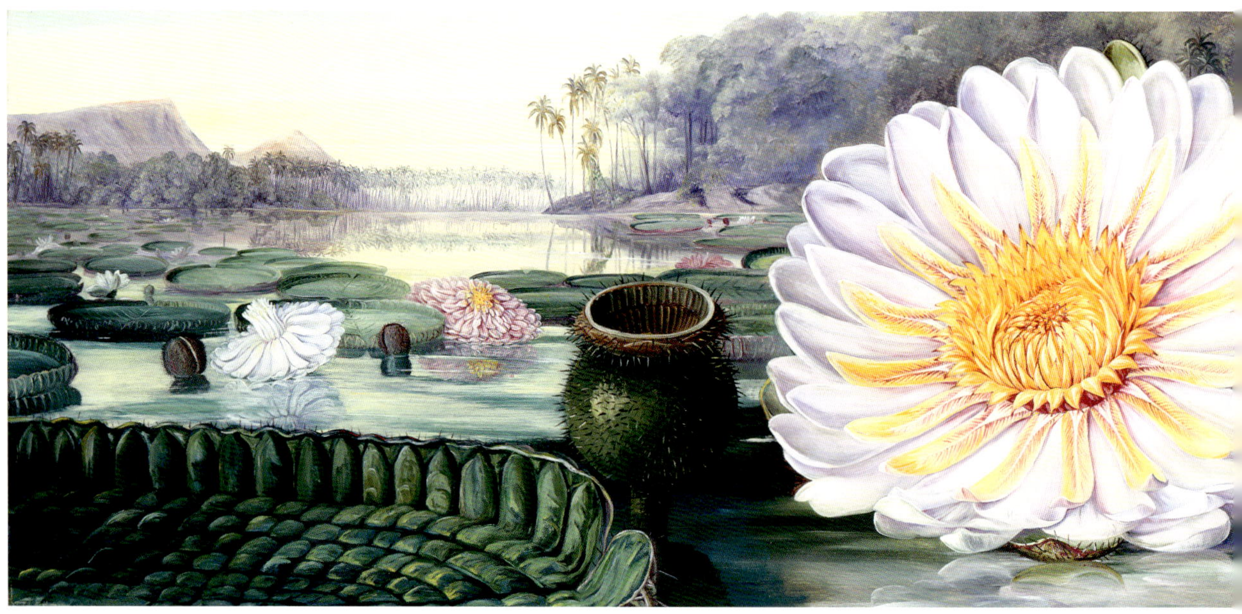

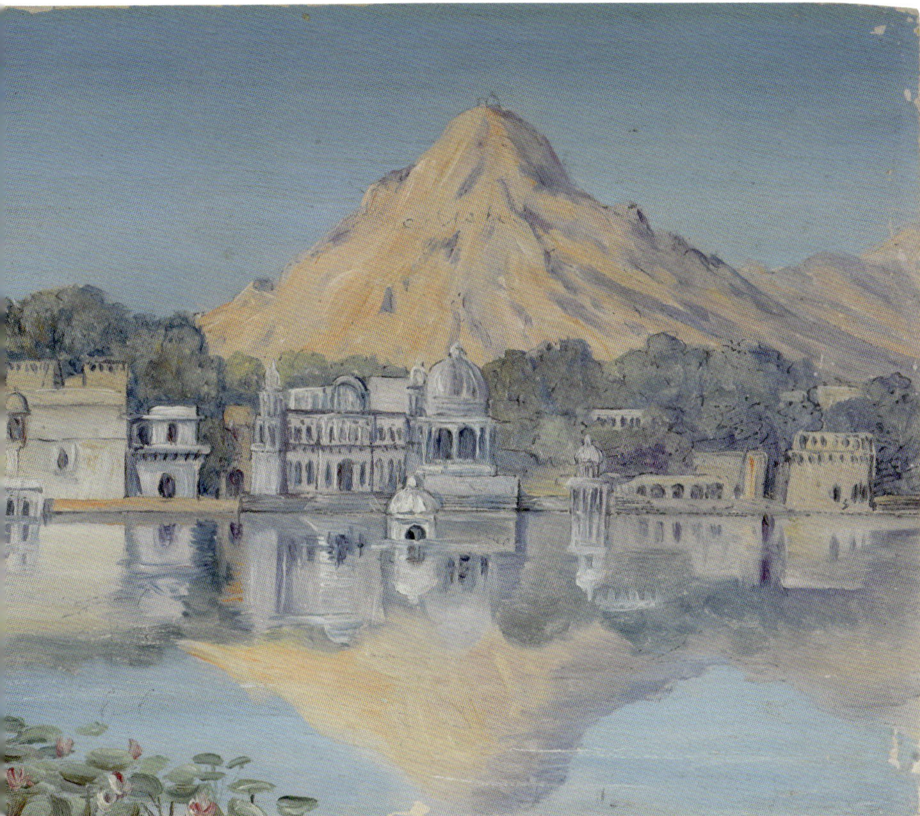

98 Marianne North, 801, *Another View at Pushkar*, oil on board, 12.2 × 34.5 cm, Royal Botanic Gardens, Kew.

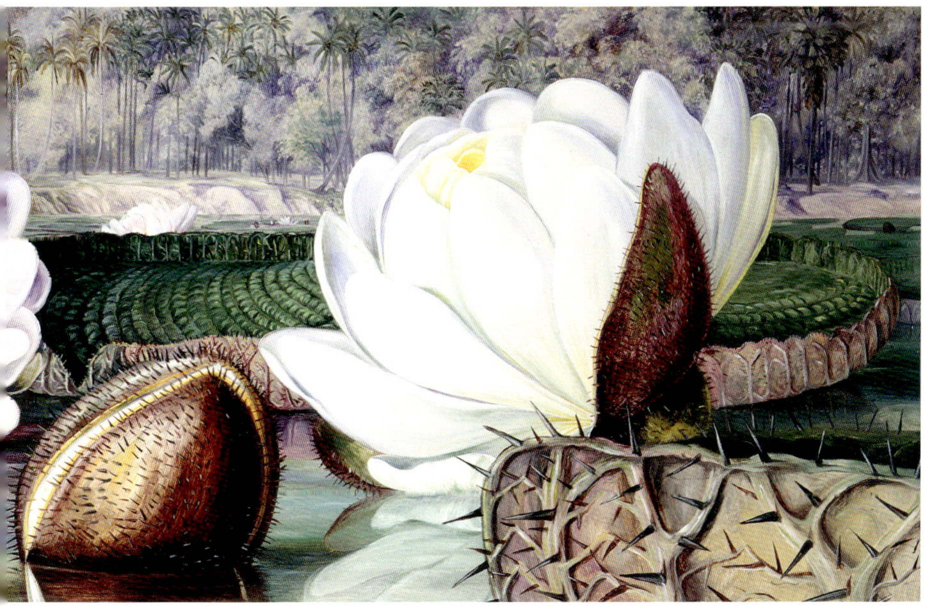

99 Marianne North, 001, *Victoria regia*, oil on board, 34.6 × 128.5 cm, Royal Botanic Gardens, Kew.

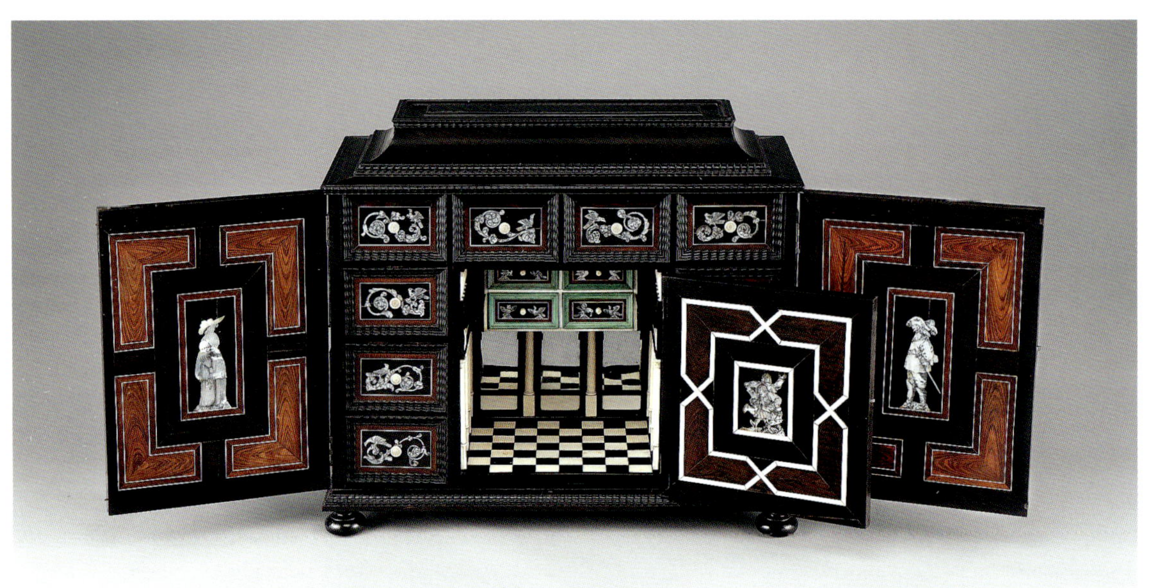

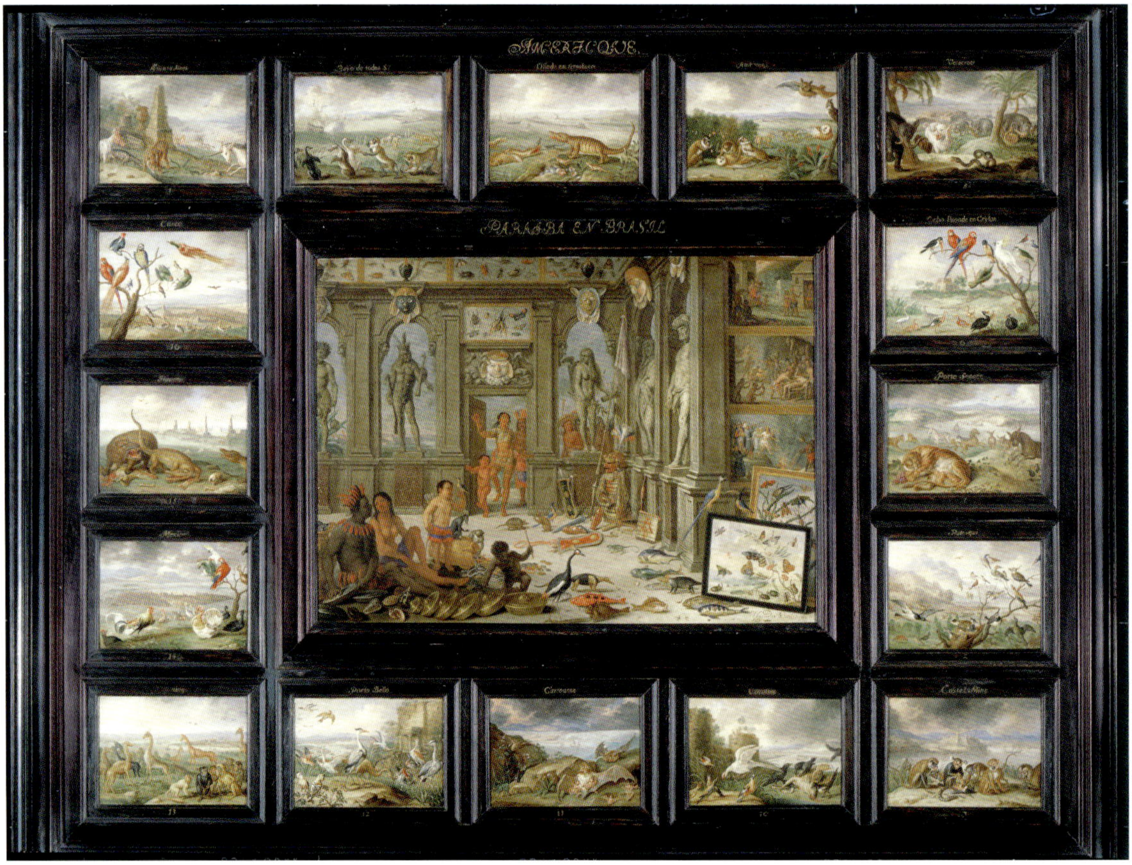

100 Herman Doomer (attributed), engraved by Salomon Saverij, figures on interior of doors after designs by Pieter Jansz Quast, figure on interior compartment door based on engraving by Albrecht Dürer, Cabinet, *c.*1640–50, oak veneered with ebony, snakewood, rosewood, kingwood, cedar and other woods, mother-of-pearl, ivory, green-stained bone, 70 × 82.1 × 40 cm, The Metropolitan Museum of Art, New York.

101 Jan van Kessel, *The Four Continents: America*, 1666, oil on copperplate, 48.5 × 67.5 cm (central panel), Alte Pinakothek, Munich.

which is also similar in style and composition to paintings by Reinagle in *The Temple of Flora*. North produced extremely elongated panorama-style sketch paintings akin to paintings by Church, Holman Hunt and Lear.

Panoramas have a further connection to pre-scientific collections known as *Wunderkammer* (wonder chambers) or cabinets of curiosities prevalent in Europe before the establishment of public museums from the late 18th century onwards (fig.100). Typically, cabinets of curiosities were used to house private collections of diverse objects and artefacts whose display was organised not in wholesale accordance with scientific principles of categorisation but, more usually, superficial relationships of formal similarity. Within cabinets of curiosities, objects taken from the natural world could often be found next to man-made artefacts and artworks at the whim of their collectors. Representations of the world as a vast, diverse and ultimately unknowable space were a recurring feature of such pre-scientific displays – as depicted by Jan van Kessel's (1626–79) allegory of *The Four Continents* (1664–6; fig.101), a painterly representation of a cabinet-like collection, with natural objects and images in black frames placed side by side, signifying the four continents of the then-known world.[91] An example of a cabinet of curiosities still in existence can be found at the Palazzo Poggi museum in Bologna.[92] In Britain the origins of such cabinets can be traced back to the time of the Jacobean court during the early part of the 17th century.[93] Examples of furniture and a room once used to house private cabinets of curiosities are still in situ at Ham House close to Kew Gardens.[94]

During North's lifetime private cabinet-like collections of 'works of art, illustrated texts and maps, coins, scientific devices, seashells, and other natural specimens' were revived and became fashionable among the middle and upper classes.[95] Given North's position within British society, it would have been highly unusual for the artist not to have been exposed to such collections. Botanical paintings on display in the North Gallery are presented as scientifically truthful and categorised rationally in accordance with identifications of regional and national geographical differences. This approach is further supported by the organisation and naming of wood samples in the gallery's dado and, at the time of the gallery's opening, the publication of an accompanying guide and explanatory catalogue. The presentation of the North Gallery's collection of paintings and objects is, however, also akin to the way in which cabinets of curiosities are organised. North's hanging of the paintings in black japanned frames alongside natural objects as a representation of vast global diversity echoes similar approaches to display during the 17th century, as depicted by van Kessel. Moreover, while North's paintings purport to be scientific, they are in fact closer in their execution to the making of high art. The North Gallery can therefore be interpreted both as a scientifically motivated display and, in part, as a latter-day cabinet of curiosities intended to instil sublime feelings of awe and wonder in the face of the unknown and ultimately unknowable.

A community celebration day 'inspired by the work of Marianne North' and supported by the UK National Heritage Lottery Fund was held at Kew Gardens on Sunday, 11 October 2009. The celebration day was intended to showcase progress on the North Gallery's restoration during Kew's 250th anniversary year. It included a programme of activities that ran from 11.00 am to 3.30 pm. Among those activities was a World Tea Party held in the Temperate House, where visitors could taste teas that North may have encountered while travelling (a knowing reversal perhaps of Joseph Hooker's views on the serving of refreshments at the North Gallery); a demonstration by volunteers from the BAPS Shri Swaminarayan Mandir, Neasden, of Rangoli, a traditional Indian cultural practice in which floral and flower-like patterns are made on floors and tabletops, using minerals and plant materials to welcome Lakshmi, the goddess of wealth and good luck; and interactive henna painting sessions also held in the Temperate House. A talk was given within the

North Gallery about Hindu sacred plants represented in paintings by North. There were also handmade banners of batik silk inspired by North's travels and the plants within Kew Gardens. The silks were provided by the Marjory Kinnon School and Feltham Arts association, together with the artist Sofie Layton. Yurts were placed around the garden in proximity to the North Gallery where visitors could paint plants as part of a workshop that encouraged participants to transform a piece of nature into an artwork inspired by North's intense colour palette. Instead of paper or canvas bark leaves, wood and other natural materials were used. Visitors to the celebration day were invited to engage with contemporary technology as part of an animation special that enabled viewers to bring North's paintings to life in the present day. This activity was accompanied by a workshop for families that made use of images from the gallery. Another talk was given by the Kew Conservation Team in the adjoining Shirley Sherwood Gallery on the restoration of the North Gallery. The main event of the day was a performance of traditional Indian dances inside the North Gallery by the Pushpalata Dance Academy, Osterley, inspired by North's travels to South Asia, which made references to entries in North's diaries.

This combined celebration of North's life and 21st-century multicultural Britain effectively raised the painter's status to one of a historical cultural icon whose legacy can be seen not only to traverse geographical boundaries but also others of gendered identity, ethnicity and culture. The upholding of North as a cultural icon in this way is not without foundation. North did not identify as a feminist, but nevertheless challenged expectations about the role and agency of women in an intensely patriarchal British Victorian society. North's undeniable cosmopolitanism also cut across rigid social and at times cultural divisions. Moreover, North's disruption of conventional ways of making and exhibiting botanical painting resonate with the multifaceted displays and varied cultural practices at the celebration day. The North Gallery, although connected to prevailing 19th-century ideas about display, was and still is a highly idiosyncratic site of transporting aesthetic experience, found, perhaps fittingly, in an unpretentious position at the edge rather than in a central part of Kew Gardens.

Conclusion

Marianne North's Legacy

Even as work started on the building of the North Gallery, North had begun to express hopes about the significance for posterity of what would be 14 years of producing paintings while travelling. Writing to Joseph Hooker on 11 August 1879, North states, 'no one can tell how soon death comes & it would be a great happiness to know my life has not been spent in vain that I can leave something behind which will add to the pleasure of others & not discredit my fathers [*sic*] old name'. North also writes in the same letter of accessing the North Gallery and its studio after no longer being able to 'wander over the other side of the world'.[1]

In 1885, North began to write of returning to Britain permanently, and by 1886 had found a new home in Alderley, Gloucestershire, 'the exact place I wished for', to retire in.[2] The house at Alderley was rented from a General Hale and had 'a ready-made old house and garden' that North intended to refashion 'away from callers and lawn tennis'.[3] After moving in, North promptly covered over the house's tennis court, planting a terraced garden in its place, and installed a pond and a rockery that was 'stocked with rare plants from all corners of the globe' (fig.102).[4] Kew furnished North with 'all sorts of foreign rarities' for the garden at Alderley, and North's nieces collected alpine plants from Davos in Switzerland. North's friends 'Mr. Wilson, Canon Ellacombe, Miss [Gertrude] Jekyll, and many others – sent generous contributions from their famous gardens'. All were interested in North's gardening endeavours and in 'how she worked'.[5] North's sister Catherine Addington Symonds comments that 'The good taste' of the 'artist's mind helped her to utilise the things she found ready to her hand; instead of cutting down, she adapted what was there before'.[6] Many of North's old friends visited the house at Alderley, including the Asa Grays and Joseph Hooker.[7]

Despite North having been socially and professionally well connected, the artist's achievements were never formally honoured by the British state. On 28 August 1884, Henry F. Ponsonby, private secretary to Britain's Queen Victoria, wrote an official letter to North from Osborne House on the Isle of Wight. Ponsonby's letter conveyed the Queen's thanks for North's 'generous conduct in presenting to the nation, at Kew, your valuable collection of botanical paintings, in a gallery erected by yourself'. Ponsonby also apologies

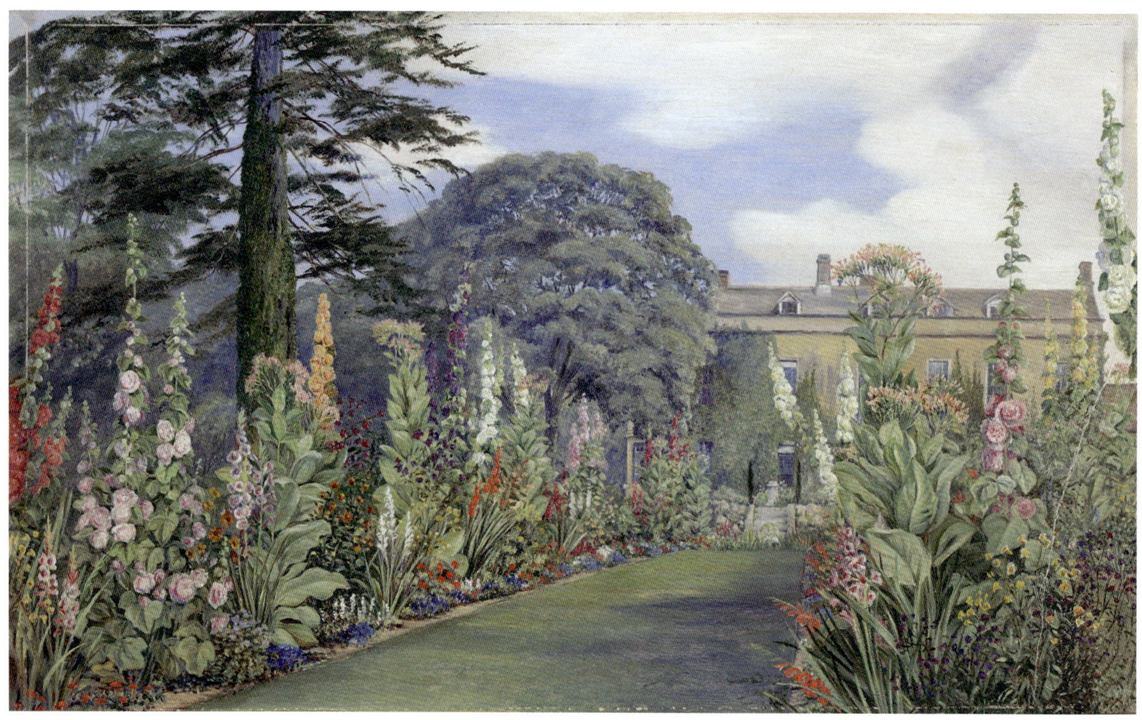

102 Marianne North, S52, *Alderley Garden, Gloucestershire, England*, oil on paper, 31 × 50.6 cm, Royal Botanic Gardens, Kew.

on behalf of the Queen, who could not recommend any 'mode of publicly recognising' North's 'liberality'. The letter was accompanied by a photograph of the Queen.[8]

From the early 1880s, North became increasingly unwell and was 'never quite free from discomfort'. Addington Symonds acknowledges the 'indomitable strength which had seemed never to flag [. . .] through poisonous climates, never breaking down under incessant work, fatigue, bad food, and all the hardships which few women, travelling absolutely alone, would have dared to face'.[9] Addington Symonds also writes of 'The "enemy" of her last two voyages' throughout which 'weary, constant noises never ceased' in North's head. Addington Symonds conjectures that the noises were the result of an 'overtired brain' which translated them 'into human voices, whose words were often taunts' and that North's 'deafness was of course responsible for this', adding that the artist's 'brave common-sense recognised that the voices were delusions'.[10] Addington Symonds indicates that in 'the autumn of 1888 a deep-seated disease of the liver, brought on originally, no doubt, by long exposure to all sorts of bad climatic influences, declared itself', adding, the 'unkind voices fled, and the relief was immense'. North's last letter to Addington Symonds is dated 11 June 1890. The artist died on 30 August and 'was buried in the quiet green churchyard at Alderley'.[11]

Writing in a valedictory tone after North's death, Addington Symonds observes that the 'principle of unostentatious kindness' had been North's 'rule through life, making her often seem indifferent to other people's wider schemes and charities'. The artist was 'intolerant of "Rules" in all things (except perhaps music)', and 'exceedingly and scornfully sceptical as to rules in art: for instance, the limitations and laws of composition in painting'. In Addington Symonds's opinion, North 'painted as a clever child' who 'had scarcely ever any artistic teaching'.[12] Addington Symonds concludes that when North 'began to study plant-life, she read much and constantly about the trees and flowers she drew and cultivated' and 'always with special regard to their out-door habits and characteristics'.[13] These comments, although sparse, are in many ways an accurate summary of North's personality and approach to botanical painting.

As an unmarried woman with no children, North's legacy lies principally with the North Gallery and the paintings contained within it, in addition to the three volumes of posthumously published diaries edited by Addington Symonds. North's style and techniques as a botanical painter were the result of borrowings from several sources, scientific and artistic. The paintings are nevertheless highly innovative in their traversing of artistic and scientific boundaries and, especially, of adapting artistic compositional tropes to scientific purposes; not least the pictorial representation of plants in their natural settings observed at first hand. Although their innovatory scientific value is not as well appreciated today as it was in the 19th century, North's paintings nevertheless retain a strong appeal both aesthetically and as a record of scientific and artistic endeavour connected to travel. Learning from the work of others is, of course, a normal aspect of artistic development. The most celebrated British painter of the 19th century, J.M.W. Turner, for example, spent a lifetime producing paintings in dialogue with those of Claude Lorrain.[14]

The complex boundary-crossing construction of North's paintings is in many respects in keeping with postmodernist and contemporary artistic sensibilities. However, North's paintings continue to be overlooked by art-historical scholarship. A likely reason for this oversight is that the artist died on the cusp of the emergence of the European art movements that would initiate 20th-century modernism. From that perspective North's work seems highly Victorian and therefore retrogressive; and this despite the influence that some artists of the time, such as Charles Algernon Swinburne, had on the development of English modernist aesthetics. While still a pupil at Eton College, the English novelist Evelyn Waugh (1903–66) was a member of a group known as the 'Eton Candle' (Eton Scandal) that discussed art, interior decoration and the work of Swinburne, to whose memory the group was dedicated.[15] Transitionary musings of this kind between Victorian and 20th-century aesthetic sensibilities were eventually overtaken by continental avant-garde modernism and its repudiation of anything with historicist leanings. As the cultural historian Matthew Sweet indicates, the English modernist Bloomsbury Group conducted a 'persuasive and witty debunking' of 19th-century worthies not least through Lytton Strachey's (1880–1932) satirical book *Eminent Victorians* (1818).[16] Historian of visual culture Jonathan Crary sees the marginalisation of Victorian painting by modernism as ironic, given that both have their origins in the 'same nineteenth-century milieu'.[17]

North was also overlooked by early 20th-century publications representative of Kew Gardens and its history. English illustrator Edward Bawden (1903–89) – producer of numerous illustrations of Kew Gardens over many years – proposed *A General Guide of the Royal Botanical Gardens, Kew* for spring and Easter 1923 that does not contain a single reference to the North Gallery, not even on the visitor map identifying the garden's diverse array of buildings and follies.[18] Writing about Kew in the 1970s, arch-modernist Wilfrid Blunt criticised displays there for their 'tendency to overcrowding',[19] adding, 'I know I have somewhat viciously attacked the obsolete method of display adopted in the museums at Kew [. . .] all I wrote of them really applies equally to the North Gallery [. . .] Nothing could be more outmoded'. Blunt goes on to describe the hanging of the paintings within the North Gallery as 'absurd'.[20] By contrast, the garden historian Guy Brett argues that 'before we try to define' North and 'decide whether it [the North Gallery] belongs primarily to science or to art (or whether such a distinction is meaningful or useful)' we should assess the gallery 'in the result of all its circumstances'.

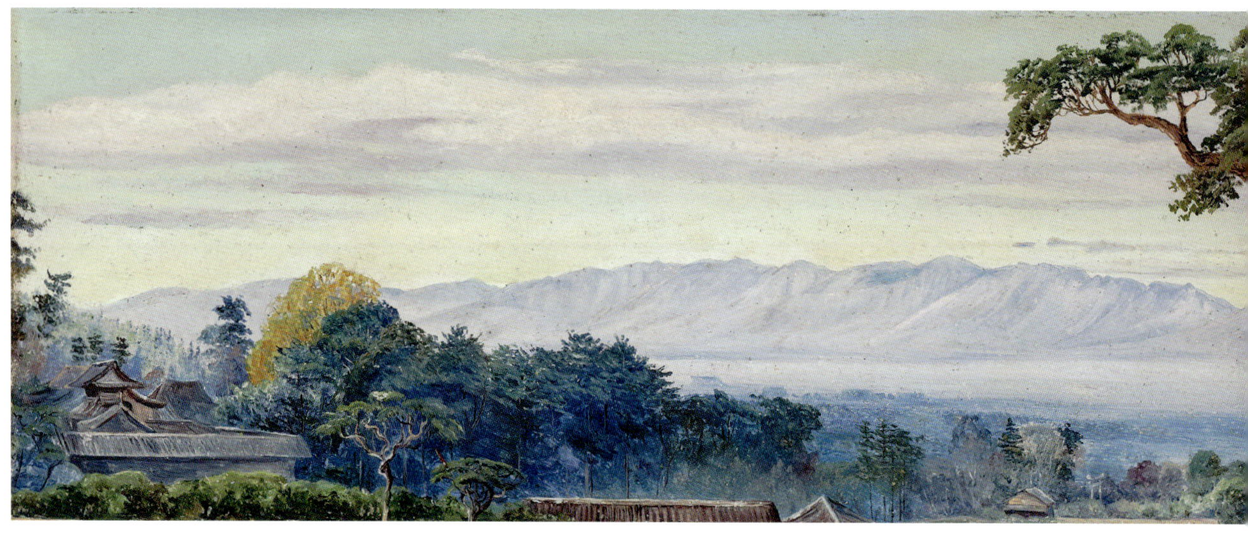

103 Marianne North, 657, *View of the City of Kioto, Japan in the Morning Mist*, oil on board, 18.4 × 91 cm, Royal Botanic Gardens, Kew.

Brett continues, 'The whole project still holds its charge of eccentricity [...] outside the professional contexts of both science and art of the time.'[21] Many contemporary artworks involve similar combinations of science and art. The American artist Chris Burden (1946–2015), for example, has described their own work as a performance artist and sculptor as 'a little bit like science experiments. You don't know the outcome necessarily but you're very precise when it comes to the input.'[22]

Other artists have been able to successfully negotiate differing pre-avant-garde and more recent cultural sensibilities while avoiding disdain for the former. According to the art writer Martin Harrison, the Irish designer and painter Francis Bacon (1909–92) 'retained many of the attitudes as well as demeanour of an Edwardian aristocrat' whilst having 'partly reinvented himself as a bohemian.'[23] Like North, Bacon was connected to Charles Kingsley, and Bacon's great aunt Eliza Mitchell's art collection included works by Frederic Leighton.[24] Bacon's studio was famously littered with photographs and photographic reproductions from books and magazines used as sources for the making of paintings.[25] North's likely use of photography as an aid to painting was shared not only by Victorian-era painters such as William Holman Hunt and Edgar Degas (1834–1917) but also more conspicuously by numerous modernist and postmodernist artists. At the time North was painting, the process of making a realistic rendering from photographs by engravers and printers was commonplace. Others using the same methods include James Fergusson, whose publications display illustrations engraved from photographs.[26] Crary writes that up until the mid-1800s 'the artist operated within conditions of relative equilibrium between the imperatives of external rules and techniques'. The intensification of new technologies being used to make artworks in the late 19th century 'triggered the erosion of this reciprocity between individual experience and exterior processes and instruments.'[27] Early modernist painters such as Édouard Vuillard (1868–1940) and Pierre Bonnard (1867–1947) were 'keen amateur photographers' and used the photographs they took as 'preliminary sketches' for their paintings, even if viewers who were still attached to early 19th-century attitudes saw uses of this kind as anathema to art.[28] As Harrison

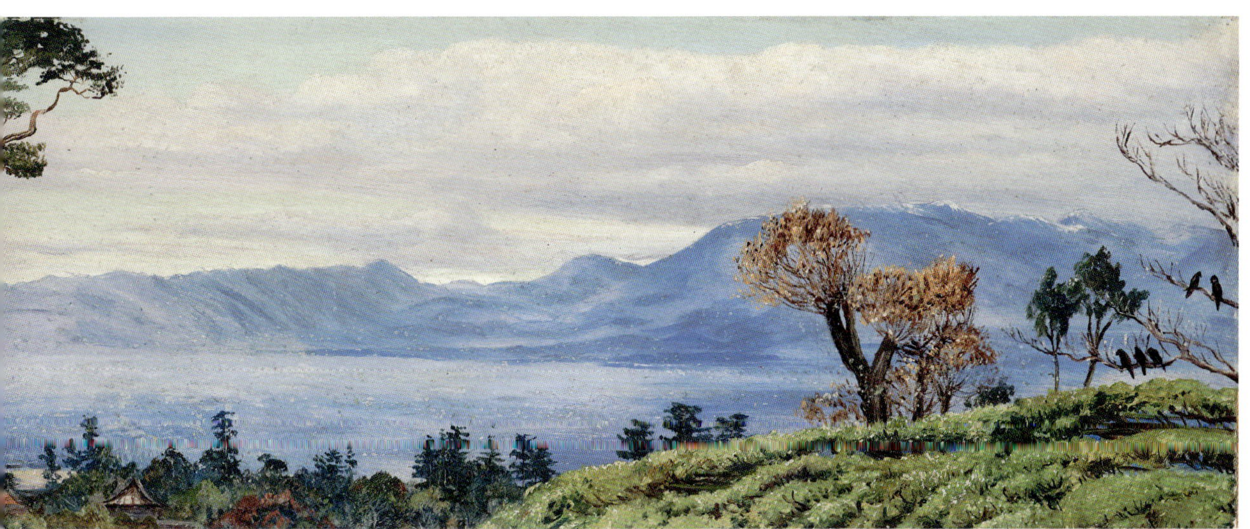

explains, in the context of postmodernity 'it became widely accepted that no art form had an independent, autonomous existence, and photography was adopted as a medium by artists who had never held a paintbrush'.[29]

Crary asserts that we are now 'in a material environment where earlier 20th-century models of spectatorship, contemplation and experience are inadequate for understanding the conditions of cultural creation and reception', and that some of this 'experimental activity involves the creation of unanticipated spaces and environments in which our visual and intellectual habits are challenged or disrupted. The processes through which sensory information is consumed become the object of various strategies of de-familiarization.'[30] A key index of the shift described by Crary is the proliferation since the 1960s of various forms of installation art and immersive art experiences, the most recent variation on which is the use of virtual reality and artificial intelligence in artistic contexts. This, to some extent, returns artists to the cultural conditions of the mid- to late 19th century where science and art were both considered 'part of a single interlocking field of knowledge and practice'.[31]

The North Gallery's embodiment of the Humboldtian panorama is arguably prescient of later developments in modernist and postmodernist spectatorship. In the view of the historian of botanical painting Marion Arnold, the North Gallery constitutes 'an idiosyncratic installation conceived decades before Claude Monet's famous *Waterlilies* series at the Orangerie, Paris, which also depicts relationships between plants and their habitats'.[32] While it would be misleading to describe the North Gallery as postmodernist, as Arnold indicates the immersive experience it gives rise to is undeniably resonant with the installation art of the last half century. The art historian and theorist Claire Bishop defines a work of installation art as involving a 'theatrical' or 'immersive' space that the audience/viewer must physically enter. As Bishop indicates, such a capacious definition extends, within the context of postmodernist and contemporary defamiliarisation, even to the relatively conventional 'display of paintings on a wall'. Today, Bishop's definition might also be further extended to include virtual spaces. In Bishop's view, an 'installation of art is secondary in importance to the individual works it contains, while in a work of installation art, the space, and the ensemble of elements within it, are regarded in their entirety as a singular entity'; but 'the distinction between an installation of works of art and "installation art" proper has become increasingly blurred'. Bishop concludes

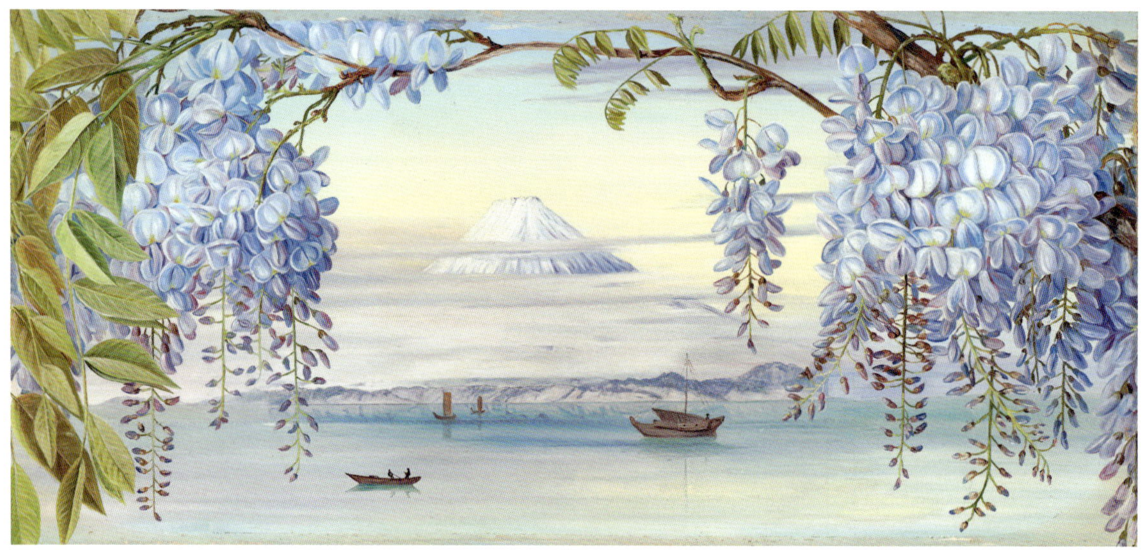

104 Marianne North, 658, *Distant View of Mount Fujiyama, Japan, and Wistaria*, oil on board, 29.4 × 63.1 cm, Royal Botanic Gardens, Kew.

that what 'both terms have in common is a desire to heighten the viewer's awareness of how objects are positioned [installed] in a space, and of our bodily response to this.'[33]

The North Gallery at Kew is not an intentional work of installation art. However, there is clearly an interrelationship between North's paintings and the way they are installed that resonates with Bishop's definition. Within the North Gallery, viewers shuttle continually between North's paintings, viewed singly or in groups, and the gallery's interior as a *Gesamtkunstwerk* (total artwork)-like combination of painting and architectural space. Confirmation of this resonance can be found in Bishop's assertion that installation art involves 'using an entire space that must be circumnavigated to be seen' that provides 'a direct analogy for the desirability of multiple perspectives on a single situation.'[34]

Bishop's definition of installation art is in many ways consonant with the Humboldtian notion of an artistic/scientific panorama. Alexander von Humboldt recognised the capacity of landscape painters to communicate contextual information about the natural world with an accuracy and immediacy denied to writers.[35] North travelled further than most other painters and botanical illustrators in trying to realise the Romantic vision set out by Humboldt. As the botanical historian Kate Teltscher explains, Humboldt encouraged landscape painters to view plants 'not merely in hot-houses or in the descriptions of botanists, but in their native grandeur in the tropical zone.'[36] Humboldt collaborated with the Bavarian botanist Carl Friedrich Philipp von Martius (1794–1868),[37] whose illustrations of plants are at times similar in composition and style to some of North's paintings. North's awareness of the impact on the natural environment of 19th-century capitalism gives further weight to a projection of this combination of science and art onto the present.

Cinema, the internet and virtual reality may have technically eclipsed Humboldt's idea of the panorama,

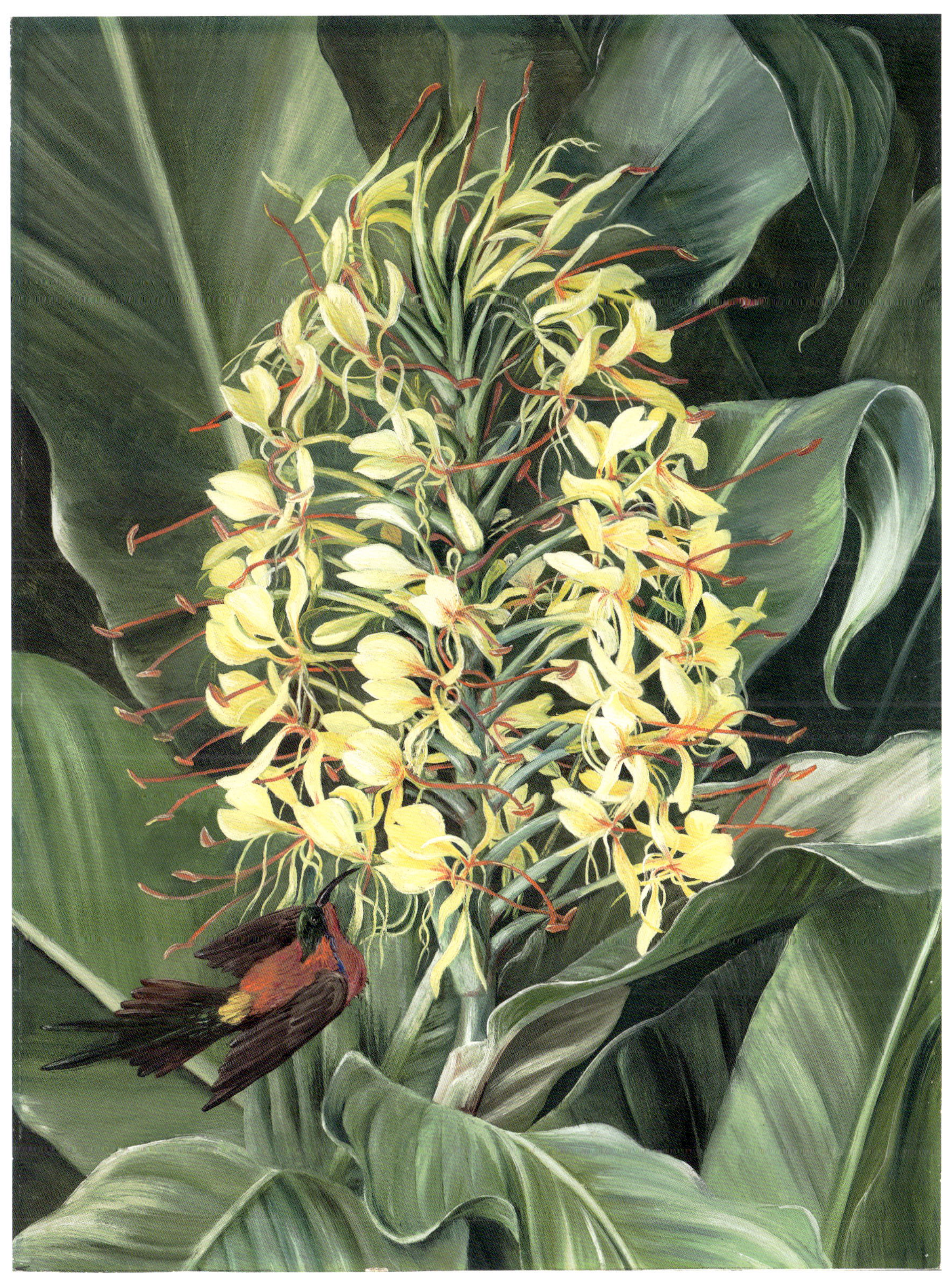

105 Marianne North, 345, *Hedychium gardnerianum and Sunbird, India*, oil on board, 45.6 × 35.4 cm, Royal Botanic Gardens, Kew.

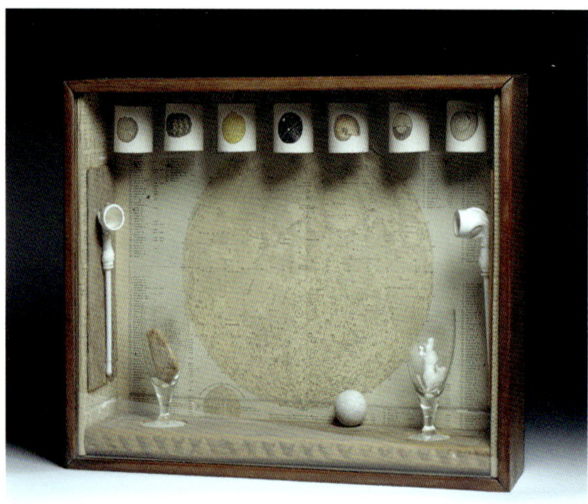

106 Joseph Cornell, *Soap Bubble Set*, 1949–50, glasses, pipes, printed paper and other media in a glass-fronted wooden box, dimensions unknown, Smithsonian American Art Museum.

but the intertextual traces of that idea can nevertheless be seen to persist in the context of installation art. The North Gallery is an embodiment of the Humboldtian panorama, and a conspicuous and deliberate amalgam of art and science. It also represents North's first-hand engagement with nature in multiple locations in contrast to more conventional panoramas that simply show a single scene in the round, such as Robert Barker's 'panorama studio' in Southwark, London, opened in 1827.[38] The North Gallery includes individual landscape panoramas and dioramas in addition to close-up paintings of plants (figs 103–105). Examples of 19th-century display closer in conception to the multiple perspectives of the North Gallery include 'moving panoramas' open to the public from the early 1830s in which audiences sat in carriages to watch images on moving canvases flash by.[39]

The mutual interdependence of artworks and the sites of their display was recognised by James Fergusson, the architect of the North Gallery. Fergusson writes of the interdependence of architecture and painting, adding, 'it is evident that the effect of even [the celebrated Renaissance painter] Giotto's frescoes would have been heightened by architectural mouldings being interspersed with them'. Fergusson observes that '[a]s usual the truth is, [. . .] perfection lies between the two extremes' since '[t]he Italians of that age despised architecture as an internal decoration [. . .] We on the contrary, neglected painting, in order to display mechanical skills.'[40]

There are also strong resonances between the North Gallery's bricolaging of various objects – paintings, wood samples, decorative motifs and furnishings – and the defamiliarising modes of display characteristic of avant-garde modernist and postmodernist art. An indicative example of artistic defamiliarisation similar in its eclectic scope to the North Gallery is the work of the early to mid-20th-century American artist Joseph Cornell (1903–72). Cornell made assemblages, often contained in boxes under glass, redolent of cabinets of curiosities with their presentations of natural and other objects. Cornell's assemblages often include found objects and fragments of images appropriated from scientific and popular sources whose relationships and significance are open to poetical interpretation. In doing so, Cornell can be understood to extend forms of collage-montage pioneered by European Dada and surrealism intended to challenge settled meaning through the open-ended proliferation of possible readings. In works such as *Cabinet of Natural History: Object* (1934 and 1936–40) and *Soap Bubble Set* (1949–50; fig.106), Cornell often hints at ideas and practices associated with 18th- and 19th-century natural philosophy and science alongside surrealistic dreamlike representations of the uncanny and the occult.

Technically similar approaches can be found throughout avant-garde modernist, postmodernist and contemporary art. Approaches of this sort that resonate with the North Gallery in the context of postmodernist and contemporary art include works by the American artist Mark Dion (b.1961). In installation works such as *Tate Thames Dig* (1999), Dion presents what the art historian Ruth Erickson has described as a 'preservation, classification, and display' like that of a *Wunderkammer* or cabinet of curiosities with poetical-artistic intent. Erickson also comments that Dion is 'conscious of the correspondences between the birth of the modern museum and the contemporaneous emergence of biology, ethnography, and archaeology as coherent and defined disciplines' and that Dion's work intervenes with the supposed limits of artistic and scientific museological display.[41] Like North's, Dion's work makes intentional use of scientific and artistic modes of representation and display.

This is not to claim North as an avant-garde, postmodernist or contemporary artist *avant la lettre*; the prevailing discourses of the mid- to late 19th century with which North was entangled did not encompass a full consciousness of the effects of defamiliarisation that have come to define the progressive art and visual culture of the 20th and 21st centuries. It is, however, to recognise a continuum of combinatory techniques that are open to changing interpretation over time. Wilfrid Blunt's description of the viewing experience at the North Gallery as akin to looking at 'a gigantic botanical postage-stamp album'[42] is clearly intended to be pejorative in its allusion to a minor, often amateurish form of visual taxonomical organisation. That same description is open to a more positive reading from the standpoint of postmodernist and contemporary visual sensibilities.

Despite being celebrated in the 19th century, and unlike other female painters of the 20th century such as Frida Kahlo and Georgia O'Keeffe (1887–1986), whose work includes representations of plants and flowers, North is not widely recognised by the contemporary artworld. As the historian of botanical painting Guy Brett indicates, '[l]ittle consideration has been given' to North's paintings as works of art, since their 'presence at Kew Gardens has ensured that [they are] [...] seen in a botanical context'.[43] The openness of North's painting to scientific and aesthetic appreciation nevertheless casts a shadow over the work of present-day botanical illustrators. British botanical illustrators Pandora Sellars and Margaret Mee were both trained initially as designers and artists. Mee, whose work focuses on plants in the Brazilian Amazon seen at first hand and depicted in their natural contexts, has been referred to as an artist rather than as an illustrator.[44] The historian of Kew Gardens Ray Desmond writes that Mee's work can be compared with North's since both sometimes include birds or small animals in their paintings.[45] Sellars's paintings have a strong sense of compositional design that also bears comparison with North's. The pictorial innovations pioneered by North have now been assimilated by mainstream scientific botanical illustration.

The North Gallery has arguably had some impact on the world of present-day botanical illustration. The Shirley Sherwood Gallery, which opened next to the North Gallery in 2008, stages exhibitions of contemporary and historical botanical illustration. Works exhibited at the Sherwood Gallery include Susan Ogilvy's *Snowdrops, Churchyard: Galanthus nivalis* (2000; fig.107) – which is similar in its subject matter and composition to North's painting 192, *Wild Flowers from the Neighbourhood of New York* (fig.108) – and Carol Reddick's *Black Bird-Berry – Psychotria capensis* (2016; fig.109) – which echoes North's painting 155, *Foliage and Fruit of the Loquat, or Japanese Medlar, Brazil* (fig.110). Bryan Poole's illustration *Heliconia bihai, Eulampis jugularis* (2008; fig.111), also exhibited at the Sherwood Gallery, carries formal traces of works by North, such as 047, *Flowers of Datura and Humming Birds, Brazil* (fig.46 above) and by association paintings by Martin Johnson Heade and Philip Reinagle.

The Sherwood Gallery also showcases exhibitions of artworks representative of the natural world. A recent example of the latter is an installation by the Australian artist Tanya Schultz, otherwise known as Pip & Pop, titled *When Flowers Dream* (2022). In preparation for the installation Schultz researched botanical illustrations held in the Kew Archive and Library over a four-week period.[46] Various materials were used in the making the installation, including 'sugar in various forms [...] modelling clay, textiles, papier maché and craft materials like pompoms, beads, bio-glitter, and

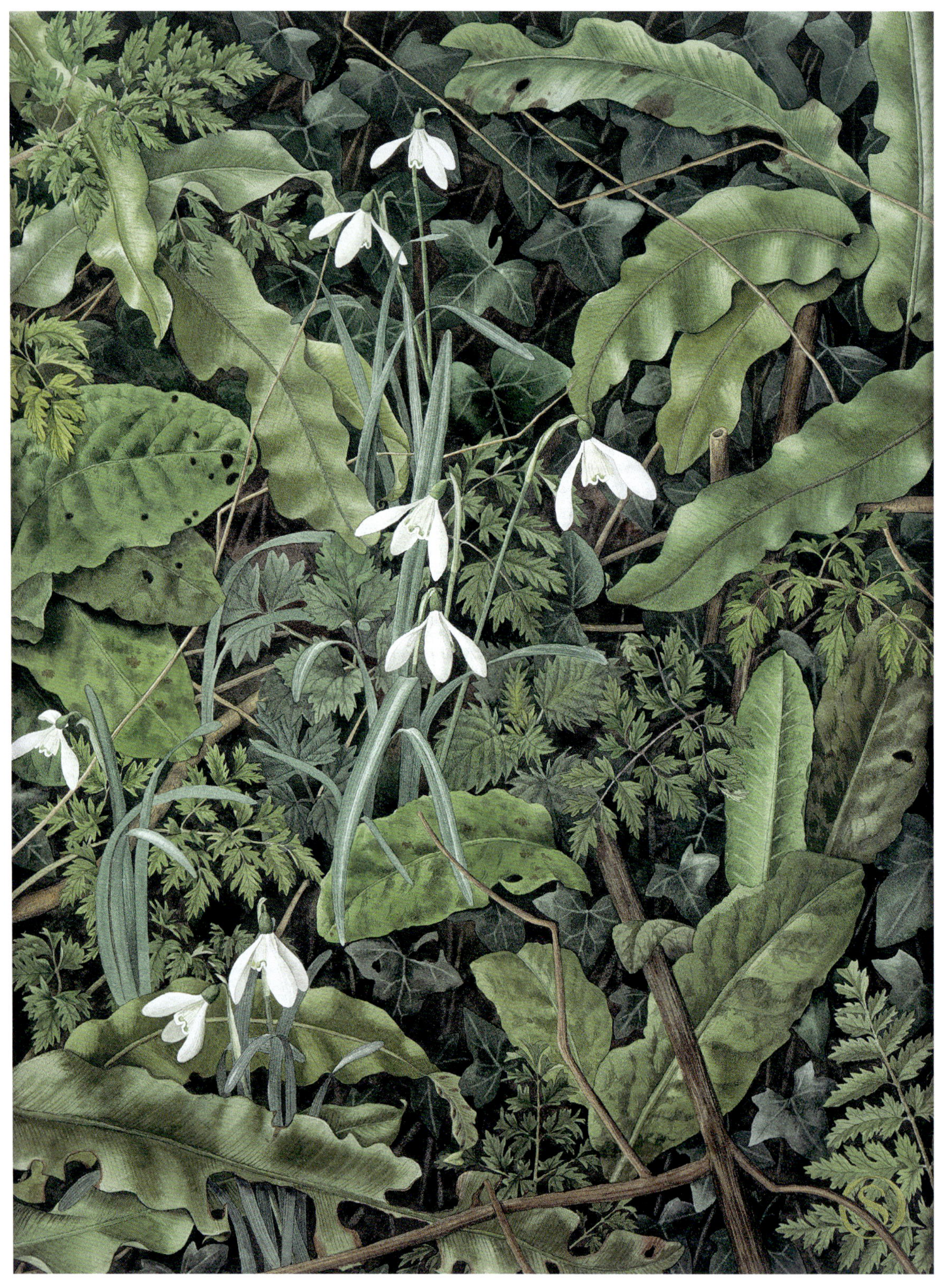

107 Susan Ogilvy, *Snowdrops, Churchyard: Galanthus nivalis*, 2000, watercolour on paper, 45.7 × 35 cm, The Shirley Sherwood Collection.

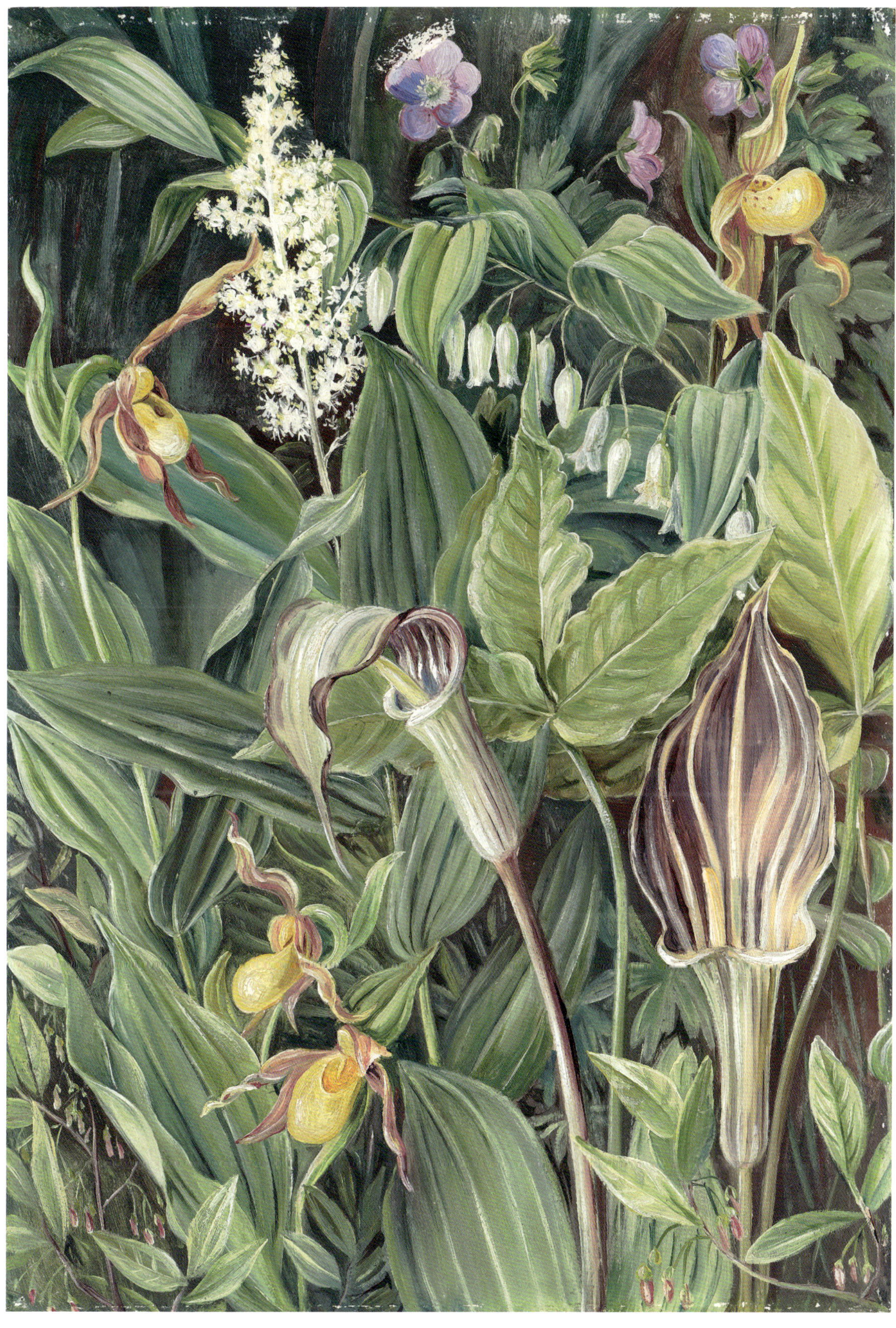

108 Marianne North, 192, *Wild Flowers from the Neighbourhood of New York*, oil on board, 35 × 25 cm, Royal Botanic Gardens, Kew.

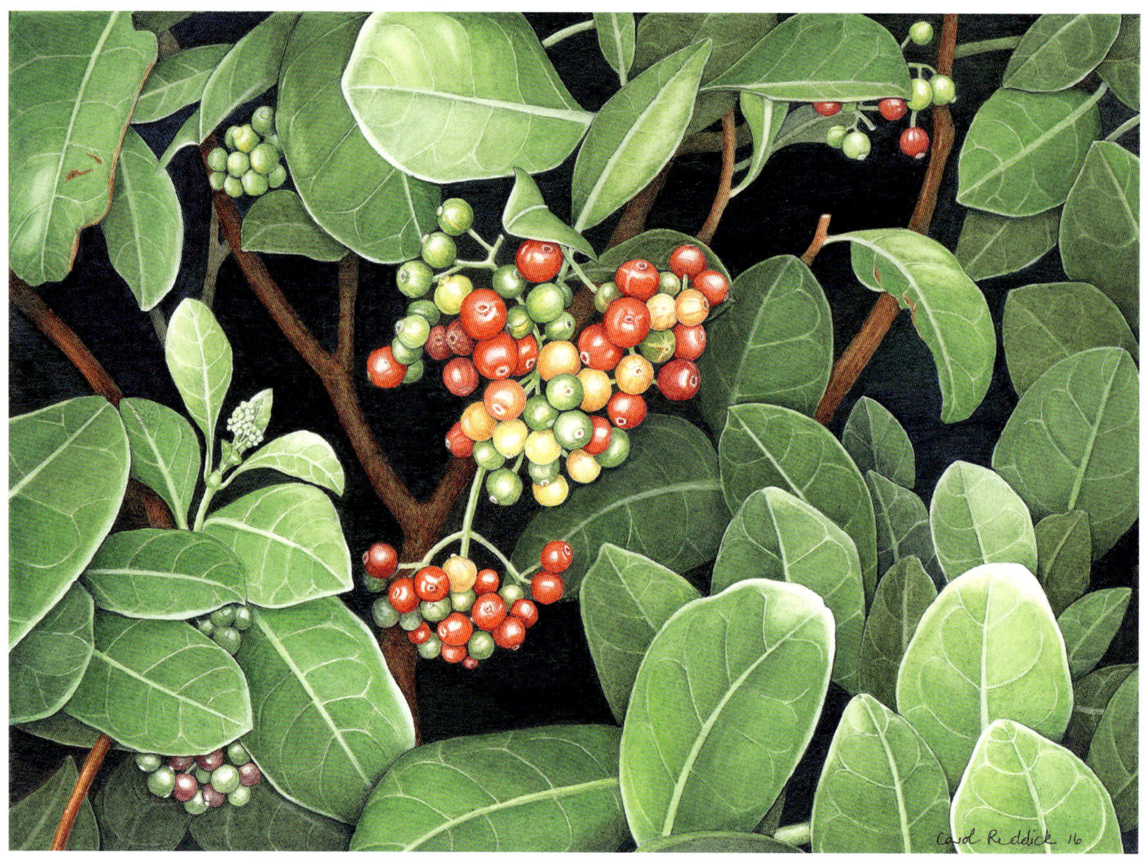

109 Carol Reddick, *Black Bird-Berry – Psychotria capensis*, 2016, watercolour on paper, 23 × 32 cm, The Shirley Sherwood Collection.

coloured string' that were sourced and then reconfigured or further embellished.[47] Schultz declares in a podcast for Kew that 'I'm fascinated by fictional geographies and paradise mythologies, places where we can escape our earthly realities.' '[T]hese places may or may not exist' and 'are often found by chance, and are impossible to locate again once you leave'.[48] Schultz's installation was accompanied by a video, involving a 'kaleidoscopic moving image' of food plants that 'swirl and spin and float around'.[49] Schultz states that they created their 'own version of many of these plants' and that 'some are completely fictional'.[50] Part of the installation presented a 'large digital collage created from hundreds of images of edible plants, fruits, and seeds' as well as images taken from the Shirley Sherwood Collection but 're-coloured' so that they are 'saturated and a bit otherworldly'.[51] The relationship to the North Gallery is undeniable.

Marianne North worked across the boundaries between differing artistic styles, techniques and genres. That diversity of approach appeals to the ideas and working methods of contemporary art-making and curatorial practice today. A close attention to North's botanical painting and its installation at the North Gallery reveals a depth of painterly skill and engagement with progressive thinking that is extraordinary as well as compelling. In both one can observe not only a significant disciplinary eclecticism and forward-looking interests in environmentalism but also the likely use of innovative technologies.

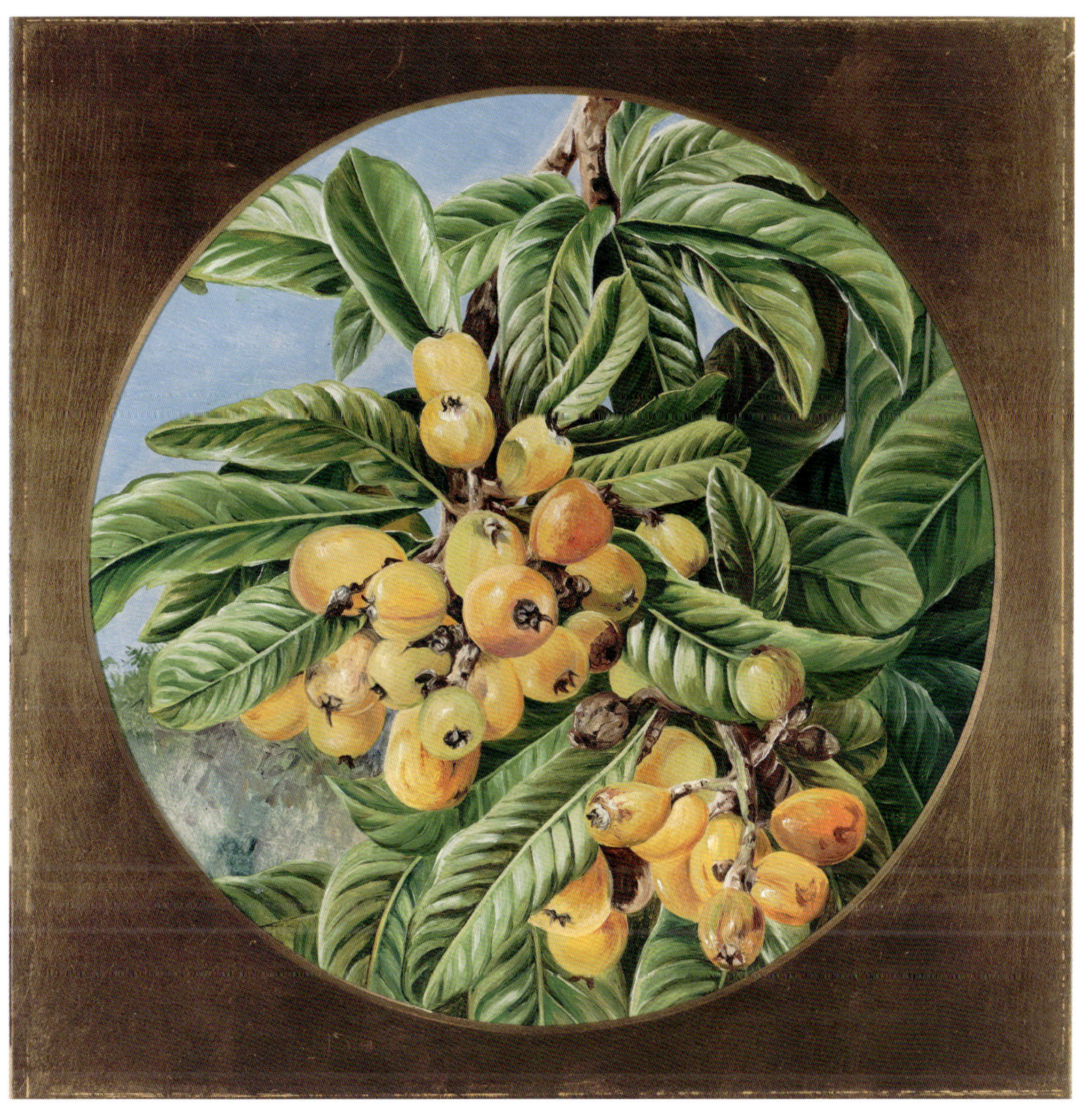

110 Marianne North, 155, *Foliage and Fruit of the Loquat, or Japanese Medlar, Brazil,* oil on board, 36 × 35 cm, Royal Botanic Gardens, Kew.

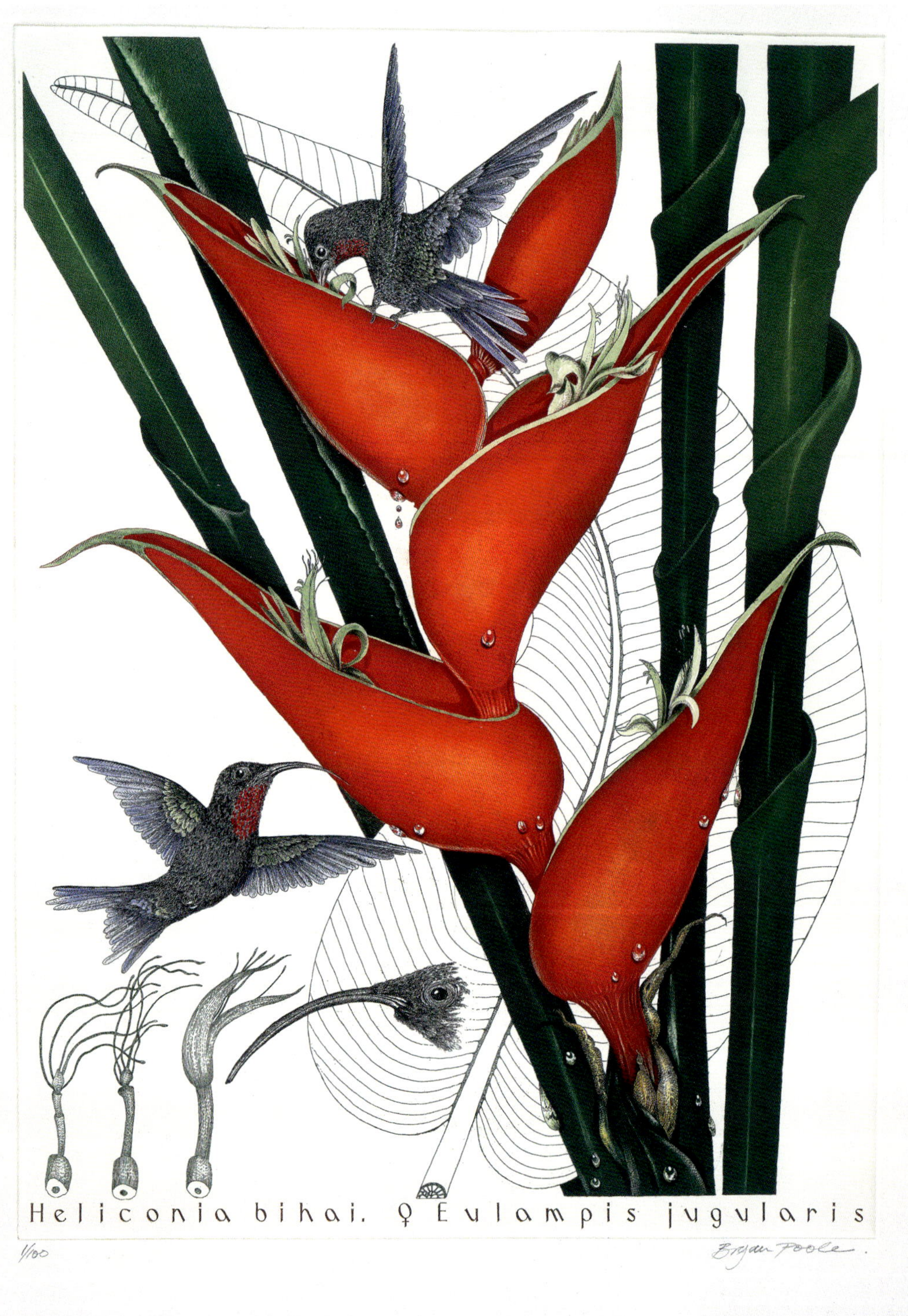

111 Bryan Poole, *Heliconia bihai, Eulampis jugularis*, 2008, etching and engraving 1/100, 75 × 55 cm, The Shirley Sherwood Collection.

Notes

1 EARLY LIFE

1 Marianne North, 'Early Days and Home Life', in *Recollections of a Happy Life*, ed. Catherine Addington Symonds, 2 vols, Macmillan & Co., London and New York, 1892, vol.I, p.1.
2 ibid., p.2.
3 F. O'Gorman, '"More Interesting than all the books, save one": Charles Kingsley's Construction of Natural History', in Juliet John and Alice Jenkins (eds), *Rethinking Victorian Culture*, Macmillan Press Ltd, Basingstoke, Hampshire, UK, 2000, p.146.
4 ibid., p.147.
5 North, 'Canada and United States', in *Recollections*, vol.I, p.39.
6 North, 'Early Days and Home Life', in *Recollections*, vol.I, p.4.
7 ibid., p.5.
8 ibid., pp 5–6.
9 Suzanne Le-May Sheffield, 'Finding a New Life: Marianne North as Daughter, Patron and Traveller', in *Revealing New Worlds: Three Victorian Women Naturalists*, Routledge, London and New York, 2001, p.79.
10 North, 'Early Days and Home Life', in *Recollections*, vol.I, pp 5–6.
11 ibid., p.7.
12 ibid., pp 10–11.
13 ibid., p.12.
14 ibid., p.8.
15 ibid.
16 James Nasmyth, cited in John Gage, 'The Vision of Landscape', in Robert Hoozee, John Gage and Timothy Hyman, *British Vision: Observation and Imagination in British Art 1750–1950*, exh.cat., Mercatorfonds, Brussels, and Thames & Hudson, London, 2008, p.39.
17 Gage, 'The Vision of Landscape', p.39.
18 ibid., p.38.
19 Edmund Burke, *A Philosophical Enquiry into the Origin of our Ideas of the Sublime and Beautiful* [1757], Penguin, London, 1999.
20 William Chambers, cited in John Dixon-Hunt and Peter Willis (eds), *The Genius of the Place: The English Landscape Garden 1620–1820*, Paul Elek Ltd, London, 1975, p.320.
21 North, 'Early Days and Home Life', in *Recollections*, vol.I, p.12.
22 ibid., p.9.
23 Tabitha Barber, 'The Natural World', in Alison Smith (ed.), *Watercolour*, exh.cat., Tate Publishing, London, 2011, p.57.
24 ibid.
25 North, 'Early Days and Home Life', in *Recollections*, vol.I, p.12.
26 ibid., p.9.

27 ibid., p.13.
28 ibid., p.15.
29 ibid., pp 19–20.
30 ibid., pp 16–17.
31 ibid.
32 ibid., p.22.
33 ibid.
34 ibid.
35 ibid., pp 19–20.
36 ibid., p.26.
37 ibid., p.27.
38 ibid.
39 Sheila Fletcher, '10 May', in *Victorian Girls: Lord Lyttelton's Daughters*, The Hambledon Press, London and Rio Grande, Brazil, 1997, p.164.
40 North, 'Early Days and Home Life', in *Recollections*, vol.I, p.27.
41 ibid., pp 26–7.
42 Laura Ponsonby, 'Early Years', in *Marianne North at Kew Gardens* [1996], Royal Botanic Gardens, Kew, Surrey, UK, 2002, p.14.
43 North, 'Early Days and Home Life', in *Recollections*, vol.I, pp 27–8.
44 Sheffield, 'Painting Outside the Lines: Marianne North's Botanical Art', in *Revealing New Worlds*, p.110.
45 North, 'Early Days and Home Life', in *Recollections*, vol.I, pp 27–8.
46 ibid.
47 Pam Hirsch, 'The Early Years', in *Barbara Leigh Smith Bodichon: Feminist, Artist and Rebel* [1998], Pimlico, London, 1999, p.19.
48 ibid.
49 North, 'Early Days and Home Life', in *Recollections*, vol.I, p.28.
50 Hirsch, 'The Early Years', *Barbara Leigh Smith Bodichon*, p.19.
51 ibid., p.21.
52 John Ruskin, cited in Lionel Lambourne, 'Oils versus Watercolours: Landscape Painting', in *Victorian Painting* [1999], Phaidon, London and New York, 2005, p.115.
53 North, 'Early Days and Home Life', in *Recollections*, vol.I, pp 27–8.
54 ibid., p.29.
55 ibid.
56 John Lehmann, *Edward Lear and His World*, Thames & Hudson, London, 1977, p.48.
57 Marianne North, cited in Ponsonby, 'Early Years', in *Marianne North at Kew Gardens*, p.15.
58 North, 'Early Days and Home Life', in *Recollections*, vol.I, pp 29–30.
59 ibid., pp 30–31.
60 ibid., pp 32–3.
61 ibid.
62 Sheffield, 'Finding a New Life', in *Revealing New Worlds*, p.81.
63 North, 'Early Days and Home Life', in *Recollections*, vol.I, pp 34–5.
64 ibid.
65 Sheffield, 'Finding a New Life', in *Revealing New Worlds*, p.83.
66 ibid., p.81.
67 North, 'Early Days and Home Life', in *Recollections*, vol.I, p.35.
68 ibid., p.37.
69 ibid., p.38.
70 ibid.
71 ibid.
72 Marianne North, 'Mentone and Sicily, 1869–1870', in *Some Further Recollections of a Happy Life*, ed. Catherine Addington Symonds, Macmillan & Co., London and New York, 1893, p.231.
73 North, 'Early Days and Home Life', in *Recollections*, vol.I, p.38.
74 North, 'Canada and United States', in *Recollections*, vol.I, p.39.

2 SOCIAL, SCIENTIFIC AND ARTISTIC CONNECTIONS

1 Laura Ponsonby, 'Early Years', in *Marianne North at Kew Gardens* [1996], Royal Botanic Gardens, Kew, Surrey, UK, 2002, p.15.
2 North, 'Syracuse and its Neighbourhood – Taormina, Monte Generoso, and Trafoi, 1870', in *Further Recollections*, p.313.
3 Marianne North Papers, Archives of the Royal Botanic Gardens, Kew, MN/1/1, Letters to Dr Arthur Coke Burnell, 1878, letter 16.
4 MN/1/1, Letters to Dr Arthur Coke Burnell, 1878, letter 58, pp 59–60.
5 MN/1/1, Letters to Dr Arthur Coke Burnell, 1878, letter 72, pp 62–3.
6 John Addington Symonds, cited in Ponsonby, 'The Travels', in *Marianne North at Kew Gardens*, p.17.

7 Suzanne Le-May Sheffield, 'Painting Outside the Lines: Marianne North's Botanical Art', in *Revealing New Worlds: Three Victorian Women Naturalists*, Routledge, London and New York, 2001, p.125.

8 Pam Hirsch, 'Preface', in *Barbara Leigh Smith Bodichon: Feminist, Artist and Rebel* [1998], Pimlico, London, 1999, p.vii.

9 John Ruskin, cited in Hirsch, 'Love and Loss', in *Barbara Leigh Smith Bodichon*, p.164.

10 Lionel Lambourne, 'Women Artists', in *Victorian Painting* [1999], Phaidon, London and New York, 2005, p.315.

11 Tim Barringer, 'A Radical Legacy: The British Pre-Raphaelites and Global Pre-Raphaelitism', in Linda S. Ferber and Nancy K. Anderson (eds), *The American Pre-Raphaelites: Radical Realists*, exh.cat., National Gallery of Art, Washington, in association with Yale University Press, New Haven, MA, and London, 2019, p.27.

12 ibid., p.28.

13 ibid., p.19.

14 Sheffield, 'Finding a New Life: Marianne North as Daughter, Patron and Traveller', in *Revealing New Worlds*, p.96.

15 MN/1/1, Letters to Dr Arthur Coke Burnell, 1878, letter 141, pp 141–2.

16 North, 'Borneo and Java', in *Recollections*, vol.I, p.249.

17 MN/1/1, Letters to Dr Arthur Coke Burnell, 1878, letter 72, p.72.

18 Colin Ford, 'Ceylon', in *Julia Margaret Cameron: 19th-Century Photographer of Genius*, exh.cat., National Portrait Gallery, London, 2003, p.78.

19 Barringer, 'A Radical Legacy', in Ferber and Anderson (eds), *The American Pre-Raphaelites*, p.34.

20 Carol Jacobi, 'New Truths', in Carol Jacobi and Hope Kingsley, *Painting with Light: Art and Photography from the Pre-Raphaelites to the Modern Age*, exh.cat., Tate Publishing, London, 2016, p.23.

21 Diane Waggoner, '"The Perfect Observance of Truth": Photography and American Pre-Raphaelitism', in Ferber and Anderson (eds), *The American Pre-Raphaelites*, p.98.

22 William James Stillman, cited in Waggoner, '"The Perfect Observance of Truth"', in Ferber and Anderson (eds), *The American Pre-Raphaelites*, p.95.

23 Stephen Calloway, 'The Search for a New Beauty', in Stephen Calloway, Lynn Federle Orr and Esmé Whittaker, *The Cult of Beauty: The Aesthetic Movement 1860–1900*, exh.cat., V&A Publishing, London, 2011, p.13.

24 Caroline Dakers and Daniel Robbins, *George Aitchison: Leighton's Architect Revealed*, Leighton House Museum, London, 2011, p.14.

25 ibid., p.73.

26 Carol Jacobi, 'Whisper of the Muse', in Jacobi and Kingsley, *Painting with Light*, p.73.

27 Lambourne, 'Women Artists', in *Victorian Painting*, p.325.

28 John Holmes, 'Fault Lines: Pre-Raphaelitism and Science after 1859', in *The Pre-Raphaelites and Science*, Yale University Press in association with the Paul Mellon Centre for Studies in British Art, New Haven, MA, and London, 2018, p.163.

29 ibid., p.167.

30 ibid., p.179.

31 ibid., p.200.

32 MN/1/1, Letters to Dr Arthur Coke Burnell, 1878, letter 103, p.108.

33 Marianne North, 'Second Visit to Borneo – Australia 1880–81', in Anthony Huxley, J.P.M. Brenan and Brenda E. Moon, *A Vision of Eden: The Life and Work of Marianne North* [1993], Royal Botanic Gardens, Kew, Surrey, UK, 2002, p.151.

34 Charles Darwin, cited in North, 'Western Australia – Tasmania – New Zealand', in *Recollections*, vol.II, p.216.

35 Charles Darwin, cited in North, 'Second Visit to Borneo – Australia', in Huxley et al., *A Vision of Eden*, p.151.

36 North, 'Western Australia – Tasmania – New Zealand', in *Recollections*, vol.II, p.215.

37 Charles Darwin, cited in North, 'Western Australia – Tasmania – New Zealand', in *Recollections*, vol.II, p.216.

38 Ray Desmond, 'An Uncertain Future', in *Sir Joseph Hooker: Traveller and Plant Collector* [1999], Antiques Collectors' Club with Royal Botanic Gardens, Kew, Surrey, UK, 2006, pp 207–8.

39 MN/3/1, Note from Alfred Russell Wallace, 27 July 1883.

40 Desmond, 'An Uncertain Future', in *Sir Joseph Hooker*, p.202.

41 Sheffield, 'Finding a New Life', in *Revealing New Worlds*, p.94.

42 Katherine E. Manthorne, 'Olana, Salon for Jamaican Journeyers', in Elizabeth Mankin Kornhauser and Katherine E. Manthorne, *Fern Hunting among These Picturesque Mountains: Frederic Edwin Church in Jamaica*, exh.cat., Cornell University Press, Ithaca, NY, and London, 2010, p.63.

43 North, 'Canada and United States', in *Recollections*, vol.I, pp 73–4.

44 Edward Waldo Emerson, '1856 Louis Agassiz', in *The Early Years of the Saturday Club 1855–1870* [1918], The Riverside

Press, Cambridge, MA, n.d.; Kessinger Publishing's Rare Reprints, n.d., p.30.
45 Emerson, 'The Attraction', in *The Early Years of the Saturday Club*, n.p.
46 Barbara Novak, 'Grand Opera and the Still Small Voice', in *Nature and Culture: American Landscape and Painting, 1825–1875* [1980], Oxford University Press, New York and Toronto, 1981, p.28.
47 John K. Howat, 'Newfoundland and Labrador', in *Frederic Church*, Yale University Press, New Haven, CT, and London, 2005, pp 91–2.
48 Novak, 'Grand Opera and the Still Small Voice', in *Nature and Culture*, p.28.
49 Novak, 'Introduction: The Nationalist Garden and the Holy Book', in *Nature and Culture*, p.15.
50 J.F. Cropsey, cited in Novak, 'Introduction', in *Nature and Culture*, p.5.
51 North, 'Canada and United States', in *Recollections*, vol.I, p.71.
52 ibid., p.68.
53 ibid., p.65.
54 ibid., p.68.
55 Howat, 'Humboldt's Gift and a Trip to South America', in *Frederic Church*, p.51.
56 ibid., p.44.
57 Iain McCalman, 'The Philosopher at Sea', in *Darwin's Armada*, Simon & Schuster, London, 2010, p.44.
58 Howat, 'Humboldt's Gift and a Trip to South America', in *Frederic Church*, pp 44–5.
59 ibid., p.45.
60 Frederic Church, cited in Howat, 'Humboldt's Gift and a Trip to South America', in *Frederic Church*, pp 45–6.
61 Novak, 'Introduction', in *Nature and Culture*, p.9.
62 Marianne North, 'Teneriffe – California – Japan – Singapore 1875–77', in Huxley et al., *A Vision of Eden*, pp 81–3.
63 McCalman, 'The Philosopher at Sea', in *Darwin's Armada*, pp 41–2.
64 ibid., p.44.
65 Howat, 'Rebuilding a Family and Pilgrimage to the Near East', in *Frederic Church*, p.133.
66 Jane Munro, '"More a Work of Art than Nature": Darwin, Beauty and Sexual Selection', in Diana Donald and Jane Munro, *Endless Forms: Charles Darwin, Natural Science and the Visual Arts*, Fitzwilliam Museum in association with the Yale Center for British Art, Yale University Press, New Haven, CT, 2009, p.263.
67 Manthorne, 'Olana, Salon for Jamaican Journeyers', in Kornhauser and Manthorne, *Fern Hunting*, p.47.
68 Archives of the Royal Botanic Gardens, Kew, HEM/1/2, Letters to W.B. Hemsley MOO–ZAH, vol.2, letter 24.
69 Marianne North, cited in Ponsonby, 'Australia', 'The Travels', in *Marianne North at Kew Gardens*, pp 83–90.
70 North, 'Western Australia – Tasmania – New Zealand', in *Recollections*, vol.II, p.149.
71 Patricia Fullerton, *The Flower Hunter: Ellis Rowan*, The National Library of Australia, Canberra, 2002, p.5.
72 Ellis Rowan, cited in Fullerton, *The Flower Hunter: Ellis Rowan*, p.5.
73 Ponsonby, 'Australia', 'The Travels', in *Marianne North at Kew Gardens*, pp 83–90.
74 Marianne North, 'Second Visit to Borneo – Australia', in Huxley et al., *A Vision of Eden*, p.171.
75 Judith McKay, 'Plants', in *Ellis Rowan: A Flower-Hunter in Queensland*, Queensland Museum, Australia, 1990, p.61.
76 ibid., pp 60–61.
77 McKay, 'Techniques', in *Ellis Rowan*, p.58.
78 Huxley, 'Introduction', in Huxley et al., *A Vision of Eden*, p.13.
79 North, 'Second Visit to Borneo – Queensland – New South Wales', in *Recollections*, vol.II, pp 141–3.
80 Alfred W. Crosby, 'Weeds', in *Ecological Imperialism: The Biological Expansion of Europe, 900–1900* [1986], Cambridge University Press, Cambridge, UK, 2006, p.165.
81 Marianne North, cited in Sheffield, 'Painting Outside the Lines', in *Revealing New Worlds*, p.132.
82 North, 'Second Visit to Borneo – Queensland – New South Wales', in *Recollections*, vol.II, p.120.
83 Marianne North, 'Second Visit to Borneo – Australia', in Huxley et al., *A Vision of Eden*, p.167.
84 ibid., p.177.
85 Crosby, 'Weeds', in *Ecological Imperialism*, p.170.
86 Marianne North, 'Second Visit to Borneo – Australia', in Huxley et al., *A Vision of Eden*, p.174.
87 Marianne North, cited in Brenda E. Moon, 'Marianne North 1830–90', in Huxley et al., *A Vision of Eden*, p.238.
88 North, 'South Africa', in *Recollections*, vol.II, p.218.
89 Marianne North, 'Canada and the United States', in Huxley et al., *A Vision of Eden*, p.44.
90 Marianne North, 'Brazil 1872–73', in Huxley et al., *A Vision of Eden*, pp 71–2.
91 ibid., p.72.
92 ibid., p.68.
93 Lys de Bray, 'Kew: Heart of the Botanical World

1760–1900', in *The Art of Botanical Illustration: The Classic Illustrators and Their Achievements from 1550 to 1900* [1989], Quantum Books, Knickerbocker Press, New York, 1997, p.152.

94 Richard H. Grove, 'Stephen Hales and Climatic Environmentalism', in *Green Imperialism: Colonial Expansion, Tropical Island Edens and the Origins of Environmentalism, 1600–1860* [1995], Cambridge University Press, Cambridge, UK, 1997, p.157.

95 Grove, 'Edens, Islands and Early Empires', in *Green Imperialism*, p.51.

96 Grove, 'Introduction', in *Green Imperialism*, p.11.

97 Holmes, 'To Know What Has Grown: The Ecological Vision of Pre-Raphaelite Art', in *The Pre-Raphaelites and Science*, p.52.

98 Joseph Dalton Hooker, 'Preface to the First Edition', *Royal Gardens, Kew. Official Guide to the North Gallery* [1882], 6th edn [1914], Royal Botanic Gardens, Kew, Surrey, UK, 2009, pp iii–iv.

3 PAINTINGS, STYLES AND INFLUENCES

1 Wilfrid Blunt and William T. Stearn, 'The Botanical Artist', in *The Art of Botanical Illustration* [1995], Antique Collectors' Club, in association with Royal Botanic Gardens, Kew, Surrey, UK, 2000, p.23.

2 William A. Emboden, 'Leonardo Di Ser Piero Da Vinci's Ideas on Nature', in *Leonardo da Vinci on Plants and Gardens* [1987], Dioscorides Press, Portland, OR, 1988, p.105.

3 David Hockney, *Secret Knowledge: Rediscovering the Lost Techniques of the Old Masters* [2001], Thames & Hudson, London, 2006, p.143.

4 ibid., p.103.

5 Paul Taylor, 'Postscript: Looking at Floral Still Lifes in Golden Age Holland', in *Dutch Flower Painting 1600–1720*, Yale University Press, New Haven, CT, and London, 1995, pp 194–6; Hockney, *Secret Knowledge*, p.108.

6 Martin Kemp, 'Machine and Mind', in *The Science of Art: Optical Themes in Western Art from Brunelleschi to Seurat*, Yale University Press, New Haven, CT, and London, 1990, p.192.

7 Brian Ford, 'Herbs, Herbals and the Birth of Botany', in *Images of Science: A History of Scientific Illustration*, Oxford University Press, New York, 1993, p.91.

8 Andrea Wulf, 'Commonwealth of Botany', in *The Brother Gardeners and the Birth of an Obsession*, William Heineman, London, 2008, p.113.

9 ibid., p.115.

10 Blunt and Stearn, 'Francis and Ferdinand Bauer', in *The Art of Botanical Illustration*, p.224.

11 Keith West, 'Watercolour and Gouache', in *How to Draw Plants: The Techniques of Botanical Illustration* [1983], The Herbert Press, in association with British Museum (Natural History), London, 1999, p.122.

12 Marion Arnold, 'Petals and Stigmas: Reflections on Plant Portraiture', in Marion Arnold and John P. Rourke, *South African Botanical Art: Peeling back the Petals*, Fernwood Press in association with Art Link, Vlaeburg, South Africa, 2001, p.165.

13 Tabitha Barber, 'The Natural World', in Alison Smith (ed.), *Watercolour*, exh.cat., Tate Publishing, London, 2011, p.56.

14 Arnold, 'Petals and Stigmas', in Arnold and Rourke, *South African Botanical Art*, p.164.

15 Archives of the Royal Botanic Gardens, Kew, HEM/1/2, Letters to W.B. Hemsley MOO–ZAH, vol.2, letter 33; North references John Gerard's *The Herball or Generall Historie of Plantes*, J. Norton, London, 1597; 'enlarged and amended' by Thomas Johnson in a second edition of 1633.

16 HEM/1/2, Letters to W.B. Hemsley MOO–ZAH, vol.2, letter 34.

17 HEM/1/2, Letters to W.B. Hemsley MOO–ZAH, vol.2, letter 59.

18 Archives of the Royal Botanic Gardens, Kew, J.D. Duthie Letters, vol.2, letter 126, p.126.

19 MN/1/1, Letters to Dr Arthur Coke Burnell, 1878, letter 143, p.143.

20 MN/1/1, Letters to Dr Arthur Coke Burnell, 1878, letter 151, p.151.

21 Blunt and Stearn, 'The Second Half of the Nineteenth Century', in *The Art of Botanical Illustration*, pp 276–7.

22 Hope Kingsley, 'Photography and the Art of the Past', in Hope Kingsley and Christopher Riopelle, *Seduced by Art: Photography Past and Present*, exh.cat., National Gallery, distributed by Yale University Press, New Haven, CT, and London, 2012, p.28.

23 MN/1/1, Letters to Dr Arthur Coke Burnell, 1878, letter 137, p.138.

24 Kingsley, 'Photography and the Art of the Past', in Kingsley and Riopelle, *Seduced by Art*, p.28.

25 Suzanne Le-May Sheffield, 'Finding a New Life: Marianne North as Daughter, Patron and Traveller', in *Revealing New Worlds: Three Victorian Women Naturalists*, Routledge, London and New York, 2001, p.106.

26 ibid., p.108.
27 Arnold, 'Petals and Stigmas', in Arnold and Rourke, *South African Botanical Art*, p.155.
28 Sheffield, 'Painting Outside the Lines: Marianne North's Botanical Art', in *Revealing New Worlds*, p.108.
29 John Gage, 'Colour under Control: The Reign of Newton', in *Colour and Culture Practice and Meaning from Antiquity to Abstraction* [1993], Thames & Hudson, London, 2001, p.169.
30 ibid., p.173.
31 MN/1/1, Letters to Dr Arthur Coke Burnell, 1878, letter 127, p.128.
32 HEM/1/2, Letters to W.B. Hemsley MOO–ZAH, vol.2, letter 25.
33 HEM/1/2, Letters to W.B. Hemsley MOO–ZAH, vol.2, letter 26.
34 North, 'In the Pyrenees and Spain, 1859–1860', in *Further Recollections*, p.9.
35 North, 'Second Visit to Borneo – Queensland – New South Wales', in *Recollections*, vol.II, p.100.
36 North, 'Jamaica', in *Recollections*, vol.I, p.100.
37 Anthony Huxley, 'Introduction', in Anthony Huxley, J.P.M. Brenan and Brenda E. Moon, *A Vision of Eden: The Life and Work of Marianne North* [1993], Royal Botanic Gardens, Kew, Surrey, UK, 2002, p.13.
38 Patricia Fara, *Sex, Botany & Empire: The Story of Carl Linnaeus and Joseph Banks*, Icon Books, Thriplow, UK, 2004, pp 44–5.
39 Robert Thornton, *The Temple of Flora*, for the author, London, 1812, frontispiece.
40 Judith McKay, 'Techniques', in *Ellis Rowan: A Flower-Hunter in Queensland*, Queensland Museum, Australia, 1990, p.58.
41 Lys de Bray, 'Kew: Heart of the Botanical World 1760–1900', in *The Art of Botanical Illustration: The Classic Illustrators and Their Achievements from 1550 to 1900* [1989], Quantum Books, Knickerbocker Press, New York, 1997, p.148.
42 North, 'Palestine and Syria, 1866', in *Further Recollections*, p.163.
43 Tim Barringer, 'Radical Realism', in Martin Ellis, Victoria Osbourne and Tim Barringer (eds), *Victorian Radicals: From the Pre-Raphaelites to the Arts & Crafts Movement*, exh.cat., American Federation of Arts and Prestel Delmonico Books, New York and Munich, 2018, p.41.
44 Lionel Lambourne, 'The Pre-Raphaelites', in *Victorian Painting* [1999], Phaidon, London and New York, 2005, p.246.
45 Wilfrid Blunt, '"Aunt Pop" and other Matters', in *In for a Penny: A Prospect of Kew Gardens*, Hamish Hamilton in association with Tyron Gallery, London, 1978, p.186.
46 *The Gardeners' Chronicle*, London, 10 June 1882, pp 763–5.
47 John Gage, 'The Vision of Landscape', in Robert Hoozee, John Gage and Timothy Hyman, *British Vision: Observation and Imagination in British Art 1750–1950*, exh.cat., Mercatorfonds, Brussels, and Thames & Hudson, London, 2008, p.42.
48 James Parry, 'Image', in *Orientalist Lives: Western Artists in the Middle East 1830–1920*, American University in Cairo Press, New York and Cairo, 2018, p.153.
49 Carol Jacobi, 'New Truths', in Carol Jacobi and Hope Kingsley, *Painting with Light: Art and Photography from the Pre-Raphaelites to the Modern Age*, exh.cat., Tate Publishing, London, 2016, pp 36–7.
50 ibid., p.40.
51 Robert Hoozee, 'Observations of Landscape', in Hoozee et al., *British Vision*, p.181.
52 HEM/1/2, Letters to W.B. Hemsley MOO–ZAH, vol.2, letter 46.
53 HEM/1/2, Letters to W.B. Hemsley MOO–ZAH, vol.2, letter 56.
54 Sacheverell Sitwell, 'The Romance of the Flower Book', in *Great Flower Books, 1700–1900*, H.F. & G. Witherby Ltd, London, 1990, p.25.
55 West, 'Basic Equipment', in *How to Draw Plants*, p.23.
56 West, 'Photography', in *How to Draw Plants*, p.143.
57 Hockney, *Secret Knowledge*, p.14.
58 Archives of the Royal Botanic Gardens, Kew, J.D. Duthie Letters, 1886, vol.2, letter 127, p.127.
59 Christopher Newell, 'Buildings', in *Ruskin: Artist and Observer*, Paul Holberton Publishing, London, and National Gallery of Ottawa, Canada, 2014, p.134.
60 Jacobi, 'New Truths', in Jacobi and Kingsley, *Painting with Light*, p.23.
61 Jacobi, 'Painting with Light', in Jacobi and Kingsley, *Painting with Light*, p.11.
62 ibid., p.18.
63 Barbara Novak, 'The Geographical Timetable: Rocks', in *Nature and Culture: American Landscape and Painting, 1825–1875* [1980], Oxford University Press, New York and Toronto, 1981, p.70.
64 Katherine. E. Manthorne, 'Olana, Salon for Jamaican Journeyers', in Elizabeth Mankin Kornhauser and Katherine E. Manthorne, *Fern Hunting among These Picturesque Mountains: Frederic Edwin Church in Jamaica*,

exh.cat., Cornell University Press, Ithaca, NY, and London, 2010, p.58.

65 Katherine Bourguignon and Christopher Riopelle, 'Catalogue', in Andrew Wilton, Katherine Bourguignon and Christopher Riopelle, *Frederic Church and the Landscape Oil Sketch*, exh.cat., National Gallery, London, and Yale University Press, New Haven, CT, and London, 2013, p.41.

66 Parry, 'Image', in *Orientalist Lives*, p.157.

67 ibid.

68 North, 'Ceylon and Home', in *Recollections*, vol.I, p.315.

69 Addington Symonds, in North, 'Syracuse and its Neighbourhood – Taormina, Monte Generoso, and Trafoi, 1870', in *Further Recollections*, p.315.

70 Andy McRob, Photographer, Interview with author, Royal Botanic Gardens, Kew, Surrey, UK, 2007.

71 Colin Ford, 'Ceylon', in *Julia Margaret Cameron: 19th-Century Photographer of Genius*, exh.cat., National Portrait Gallery, London, 2003, p.79.

4 TRAVELS AS A BOTANICAL PAINTER

1 James Parry, 'Appendix One', in *Orientalist Lives: Western Artists in the Middle East 1830–1920*, American University in Cairo Press, New York and Cairo, p.254.

2 Parry, 'Epilogue', in *Orientalist Lives*, p.247.

3 Addington Symonds, in North, 'Syracuse and its Neighbourhood – Taormina, Monte Generoso, and Trafoi, 1870', in *Further Recollections*, pp 315–16.

4 MN/1/1, Letters to Dr Arthur Coke Burnell, 1878, letter 137, p.138.

5 North, 'Canada and United States', in *Recollections*, vol.I, pp 48–9.

6 Jonathan Farley, Head of Conservation, Interview, Royal Botanic Gardens, Kew, Surrey, UK, 2011.

7 North, 'Borneo and Java', in *Recollections*, vol.I, p.236.

8 Laura Ponsonby, 'The Travels', in *Marianne North at Kew Gardens* [1996], Royal Botanic Gardens, Kew, Surrey, UK, 2002, p.46.

9 Jane Robinson, 'Travel', in *Unsuitable for Ladies: An Anthology of Women Travellers*, Oxford University Press, Oxford and New York, 1994, p.315.

10 Margaret Brooke, cited in Robinson, 'The Indian Subcontinent', in *Unsuitable for Ladies*, p.319.

11 Ponsonby, 'The Travels', in *Marianne North at Kew Gardens*, p.46.

12 North, 'Borneo and Java', in *Recollections*, vol.I, pp 240–41.

13 Margaret Brooke, cited in Robinson, 'The Indian Subcontinent', in *Unsuitable for Ladies*, p.319.

14 North, 'Borneo and Java', in *Recollections*, vol.I, p.237.

15 Ponsonby, 'The Travels', in *Marianne North at Kew Gardens*, p.51.

16 North, 'Borneo and Java', in *Recollections*, vol.I, p.240.

17 Marianne North, 'Brazil 1872–73', in Anthony Huxley, J.P.M. Brenan and Brenda E. Moon, *A Vision of Eden: The Life and Work of Marianne North* [1993], Royal Botanic Gardens, Kew, Surrey, UK, 2002, p.80.

18 Ponsonby, 'The Travels', in *Marianne North at Kew Gardens*, p.51.

19 ibid., p.54.

20 Robinson, 'The Indian Subcontinent', in *Unsuitable for Ladies*, p.319.

21 North, 'Borneo and Java', in *Recollections*, vol.I, pp 242–3.

22 Margaret Brooke, cited in Robinson, 'The Indian Subcontinent', in *Unsuitable for Ladies*, p.319.

23 North, 'Borneo and Java', in *Recollections*, vol.I, p.238.

24 ibid., p.251.

25 ibid., p.249.

26 North, 'Ceylon and Home', in *Recollections*, vol.I, p.315.

27 Lionel Lambourne, 'The Good and the Great: Portrait Painting', in *Victorian Painting* [1999], Phaidon, London and New York, 2005, p.78.

28 Quentin Bajac, 'The Realm of Art', in *The Invention of Photography: The First Fifty Years*, Thames & Hudson, London, 2002, p.108.

29 Carol Jacobi, 'New Truths', in Carol Jacobi and Hope Kingsley, *Painting with Light: Art and Photography from the Pre-Raphaelites to the Modern Age*, exh.cat., Tate Publishing, London, 2016, p.23.

30 North, 'Ceylon and Home', in *Recollections*, vol.I, p.315.

31 Christine Riding, 'Travellers and Sitters: The Orientalist Portrait', in Nicholas Tromans (ed.), *The Lure of the East: British Orientalist Painting*, exh.cat., Tate Publishing, London, 2008, p.48.

32 ibid., p.54.

33 ibid., p.48.

34 ibid., p.55.

35 Parry, 'Arrival', in *Orientalist Lives*, p.68.

36 Riding, 'Travellers and Sitters', in Tromans (ed.), *The Lure of the East*, p.56.

37 North, 'Western Australia – Tasmania – New Zealand', in *Recollections*, vol.II, p.208.

38 Cited in Katherine E. Manthorne, 'Olana, Salon for Jamaican Journeyers', in Elizabeth Mankin Kornhauser

and Katherine E. Manthorne, *Fern Hunting among These Picturesque Mountains: Frederic Edwin Church in Jamaica*, exh.cat., Cornell University Press, Ithaca, NY, and London, 2010, p.45.

39 North, 'Western Australia – Tasmania – New Zealand', in *Recollections*, vol.II, p.208.

40 Manthorne, 'Olana, Salon for Jamaican Journeyers', in Kornhauser and Manthorne, *Fern Hunting*, p.65.

41 North, 'Western Australia – Tasmania – New Zealand', in *Recollections*, vol.II, p.209.

42 ibid.

43 John K. Howat, 'Humboldt's Gift and a Trip to South America', in *Frederic Church*, Yale University Press, New Haven, CT, and London, 2005, p.47.

44 Nicholas Tromans, 'The Orient in Perspective', in Tromans (ed.), *The Lure of the East*, p.104.

45 Richard Neville, 'Introduction', in State Library of New South Wales, *Grand Vistas: Panoramas from the Collection*, exh.cat., State Library of New South Wales, Sydney, 2022, p.6.

46 Howat, 'Humbolt's Gift and a Trip to South America', in *Frederic Church*, p.46.

47 ibid.

48 Neville, 'Introduction', in State Library of New South Wales, *Grand Vistas*, p.6.

49 Neville, 'Hidden Sketches', in State Library of New South Wales, *Grand Vistas*, p.14.

50 John Rae, cited in Neville, 'Hidden Sketches', in State Library of New South Wales, *Grand Vistas*, p.16.

51 Parry, 'Image', in *Orientalist Lives*, p.155.

52 Cited in Howat, 'The Heart of Andes', in *Frederic Church*, p.89.

53 North, 'Early Days and Home Life', in *Recollections*, vol.I, p.29.

54 Lambourne, 'Oils versus Watercolours: Landscape Painting', in *Victorian Painting*, p.105.

55 Tromans, 'The Orient in Perspective', in Tromans (ed.), *The Lure of the East*, pp 105–6.

56 Lambourne, 'Oils versus Watercolours', in *Victorian Painting*, p.105.

57 Riding, 'Travellers and Sitters', in Tromans (ed.), *The Lure of the East*, p.53.

58 Parry, 'Influence', in *Orientalist Lives*, p.225.

59 North, 'Palestine and Syria, 1866', in *Further Recollections*, p.196.

60 Lambourne, 'Colonial Ties: Painters in a Wider World', in *Victorian Painters*, pp 435–7.

61 Marion Arnold, 'Petals and Stigmas: Reflections on Plant Portraiture', in Marion Arnold and John P. Rourke, *South African Botanical Art: Peeling back the Petals*, Fernwood Press in association with Art Link, Vlaeburg, South Africa, 2001, p.153.

62 ibid.

63 Parry, 'Image', in *Orientalist Lives*, p.157.

64 Quentin Bajac, '1855–80: An Objective Medium?', in *The Invention of Photography*, pp 71–2.

65 James Kay, Library and Archive, Interview with author, Royal Botanic Gardens, Kew, Surrey, UK, 2007.

66 ibid.; photograph situated in C Wing.

67 The Library and Archive, Royal Botanic Gardens, Kew, Surrey, UK, 2007, previously a part of Sir William Hooker's Museum of Economic Botany, Photographic Collection.

68 North, 'Canada and United States', in *Recollections*, vol.I, p.55.

69 North, 'Teneriffe – California – Japan – Singapore', in *Recollections*, vol.II, p.222.

70 ibid., pp 224–5.

71 Suzanne Le-May Sheffield, 'Painting Outside the Lines: Marianne North's Botanical Art', in *Revealing New Worlds: Three Victorian Women Naturalists*, Routledge, London and New York, 2001, p.126.

72 North, 'Seychelles Islands – 1883', in *Recollections*, vol.II, p.309.

73 North, 'Chili', in *Recollections*, vol.II, p.330.

5 THE MARIANNE NORTH GALLERY

1 Jonathan Farley, Head of Conservation, Interview with author, Royal Botanic Gardens, Kew, Surrey, UK, 2007.

2 Marianne North Papers, Archives of the Royal Botanic Gardens, Kew, MN/1/1, Letters to Dr Arthur Coke Burnell, 1878, letter 146, p.147.

3 ibid.

4 ibid.

5 MN/1/4, North Gallery 1879–1896, 'Acceptance', letter 3, box 1 of 2.

6 MN/1/4, North Gallery 1879–1896, 'Acceptance', letter 9, box 1 of 2

7 MN/1/4, North Gallery 1879–1896, 'Acceptance', letter 11 August 1879, box 1 of 2.

8 Colin Cunningham, 'James Fergusson's History of Indian Architecture', in Catherine King (ed.), *Views of Difference: Different Views in Art*, Open University, Milton Keynes, UK, and Yale University Press, New Haven, CT, 1999, p.42.

9 ibid., p.44.

10 North, 'Early Days and Home Life', in *Recollections*, vol.I, p.31.

11 Caroline Cornish and Felix Driver, '"Specimens Distributed": The Circulation of Objects from Kew's Museum of Economic Botany, 1847–1914', *Journal of the History of Collections*, 32(2), July 2020, pp 327–40.

12 North, 'Canada and United States', in *Recollections*, vol.I, pp 46–7.

13 MN/1/4: Kew, North Gallery 1879–1896, Letter 7.

14 Ray Desmond, *The History of the Royal Botanic Gardens, Kew* [1995], The Harvill Press, London, and Royal Botanic Gardens, Kew, Surrey, UK, 1998, p.228.

15 ibid., pp 230–32.

16 ibid., p.228.

17 Elizabeth Bonython and Anthony Burton, *The Great Exhibitor: The Life and Work of Henry Cole*, V&A Publications, London, 2003, pp 191–4.

18 ibid., pp 200–201.

19 ibid., pp 182–3.

20 Desmond, *The History of the Royal Botanic Gardens*, p.230.

21 MN/1/4, North Gallery 1879–1896, 'Erection' letter 24, box 1 of 2.

22 HEM/1/2, Letters to W.B. Hemsley MOO–ZAH, vol.2, letter 54, p.54.

23 Desmond, *The History of the Royal Botanic Gardens*, p.262.

24 MN/1/1, Letters to Dr Arthur Coke Burnell, 1878, letter 146, p.152.

25 Desmond, *The History of the Royal Botanic Gardens*, p.262.

26 Cunningham, 'James Fergusson's History of Indian Architecture', in King (ed.), *Views of Difference*, p.65.

27 J.P.M. Brenan, 'Preface', in Anthony Huxley, J.P.M. Brenan and Brenda E. Moon, *A Vision of Eden: The Life and Work of Marianne North* [1993], Royal Botanic Gardens, Kew, Surrey, UK, 2002, p.7.

28 Cunningham, 'James Fergusson's History of Indian Architecture', in King (ed.), *Views of Difference*, p.53.

29 John Ruskin, cited in Matthew Sweet, *Inventing the Victorians*, Faber & Faber, London, 2001, p.134.

30 MN/1/4, North Gallery 1879–1896, 'Erection' letter 13, box 1 of 2.

31 MN/1/4: Kew, North Gallery 1879–1896 'Erection' letter 38, box 1 of 2.

32 MN/1/4:Kew, North Gallery 1879–1896 'Erection' letter 35, box 1 of 2.

33 Royal Historical Society of Victoria, 'Portable Buildings of the Nineteenth Century: A Proposal for World Heritage Listing', at https://www.historyvictoria.org.au/portable-buildings-of-the-nineteenth-century-a-proposal-for-world-heritage-listing/; accessed 1 August 2022.

34 Prestige Wrought Iron, 'The History of Ironwork in Australia', at https://www.prestigewroughtiron.com.au/blog/the-history-of-ironwork-in-australia/; accessed 1 August 2022.

35 Ian Evans, Clive Lucas and Ian Stapleton, *More Colour Schemes for Old Australian Houses*, The Flannel Flower Press, Yeronga, Queensland, 1992, p.8.

36 ibid., p.9.

37 ibid., p.14.

38 Miles Lewis, 'The Diagnosis of Prefabricated Buildings', *Australian Historical Archaeology*, 3, 1985, p.66.

39 North, 'Western Australia – Tasmania – New Zealand', in *Recollections*, vol.II, p.210.

40 MN/1/4, North Gallery 1879–1896, 'Erection' letter 45, box 1 of 2.

41 HEM/1/2, Letters to W.B. Hemsley MOO–ZAH, vol.2, letter 43.

42 HEM/1/2, Letters to W.B. Hemsley MOO–ZAH, vol.2, letter 25.

43 Jonathan Farley, Head of Conservation, Interview with author, Royal Botanic Gardens, Kew, Surrey, UK, 2009.

44 *The Gardeners' Chronicle*, London, 10 June 1882, pp 763–5.

45 ibid.

46 *The Daily News*, London, 1882. Newspaper cutting, taken from Kew Archives, no date or page number given.

47 *The Gardeners' Chronicle*, London, 10 June 1882, pp 763–5.

48 HEM/1/2, Letters to W.B. Hemsley MOO–ZAH, vol.2, letter 44.

49 Jonathan Farley, Head of Conservation, Interview with author, Royal Botanic Gardens, Kew, Surrey, UK, 2011.

50 MN/2/3, Kew – Marianne North 1882–1938, letter 187.

51 MN/2/3, Kew – Marianne North 1882–1938, letters 82 and 205.

52 MN/2/3, Kew – Marianne North 1882–1938, letter 205.

53 Temple of Heaven, *Temple of Heaven*, CIP, Beijing, 2002, p.14.

54 Adrian Hsia and Chen Shouyi (eds), *The Vision of China in the English Literature of the Seventeenth and Eighteenth Centuries*, Chinese University Press, Hong Kong, 1998, p.339.

55 MN/1/4, North Gallery 1879–1896, 'Erection' letter 36, box 1 of 2.

56 MN/1/4, North Gallery 1879–1896, 'Erection' letter 11, box 1 of 2.

57 Brenan, 'Preface', in Huxley et al., *A Vision of Eden*, p.7.

58 Cunningham, 'James Fergusson's History of Indian Architecture', in King (ed.), *Views of Difference*, p.43.
59 Farley, Interview, 2011.
60 Bernard Andreae, *The Art of Rome*, Macmillan, London, 1973, p.116.
61 Paul Roberts, *Life and Death in Pompeii and Herculaneum*, British Museum Press, London, 2013, p.171.
62 ibid., p.172.
63 Sweet, *Inventing the Victorians*, pp 125–6.
64 Liza Picard, *Victorian London: The Life of a City*, Phoenix, London, 2005, p.161.
65 Farley, Interview with author, 2007.
66 HEM/1/2, Letters to W.B. Hemsley MOO–ZAH, vol.2, letter 32.
67 HEM/1/2, Letters to W.B. Hemsley MOO–ZAH, vol.2, letter 27.
68 Lionel Lambourne, 'Women Artists', in *Victorian Painting* [1999], Phaidon, London and New York, 2005, p.325.
69 Lambourne, 'The Good and the Great: Portrait Painting', in *Victorian Painting*, p.60.
70 North, 'Teneriffe – California – Japan – Singapore', in *Recollections*, vol.II, p.225.
71 ibid., p.220.
72 ibid., p.222.
73 Kurita Kazuhisa (dir.), *In Praise of Shadows*, television programme, NHK (Japan Broadcasting Corporation), Japan, 2020.
74 Aldous Bertram, *Dragons & Pagodas: A Celebration of Chinoiserie*, Vendrome, New York and London, 2021, p.78.
75 ibid., p.164.
76 North, 'Western Australia – Tasmania – New Zealand', in *Recollections*, vol.II, p.208.
77 North, 'Canada and United States', in *Recollections*, vol.I, p.68.
78 North, 'Western Australia – Tasmania – New Zealand', in *Recollections*, vol.II, p.209.
79 John K. Howat, 'Present at the Creation', in *Frederic Church*, Yale University Press, New Haven, CT, and London, 2005, p.163.
80 Howat, 'Rebuilding a Family and Pilgrimage to the Near East', in *Frederic Church*, p.134.
81 Barbara Novak, 'The Geological Timetable: Rocks', in *Nature and Culture: American Landscape and Painting, 1825–1875* [1980], Oxford University Press, New York and Toronto, 1981, p.71.
82 Lambourne, 'Virtual Reality: The Panorama', in *Victorian Painting*, p.154.
83 Alexander von Humboldt, cited in Howat, 'Humboldt's Gift and a Trip to South America', in *Frederic Church*, p.45.
84 ibid.
85 Lambourne, 'Virtual Reality: The Panorama', in *Victorian Painting*, p.151.
86 ibid., pp 152–3.
87 ibid., p.152.
88 Edward Lear, cited in Lambourne, 'Colonial Ties: Painters in a Wider World', in *Victorian Painting*, p.432.
89 Nicholas Tromans, 'The Orient in Perspective', in Nicholas Tromans (ed.), *The Lure of the East: British Orientalist Painting*, exh.cat., Tate Publishing, London, 2008, p.105.
90 State Library of New South Wales, *Grand Vistas: Panoramas from the Collection*, exh.cat., State Library of New South Wales, Sydney, 2022.
91 Norbert Schneider, *Still Life*, Taschen, Los Angeles, CA, 2009, pp 162–5.
92 Walter Tega (ed.), *Guide to the Museo di Palazzo Poggi Science and Art*, 2nd edn, Editrice Compositori, Bologna, n.d., pp 8–15.
93 Jason M. Kelly, *The Society of Dilettanti*, Paul Mellon Centre for Studies in British Art and Yale University Press, New Haven, CT, and London, 2009, p.4.
94 National Trust, *Welcome to Ham House: A Cabinet of Pleasures*, National Trust, Richmond, Surrey, UK, 2018.
95 L. Roscoe Hartigan, *Joseph Cornell: Navigating the Imagination*, Yale University Press, New Haven, CT, 2007, p.145.

CONCLUSION: MARIANNE NORTH'S LEGACY

1 MN/1/4, North Gallery 1879–1896, 'Acceptance' letter 3, box 1 of 2.
2 North, 'Chili', in *Recollections*, vol.II, p.330.
3 ibid., p.330.
4 Catherine Addington Symonds, in North, 'Chili', in *Recollections*, vol.II, p.331.
5 ibid., p.333.
6 ibid., p.334.
7 ibid.
8 North, 'Seychelles Islands – 1883', in *Recollections*, vol.II, pp 309–10.
9 Catherine Addington Symonds, in North, 'Chili', in *Recollections*, vol.II, p.330.
10 ibid., p.334.
11 ibid., p.335.
12 ibid., p.336.
13 ibid., p.337.

14 Tim Lewis, 'Hockney, Freud, Turner and Hirst: Art Blockbusters of 2012', The Observer Art, *The Guardian*, London, 15 January 2012, p.17.

15 Paula Byrne, 'Oxford "... her secret none can utter"', *Mad World: Evelyn Waugh and the Secrets of Brideshead*, Harper Collins, London, 2010, p.43.

16 Matthew Sweet, 'Introduction', in *Inventing the Victorians*, Faber & Faber, London, 2001, p.xvi.

17 Jonathan Crary, 'Modernity and the Problem of the Observer', in *Techniques of the Observer: On Vision and Modernity in the Twentieth Century* [1990], MIT Press, Cambridge, MA, and London, 1992, p.21.

18 Pyton Skipwith and Brian Webb, 'Preface', in *Edward Bawden's Kew Gardens*, V&A Publishing, London, in association with Royal Botanic Gardens, Kew, Surrey, UK, 2014, pp 7, 14–15.

19 Wilfrid Blunt, 'A Sudden Shower', in *In for a Penny: A Prospect of Kew Gardens*, Hamish Hamilton in association with Tyron Gallery, London, 1978, p.125.

20 Blunt, '"Aunt Pop" and other Matters', in *In for a Penny*, p.185.

21 Guy Brett, 'World Gardens', in Antonia Echenique Celis, Victoria Legassa and David Bamford, *Chilean Flora through the Eyes of Marianne North, 1884*, Pehuén, Santiago, Chile, 1999, p.33.

22 'Chris Burden: Through Life Never Softly', *Lowdown Magazine*, 66, 2009, p.61.

23 Martin Harrison, 'After Picasso', in *In Camera: Francis Bacon: Photography, Film and the Practice of Painting* [2005], Thames & Hudson, London, 2022, p.31.

24 ibid.

25 Harrison, 'In Camera', in *In Camera*, p.133.

26 James Fergusson, 'Style of Empire', in *History of the Modern Styles of Architecture*, 2nd edn, John Murray, London, 1873, p.248.

27 Jonathan Crary, 'Foreword', in Nicolas De Oliveira, Nicola Oxley and Michael Petry, *Installation Art in the New Millennium: The Empire of the Senses*, Thames & Hudson, London, 2003, p.6.

28 Harrison, 'In Camera', in *In Camera*, p.64.

29 Harrison, 'Michelangelo and Muybridge', in *In Camera*, p.55.

30 Crary, 'Foreword', in De Oliveira et al., *Installation Art in the New Millennium*, pp 6–7.

31 Crary, 'Modernity and the Problem of the Observer', in *Techniques of the Observer*, p.9.

32 Marion Arnold, 'Petals and Stigmas: Reflections on Plant Portraiture', in Marion Arnold and John P. Rourke, *South African Botanical Art: Peeling back the Petals*, Fernwood Press in association with Art Link, Vlaeburg, South Africa, 2001, p.153.

33 Claire Bishop, 'Introduction: Installation Art and Experience', in *Installation Art: A Critical History* [2008], Tate Publishing, London, 2010, p.6.

34 Bishop, 'Feminism and Multi-Perspectivalism', in *Installation Art*, p.35.

35 Ruth Pullin, 'Introduction', in *The Artist as Traveller: The Sketchbooks of Eugene von Guérard*, Art Gallery Ballarat, Victoria, Australia, 2018, p.21.

36 Kate Teltscher, 'The Prices of the Vegetable Kingdom', in *Palace of Palms: Tropical Dreams and the Making of Kew* [2020], Picador, London, and Royal Botanical Gardens, Kew, Surrey, UK, 2021, p.200.

37 ibid., pp 200–203.

38 Bernard Comment, 'Introduction', in *The Painted Panorama*, Harry N. Abrams, New York, 1999, p.18.

39 Comment, 'Four Variations: From the Diorama to the "Moving Panorama"', in *The Painted Panorama*, p.63.

40 Fergusson, 'Introduction', in *History of the Modern Styles of Architecture*, p.12.

41 Ruth Erickson, 'Into the Field', in Ruth Erickson (ed.), *Mark Dion: Misadventures of a 21st-Century Naturalist*, exh.cat., Yale University Press, New Haven, CT, and London, 2017, p.20.

42 Blunt, '"Aunt Pop" and other Matters', in *In for a Penny*, p.185.

43 Brett, 'World Gardens', in Echenique Celis et al., *Chilean Flora through the Eyes of Marianne North*, p.33.

44 Tony Morrison (ed.), *Margaret Mee: In Search of Flowers of the Amazon Forests*, Nonesuch Expeditions, Suffolk, UK, 1988, front cover.

45 Ray Desmond, *The History of the Royal Botanic Gardens, Kew* [1995], The Harvill Press, London, and Royal Botanic Gardens, Kew, Surrey, UK, 1998, plate 24.

46 Pip & Pop, *When Flowers Dream*, Shirley Sherwood Gallery of Botanical Art, Exhibition Guide, Royal Botanic Gardens, Kew, Surrey, UK, and Western Australian Government, 2021–2, p.1.

47 ibid., p.2.

48 ibid., p.1.

49 ibid.

50 ibid., p.3.

51 ibid., p.2.

Select Bibliography

Arnold, Marion, and John P. Rourke. *South African Botanical Art: Peeling back the Petals*. Fernwood Press in association with Art Link, Vlaeburg, South Africa, 2001

Bajac, Quentin. *The Invention of Photography: The First Fifty Years*. Thames & Hudson, London, 2002

Barringer, Tim. 'Radical Realism' in Martin Ellis, Victoria Osbourne and Tim Barringer (eds), *Victorian Radicals: From the Pre-Raphaelites to the Arts & Crafts Movement*. exh.cat. American Federation of Arts and Prestel Delmonico Books, New York and Munich, 2018

Bertram, Aldous. *Dragons & Pagodas: A Celebration of Chinoiserie*. Vendrome, New York and London, 2021

Blunt, Wilfrid. *In for a Penny: A Prospect of Kew Gardens*. Hamish Hamilton in association with Tyron Gallery, London, 1978

Blunt, Wilfrid, and William T. Stearn. *The Art of Botanical Illustration* [1995]. Antique Collectors' Club, in association with Royal Botanic Gardens, Kew, Surrey, UK, 2000

Bray, Lys de, *The Art of Botanical Illustration: The Classic Illustrators and Their Achievements from 1550 to 1900* [1989]. Quantum Books, Knickerbocker Press, New York, 1997

Desmond, Ray. *The History of the Royal Botanic Gardens, Kew* [1995]. The Harvill Press, London, and Royal Botanic Gardens, Kew, Surrey, UK, 1998

Desmond, Ray. *Sir Joseph Hooker: Traveller and Plant Collector* [1999]. Antiques Collectors' Club with Royal Botanic Gardens, Kew, Surrey, UK, 2006

Donald, Diana, and Jane Munro. *Endless Forms: Charles Darwin, Natural Science and the Visual Arts*. Fitzwilliam Museum in association with the Yale Center for British Art, Yale University Press, New Haven, CT, 2009

Ferber, Linda S., and Nancy K. Anderson (eds). *The American Pre-Raphaelites: Radical Realists*, exh.cat. National Gallery of Art, Washington, in association with Yale University Press, New Haven, CT, and London, 2019

Ford, Colin. *Julia Margaret Cameron: 19th-Century Photographer of Genius*, exh.cat. National Portrait Gallery, London, 2003

Fullerton, Patricia. *The Flower Hunter: Ellis Rowan*. The National Library of Australia, Canberra, 2002

Harrison, Martin. 'After Picasso' in *In Camera – Francis Bacon: Photography, Film and the Practice of Painting*. Thames & Hudson, London, 2022.

Hirsch, Pam. *Barbara Leigh Smith Bodichon: Feminist, Artist and Rebel* [1998]. Pimlico, London, 1999

Hockney, David. *Secret Knowledge: Rediscovering the Lost Techniques of the Old Masters* [2001]. Thames & Hudson, London, 2006

Holmes, John. *The Pre-Raphaelites and Science*. Yale University Press in association with the Paul Mellon Centre for Studies in British Art, New Haven, CT, and London, 2018

Hoozee, Robert, John Gage and Timothy Hyman. *British Vision: Observation and Imagination in British Art 1750–1950*, exh.cat. Mercatorfonds, Brussels, and Thames & Hudson, London, 2008

Howat, John K. 'Newfoundland and Labrador' in *Frederic Church*. Yale University Press, New Haven, CT, and London, 2005

Huxley, Anthony, J.P.M. Brenan and Brenda E. Moon. *A Vision of Eden: The Life and Work of Marianne North* [1993]. Royal Botanic Gardens, Kew, Surrey, UK, 2002

Jacobi, Carol, and Hope Kingsley. *Painting with Light: Art and Photography from the Pre-Raphaelites to the Modern Age*, exh.cat. Tate Publishing, London, 2016

King, Catherine (ed.). *Views of Difference: Different Views in Art*. Open University, Milton Keynes, UK, and Yale University Press, New Haven, CT, 1999

Kornhauser, Elizabeth Mankin, and Katherine E. Manthorne. *Fern Hunting among These Picturesque Mountains: Frederic Edwin Church in Jamaica*, exh.cat. Cornell University Press, Ithaca, NY, and London, 2010

Lambourne, Lionel. *Victorian Painting* [1999]. Phaidon, London and New York, 2005

McKay, Judith. *Ellis Rowan: A Flower-Hunter in Queensland*. Queensland Museum, Australia, 1990

Neville, Richard. *Grand Vistas: Panoramas from the Collection*. State Library of New South Wales, Sydney, 2022

North, Marianne. *Recollections of a Happy Life*, ed. Catherine Addington Symonds. 2 vols, Macmillan & Co., London and New York, 1892

North, Marianne. *Some Further Recollections of a Happy Life*, ed. Catherine Addington Symonds. Macmillan & Co., London and New York, 1893

Novak, Barbara. *Nature and Culture: American Landscape and Painting, 1825–1875* [1980]. Oxford University Press, New York and Toronto, 1981

Orr, Lynn Federle and Stephen Calloway. *The Cult of Beauty: The Victorian Avant-Garde, 1860–1900*. V&A Publishing, 2012

Parry, James. *Orientalist Lives: Western Artists in the Middle East 1830–1920*. American University in Cairo Press, New York and Cairo, 2018

Payne, Michelle. *Marianne North's Travel Writing: Every Step a Fresh Picture*. Royal Botanic Gardens, Kew, Surrey, UK, 2023

Pip & Pop. *When Flowers Dream*. Royal Botanic Gardens, Kew, Surrey, and Western Australian Government, 2021–2

Ponsonby, Laura. *Marianne North at Kew Gardens* [1996]. Royal Botanic Gardens, Kew, Surrey, UK, 2002

Pullin, Ruth. *The Artist as Traveller: The Sketchbooks of Eugene von Guerard*. Art Gallery of Ballarat in association with State Library Victoria, 2018

Robinson, Jane. *Unsuitable for Ladies: An Anthology of Women Travellers*. Oxford University Press, Oxford and New York, 1994

Sheffield, Suzanne Le-May. *Revealing New Worlds: Three Victorian Women Naturalists*. Routledge, London and New York, 2001

Skipwith, Peyton, and Brian Webb. *Edward Bawden's Kew Gardens*. V&A Publishing, London, in association with Royal Botanic Gardens, Kew, Surrey, UK, 2014

Sweet, Matthew. *Inventing the Victorians*. Faber & Faber, London, 2001

Teltscher, Kate. *Palace of Palms: Tropical Dreams and the Making of Kew* [2020]. Picador, London, and Royal Botanical Gardens, Kew, Surrey, UK, 2021

Tromans, Nicholas (ed.). *The Lure of the East: British Orientalist Painting*. exh.cat. Tate Publishing, London, 2008

West, Keith. *How to Draw Plants: The Techniques of Botanical Illustration* [1983]. The Herbert Press, in association with British Museum (Natural History), London, 1999

Image Credits

The publisher would like to thank the copyright holders for granting permission to reproduce the images illustrated. Every attempt has been made to trace accurate ownership of copyrighted images in this book. Any errors or omissions will be corrected in subsequent editions provided notification is sent to the publisher. The copyright for reproduction of photographs is listed below:

Images © The Trustees of the Royal Botanic Gardens, Kew, unless otherwise stated

Art Collection 3 / Alamy Stock Photo: fig.8

© Ashmolean Museum: figs 73, 74

Photo by Birmingham Museums Trust, licensed under CCO: fig.54

The Board of Trustees of the Royal Botanic Garden, Kew: figs, 1, 2, 3, 4,7, 9, 10, 13, 14, 15, 16, 17, 18, 20, 23, 24, 26, 28, 29, 30, 32, 33, 34, 35, 36, 40, 41, 43, 44, 45, 46, 47, 48, 49, 50, 52, 53, 57, 59, 60, 65, 66, 68, 69, 70, 71, 72, 75, 76, 77, 79, 80, 81, 82, 83, 84, 85, 87, 88, 90, 91, 92, 93, 94, 95 ,96, 98, 99, 102, 103, 104, 105, 108, 110

Blauel Gnamm-ARTOTHEK: fig.101

incamerastock / Alamy Stock Photo: fig.6

Ian Dagnall Computing / Alamy Stock Photo: fig.51

© Joseph Cornell. Artists Rights Society [ARS]/Copyright Agency, 2023: fig.106

Matt Flynn © Smithsonian Institution: figs 21, 22, 55, 56

The Metropolitan Museum of Art, New York: figs 5 (bequest of Adele L. Lehman, in memory of Arthur Lehman, 1965), 11 (Marquand Fund, 1959), 25 (gift of Albert Weatherby, 1946), 31 (Purchase, 1871), 37 (Gift of Dr. W. Bopp, 1921), 38 (Purchase, Mr. and Mrs. Richard J. Bernhard Gift, by exchange, 1980), 64 (Bequest of Margaret E. Dows, 1909), 97 (Gift of the Senate House Association, Kingston, N.Y., 1952), 100 (Purchase, Rogers Fund and Joseph Pulitzer Bequest, 2011)

Montagu Images / Alamy Stock Photo: fig.86

Reproduced with the kind permission from the North family: fig.58

The Picture Art Collection / Alamy Stock Photo: fig.19

© Peter Aaron/OTTO: figs 61, 62, 63

PhotoStock-Israel / Alamy Stock Photo: fig.67

The Print Collector / Alamy Stock Photo: fig.89

© Queensland Museum, Peter Waddington: fig.27

© Royal Geographical Society (with IBG): fig.78

The Shirley Sherwood Collection; figs 39, 42, 107, 109, 111

Tate, Bequeathed by Miss Moss 1920: fig.12

Index

Note: italic page numbers indicate figures; Marianne North is abbreviated to MN in headings and subheadings.